A CENTURY OF CALIFORNIA PUPPETRY

or

"How The West Was Strung!"

A Puppet History Brought to Life by

Kevin Menegus & Randal J. Metz

Foreword by
Tony Urbano

Edited by
Danalynne Wheeler Menegus

cp

Library and Archives Canada Cataloguing in Publication

Title: A century of California puppetry : or "How the West was strung!" / a puppet history brought to life by Kevin Menegus & Randal J. Metz ; foreword by Tony Urbano ; edited by Danalynne Wheeler Menegus.
Other titles: "How the West was strung!"
Names: Menegus, Kevin, author. | Metz, Randal J. (Randal John), 1959- author. | Urbano, Tony, writer of foreword. | Menegus, Danalynne Wheeler, editor.
Description: Includes bibliographical references and index.
Identifiers: Canadiana 20200352601 | ISBN 9780921845539 (softcover) 978-0-921845-54-6 (Hard Cover) 978-0-921845-55-3 (eBook)
Subjects: LCSH: Puppeteers—California—Biography. | LCSH: Puppet theater—California—History. |
  LCGFT: Biographies.
Classification: LCC PN1982.A2 M46 2020 | DDC 791.5/30922794—dc23 ISBN: 978-0-921845-54-6

ISBN: 978-0-921845-54-6   (Hard Cover)

Photo front cover photo: Tony Urbano Productions.

CHARLEMAGNE PRESS
4348 Coastview Drive
Garden Bay, BC, V0N 1S1 Canada
http://charlemagnepress.com

∽ ∽ ∽

"We have gathered for fellowship and to share an interest. We have made contributions. We have received inspiration, involvement, training. We have gained from giving. We have gained by receiving. We have made lasting friendships. May we continue to receive, to give, to contribute, and most of all, to elevate the art of puppetry, as friends into and through the next millennium."

—Lettie Connell Schubert, 1996.

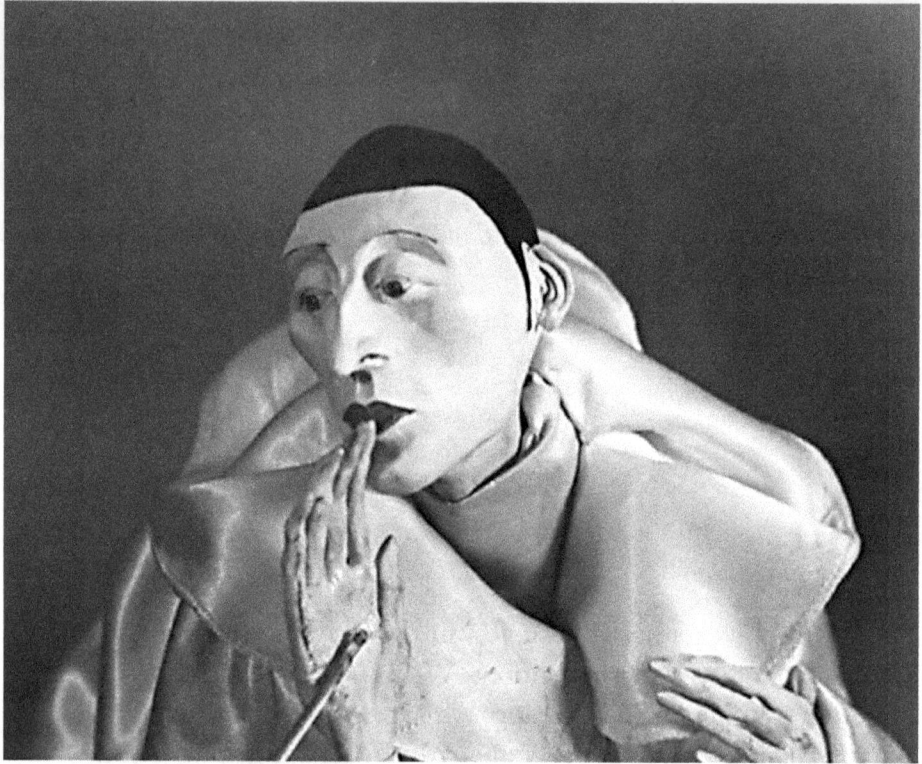

BRUCE SCHWARTZ
Pierrot
1960s

Table of Contents

Photo Credits

The authors thank the following:

- All the puppeteers who provided their photographs,
- Animation Resources for the photo of Daws Butler & Bob Clampett,
- Bob Baker Marionette Theater for the pictures of Bob Baker & Alton Wood and the Bob Baker Marionette Theater,
- Children's Fairyland for the photos of Mike and Frances Oznowicz, Bruce Sedley, Ben Blake, William S. Jones, John Gilkerson, Ray and Betty Mount, and the Storybook Puppet Theater,
- Elizabeth Luce for the pictures of Roger Mara,
- Gregory Hayes for the pictures of Lex Rudd and Bob Hartman,
- Happy Hollow Park and Zoo for the photo of the Castle Theater,
- Jim Henson Company for the photos of Jerry Juhl, Frank Oz, and Mike Quinn,
- Lettie Schubert for the photo of the Vagabond Theater,
- Lynne Jennings for the pictures of Pamelia McIntire, Ellen Galpin and Marie Hitchcock,
- Mel Birnkrant for the photo of the Hestwoods marionettes,
- Nancy Mitchell for the photo of the Showboat Theater,
- Odd Savvy for the photo of Larry Schmidt,
- Olde World Puppet Theatre for the photo of Steven M. Overton,
- Peter & Debbie Allen for the picture of Nick Lefeuvre,
- Ray Harryhausen Foundation for the photo of Ray Harryhausen,
- Ronnie Burkett for the photos of Frank Paris and Perry Dilley,
- Rose Sage Barone for the photo of Nick Barone,
- Shadow Light Productions for the photo of Larry Reed,
- Siera Salin for the picture of Wolo von Trutzschler,
- Tippett Studios for the picture of Paul Tippett,
- Puppetry Arts Institute for the picture of Robert Leroy Smith,
- Puppetry Journal for permission to reprint photographs from that publication,
- Photographers:
    - Richard Termine for the picture of Leslie Carrara-Rudolph.
    - Mike Fitelson for the photo of Randal Metz,
    - Art & Clarity for the picture of Michael and Valerie Nelson.
- The Northwest Puppet Center for permission to include the Southern Belle by Harry Burnett from the Cook/Marks Collection and the Violinist by Bob Bromley from the Charles and Elaine Taylor Collection. Both photos by Luman Coad.

Foreword

CALIFORNIA has it all!

Visitors from all over the world are drawn year 'round to enjoy California's numerous attractions: World class opera companies, symphony orchestras and the art museums, the Wine Country, the Golden Gate Bridge, Yosemite and giant sequoias. There are art colonies and music festivals strung along California's spectacular coastline, Hollywood movie studios, Disneyland, the San Diego Zoo and diverse international and local cuisine, all mixed in with the occasional pesky earthquake and wild wildfires.

And, for sure, there are the blonde, bronzed surfers riding totally awesome Pacific Ocean waves. Oh, and puppets.

Whoa, dude. Puppets?

Yes indeed. It should be no surprise that in a place with all this creative energy, the age-old art of puppetry has flourished under the California sun.

I saw my first puppet show at the 1939 Golden Gate Exposition held on Treasure Island in San Francisco Bay. It was a hand puppet show promoting the Roma Wine Company. The plot involved a beautiful young girl who was being forced to marry a rich — but evil — old man. She, of course, is in love with the poor — but handsome — gardener's son. With the help of the Roma Wine Cellar Master (the company's logo), a clever plan is devised to free her from this awful villain.

The planning process, which consisted of a lot of silly ideas and funny one-liners, brought us to the final scene. The Cellar Master, the girl and a local minister are waiting for the villain to arrive at the wedding. As the old man's elaborate carriage comes into view, the Cellar Master tricks the villain into sticking his head out of the carriage door. (Now comes the clever part!) The Cellar Master bounces across the stage and hits the old man over the head with a mop, rendering him unconscious. By the time the villain wakes up, the girl is married to the boy she adores.

OK, not terribly P.C., but to my 4½ year old mind, this was the height of wit and wisdom. I have been hooked on puppetry ever since.

I, of course, am not the only person in this most populous state in the union to have been bitten by the puppet bug, and I thank Kevin and Randal for authoring this book showcasing these artists, both the early contributors and the contemporary practitioners of puppetry in California.

The Golden State occupies the "left coast" of the North American continent. It's where people come to shake off pre-conceived notions, to be free to express themselves, to create. Those born here are raised in this culture of creative freedom, and those who migrate here revel in that same atmosphere.

For native California puppeteers, or those who have found their way here, the state motto is quite apt:

"Eureka!" (I Have Found It)

— Tony Urbano
    Los Angeles, CA
    February 2019

Tony Urbano with Phyllis Diller

Opening Thoughts on California Puppetry

"ANIMATING the Inanimate!" That is what many puppeteers consider to be the definition of puppetry. After all, how many of you have ever taken salt and pepper shakers, or napkins, from the dinner table and began to give them life and personalities of their own? If you have, then you might have the makings to be a professional puppeteer.

In his writings, puppet historian Alan Cook has suggested there are five major geographical centers of American puppetry. California has two: Los Angeles and San Francisco (the other three are Chicago, Detroit and New York). So it's no wonder the Golden State has so many puppeteers to write about. From the northern mountains to the southern deserts, puppets have found a home entertaining in one way or another. And the range of puppet styles in this state is amazing. Puppet can vary from shadows to found objects, they can be movie or television creations, they can influence through the avant-garde or political venues and they can even dazzle on the theatrical or musical stage. And of course, don't forget the many California puppet theaters and puppets in cabaret revues and amusement parks!

In the last hundred years, puppets have matured from a novelty act to gaining respected homes in libraries, films and theater. And with the ever-growing popularity of puppet slams, puppets are once again being seen as political and adult avant-garde inspirations. So … why write this book? Because: this art form has evolved from a community of artists, sharing and influencing each other's career. We are a gathering of tinkerers, willing to discuss our information with other like minds in order to create a better puppet theater. And along the way, it is easy to forget the accomplishments and the mentorship so freely given by past puppet professionals. So … we have chaptered the book and listed the biographies of the puppeteers in a way you may easily see the changes over the years, and witness how each artist influenced the next.

When we started researching the book, we discovered more than 200 respected puppet professionals who merited mentioning. That number has been reduced to what we now consider a more manageable 121, through a stringent set of criteria. And at the end of each chapter, we've added a section we call "Outstanding Ovations," where we've highlighted another 47 puppeteers whose accomplishments we feel need to be recognized, in a shorter format. We've also included a special chapter on eleven established California puppet theaters.

In addition to the requirement of the artist having lived in California at one time, we carefully subjected each name to a battery of questions. Have they mentored the careers of other puppeteers? Have they run a successful puppet theater, program or business? Have they made a huge difference in some puppetry aspect? Have they taught or worked in some form of educational puppetry? Have they made a difference in the business, or history, or guilds of puppetry? Is this someone we haven't heard about before? Were they heavily recommended by their peers and colleagues? And finally, were they a stop motion animator, ventriloquist, or other puppet-like business?

There are many more names that we missed, or did not discover, either because history has passed them by or they have been forgotten by the internet. Or maybe their careers are just beginning and they haven't made a big enough name yet for themselves. If you are reading this historic tome, and feel overlooked, we're terribly sorry. Your contribution to the puppet arts are just as significant, and your time will come. We are looking forward to the day when another historian picks up their pen (or computer) and decides to create a supplement to our volume, much like Marjorie Batchelder McPharlin did for her husband Paul's initial history *The Puppet Theatre in America: A History, 1524 to Now.*

In the meantime, sit back, relax and enjoy *"How the West Was Strung!"*

> — Randal J. Metz
> — Kevin Menegus

1850–1900

CALIFORNIA officially became the 31ˢᵗ state of the Union on September 9, 1850. Mexico had reluctantly ceded California and much of its northern territory to the United States in the Treaty of Guadalupe Hidalgo on Feb 2, 1848. The West was virgin territory for puppeteers who had already plied their trade on the East Coast since 1776. We know this because there is a reference in General George Washington's accounting journals for the payment of a *"Punch and Judy"* show, to Peter Gardiner, for the troops on November 16, 1776.

But it wasn't just the beauty and charm of this new wilderness which brought the population, it was the GOLD! Mexico might not have given this territory to the U.S. if it had known that on January 24, ten days before the treaty signing, gold had been discovered at Sutter's Mill in Coloma. It is estimated over 300,000 settlers braved the trek west and settled in California. How many might have been, or would become, puppeteers is not known. But we know *"Punch & Judy"* was there. They entertained in Sandy Bar, a rough town with buildings of pine poles and canvas near San Francisco. We also know Chinese shadow shows were popular with the miners.

It wasn't until the 1870s when the state had settled a little, before prominent puppet theater troupes traveled to the cities. Many of the more popular entertainments such as magic, ventriloquism and puppetry can trace their roots back to England and to entertainers who traveled across the pond to make their fortunes. This was partly due in fact to two brilliant (and perhaps devious) promoters, John McDonough and his partner Hartley Earnshaw. McDonough and Earnshaw were U. S. Agents responsible for bringing the puppet arts to the theaters. They joined forces with William Bullock, a puppeteer based in England, and employed his company for performances. Billed as *"Bullock's Royal Marionettes from Eng-*

land," they were able to book recognized stage theaters rather than the dime museums, circuses and beer halls where other puppeteers had languished.

A Bullock production followed a basic three act program which future puppeteers adopted as a blueprint for their own shows. Act one was a minstrel puppet show with songs and dance. Act two featured the trick marionettes of the show. This was known as the "Fantoccini," the Italian name for trick puppets. And finally, act three was a tale like *"Red Riding Hood"* or the popular *"David and Goliath."* Playing in Boston and other cities on the East Coast, the show required 10 puppeteers and an additional 10-15 performers. Bullock arrived in America in 1873, but within a few months found himself at odds with McDonough and Earnshaw.

The puppets were popular, no doubt about that. But Bullock wanted to work in both England and the United States. He departed for England and left his company in the hands of his own supervising agent, who had the power of attorney. Differences occurred over how the show was produced, threats were made, performances were halted and the puppets were produced in court. McDonough and Earnshaw wanted the puppets to extend their stay in America, as their contract read, under their supervision. The court allowed the promoters to recreate a brand new Royal Marionette show, based on Bullock's, in order to continue their tour. Bullock was further dismayed to find many of his puppeteers and puppet craftsmen stayed with the agents, who had extended their contracts to include a few years of touring on the exciting West Coast of America. And thus began the battle of the Royal Marionettes.

Bullock attempted to bring a new troupe from England to help fill the ranks of his missing original performers. That meant three Royal Marionette companies were touring the East Coast, and when other puppeteers in the splintered group eventually left McDonough and Earnshaw, they formed other Royal Marionette companies. Yet the format of the show remained the same.

Bullock and the promoters had spawned a number of competing rivals in both England and the U.S., all claiming to be the Royal Marionettes. The term "Royal" was applied to English troupes, implying they had royal approval. In America, it was used as a gimmick to create prestige. So McDonough and Earnshaw traveled to San Francisco and puppetry in the region began to flourish. Names like the Lano Family Marionettes, Royal Marionettes, Deaves Marvelous Manikins and Daniel Meader's Marionettes became popular and paved the way for future performers.

Puppet historian Gregory Williams reminds us most puppeteers of this period were considered variety artists. They performed in California with varying levels of prestige. Lower level performers found themselves entertaining in beer halls. Mid-level performers, who generally travelled with circuses and medicine shows, appeared at the dime museums. These were an offshoot of the carnival side show themes, but guaranteed a performance indoors when you couldn't get an audience on the benches due to the inclement weather. The best entertainers broke onto the vaudeville stages, which became popular in the early 1880s. The vaudeville stage catered to a thirst for the unusual, and most of their acts were. In most cases, the puppeteer was guaranteed 5 to 8 shows a day, increasing to 17 or more on weekends and holidays. Remember, there were no movies at this time. As puppet historian Alan Cook suggests, "Like Punch and Judy, puppetry struggles and thrives as an orphan child of the arts."

DAVID LANO
1940

Alberto, Oliver & David Lano
1810–1895, 1832–1902 & 1874–1957

Career: 1818–1957. The Lano family stretches across three generations of early circus puppet performers. Alberto Lano moved from Milan to the United States in 1825, and to California in 1850. He brought his street performance puppets and his skills as a one man band. Later he added a trained bear and other circus skills. His son Oliver learned the trade and, along with his wife, Annie, presented plays such as *"Punch and Judy,"* which was seen in civil war and gold mining camps, *"Faust," "Why the Sea Is Salt"* and their famous *"David and Goliath."* While his father toured the countryside, Oliver's son David and his wife, Mary, presented the Lano puppet plays along with knife-throwing and elephant acts. David's brother Burt was also a circus artist, wood carver, painter and puppet maker.

For 139 years, the three generations of the Lano Family Marionettes performed all over Europe and North America in dime museums, medicine shows, fairs and circuses, supplementing their puppet shows with other skills including knife throwing, acrobatics, animal acts, rope tricks and homemade medicine sales. One of the trademarks of the Lano shows was the red plush front curtain of a stitched scene from *"Orlando Furioso"* that Alberto had brought from Europe.

In 1957, David wrote the book *A Wandering Showman, I,* which is a loose autobiography of the trials and tribulations of his family's life on the road. David was buried in an unmarked grave in Michigan, where eventually fellow puppeteers under the direction of Rick Morse raised funds to install a proper headstone. It reads, "David Lano - PUPPETEER — It's a poor heart that never rejoices in Punch"

The Lano's are often referred to as a family of "Frontier Showmen."

WALTER DEAVES
1910s

Edwin, Walter Eugene & Harry Deaves
1809–1890, 1854–1919 & 1860–1927

Career: 1821–1920. The Deaves family, another multi-generational clan of puppeteers, performed across America for close to 100 years. Edwin Deaves saw his first puppet show in Boston in 1819. A few years later, he started making puppets for his own amusement. Puppetry soon became his profession. Prior to arriving in San Francisco in 1854, Edwin performed his puppet act with the Virginia Serenaders, an early American minstrel troupe. When promoters McDonough and Earnshaw brought their own "Royal Marionettes" show to California in 1874, they hired Edwin to help adapt the show to western standards.

Edwin's son Walter briefly worked as a principal manipulator for McDonough and Earnshaw before leaving to create his own traveling show based on the Royal Marionettes format. His brother Harry joined him on the road. Walter called his puppets "Manikins," and added "box" puppets — a mechanical set of audience members, or an orchestra. During the vaudeville days, the word "manikin" became a synonym for string puppets or marionettes. Walter's children Ada and Edwin II, as well as Harry's wife Rhetta, also joined the family business, allowing more than one company to travel at a time. The shows closed after Walter's passing.

The Deaves Marvelous Manikins marionettes were obviously influenced by William Bullock's original Royal Marionettes from England. The various Deaves performing companies travelled with a proscenium-fronted marionette theater which was set up on vaudeville stages (a stage within a stage). The stage featured miniature box seats with puppet spectators, and an orchestra pit with puppet musicians. Miniature circus acts with acrobats and animals were included in the performance, as well as the ever popular trick marionettes.

DANIEL MEADER
1880s

Daniel Meader
1856–1929

Career: 1876–1929. In 1876, while McDonough & Earnshaw's "Royal Mario-nettes" were performing in San Francisco, they discovered twenty-year-old Dan-iel Meader. Daniel had established a niche as a sculptor and fine craftsman, and was apprenticing as a prop maker for the San Francisco Opera House. He also toured in California minstrel shows. The two marionette promoters hired Daniel to do voices and singing for the puppets, which he did for the next six years.

Daniel loved to watch the puppets and often showed up to work early in order to teach himself how to make them move. One night the chief operator was too drunk to work, allowing Daniel to step in. He soon became a main manipulator for the show.

In 1882, Daniel created his own Royal Marionettes company and performed in the San Francisco area through 1898. While he did all of the traditional trick marionette acts, he often populated his shows with the ethnic characters (which we would now consider racial stereotypes) often found in the 19th century shows. His "grand turk" transformation, where one puppet turns into many, was a standout in the productions. Daniel also loved to perform stories and acts based on the puppets of French and Italian farce. After his death, many of his handbills, as well as his marionettes — which often had fully articulated heads with ani-mated eyes and mouths — were given to San Francisco puppeteer Perry Dilley by Daniel's wife.

Upper Left: DEAVES
  Sea Diver & Octopus, 1904

Lower Left: MEADER
  Harlequin, 1882

Below: LANO
  Goliath

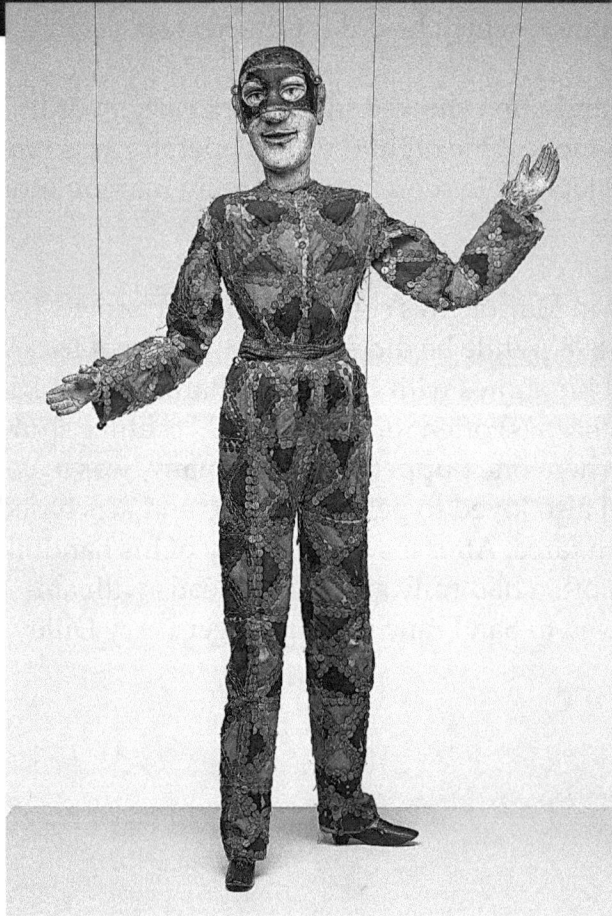

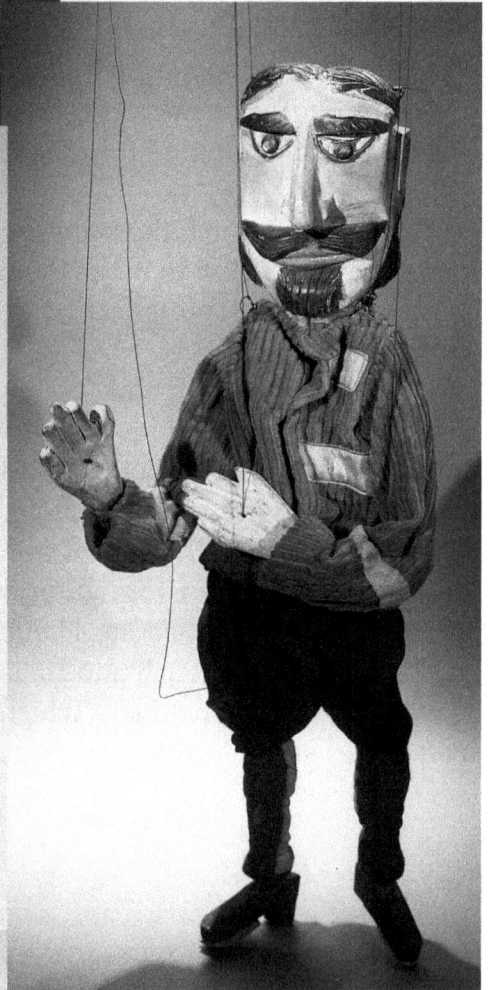

2

1901–1929

THE BEGINNING of the 20th Century brought hope and excitement to the people of the United States. In addition to vaudeville and legitimate stage presentations, the new invention of "movies" helped the populace forget the everyday drudgery of the period. French filmmakers Auguste and Louis Lumière impressed audiences with their film stylings in 1895, and Los Angeles soon had its eye on this new business opportunity.

In 1903, audiences were dazzled by the silent adventures of *"The Great Train Robbery"* and in 1927 marveled at the addition of vocals in *"The Jazz Singer."* They cheered when Walt Disney released *"Steamboat Willie,"* featuring the soon-to-become iconic Mickey Mouse, in 1928. Filming puppets and their stylized movements, particularly stop motion animation, was not far behind. California was becoming the state of dreams and imagination. And California puppeteers were up to the challenge of creating new worlds and stories of enchantment.

While Hollywood was creating movies, puppeteers were creating touring spectacles from classic novels and stories. Tony Sarg, the father of modern puppetry in America was producing puppet productions on the East Coast as early as 1917. By 1921, and through 1939, he was touring across the states presenting puppet plays and creating a training ground for young puppeteers. Those puppeteers, including Bil Baird, Rufus and Margo Rose and Sue Hastings, went on to create their own traveling theaters and inspire like-minded puppeteers in the Golden State. The puppets seen in revue shows on the vaudeville stage were being replaced by more sophisticated puppet productions such as *"Alice in Wonderland," "The Passion Play," "The Rose and the Ring," "Treasure Island," "Robin Hood"* and others. Literature brought to life!

As larger touring companies presented these grand scale classics, smaller troupes began using the puppet as an icon to create a more "intimate" theatrical experience on the theater stage. In 1908, famous theater critic Edward Gordon Craig published his most popular theory, "The Actor and the Uber-marionette." Craig, a scenic designer, author and theorist, suggested the director was the puppeteer of a production and the actors were just puppets or "uber-marionettes" in their hands. The actor should be a mask or symbol for the audience to interpret, while scenery, lighting and such were simply tools used by an inspired director to highlight his puppet-like actors and ideals. The actor *should not* spoil the performance by letting their personality or realism imprint the production. Theatrical style is only attainable through a controllable figure rather than a willful human.

Many puppeteers embraced this theory and took it to another level, in which the puppeteer became the inspired director. Marionettes imitated humanity, while lighting and sparse settings took the miniature actors to new extremes. The puppeteer/director became the actor — using the puppet to act! New York puppeteer Remo Bufano took this idea to new heights (pardon the pun), presenting *"Oedipus Rex"* with 10-foot-tall marionettes worked from scaffolding above. And in the avant-garde areas of San Francisco, the marionette actor excelled and gave main stage theater a run for its money. *"Hamlet"* was given a whole new dimension, and America was waking up to the creativity and wonder of the marionette.

Meanwhile, in Los Angeles, marionettes were being featured in a brand new style of vaudeville revue. Instead of the traditional musical selections used consistently by the trick marionettes on the vaudeville stage, original songs were being written for L.A. puppets. Puppets were also now used to characterize popular celebrities and moments from films. Jugglers, break apart skeletons, flip characters and popular gimmick marionettes were combined with puppets of well-known stars such as Greta Garbo, Jimmy Durante and other famous faces of the day. The new puppets were literally miniature "stars," lighting the way for night club acts and the puppet theaters of the future.

In 1916, Ellen Van Volkenburg, director of the Chicago Little Theater, coined the term "puppeteer" to name the manipulators of her puppet production *"A Midsummer Night's Dream."* In this era, puppet theater ranged in variety from dramatic to farce, depending on what type of performance was presented. And *"Punch and Judy"* was still being performed on the streets and at fairs, demonstrating no matter how small the puppet voice, the populace will stop and wonder at the marvel created by these animated dolls. With Perry Dilley using hand puppets to populate his stage productions in Oakland, the Yale Puppeteers changing the look of puppet theater in Los Angeles, and Ralph Chessé and Blanding Sloan's Marionette Guild in San Francisco embracing the "uber-marionette," the world of puppetry appeared to have no limits.

But one of the darkest moments in United States history was looming on the horizon. By the end of 1929, the nation would be involved in the Great Depression, which would change the face of puppetry for many years to come.

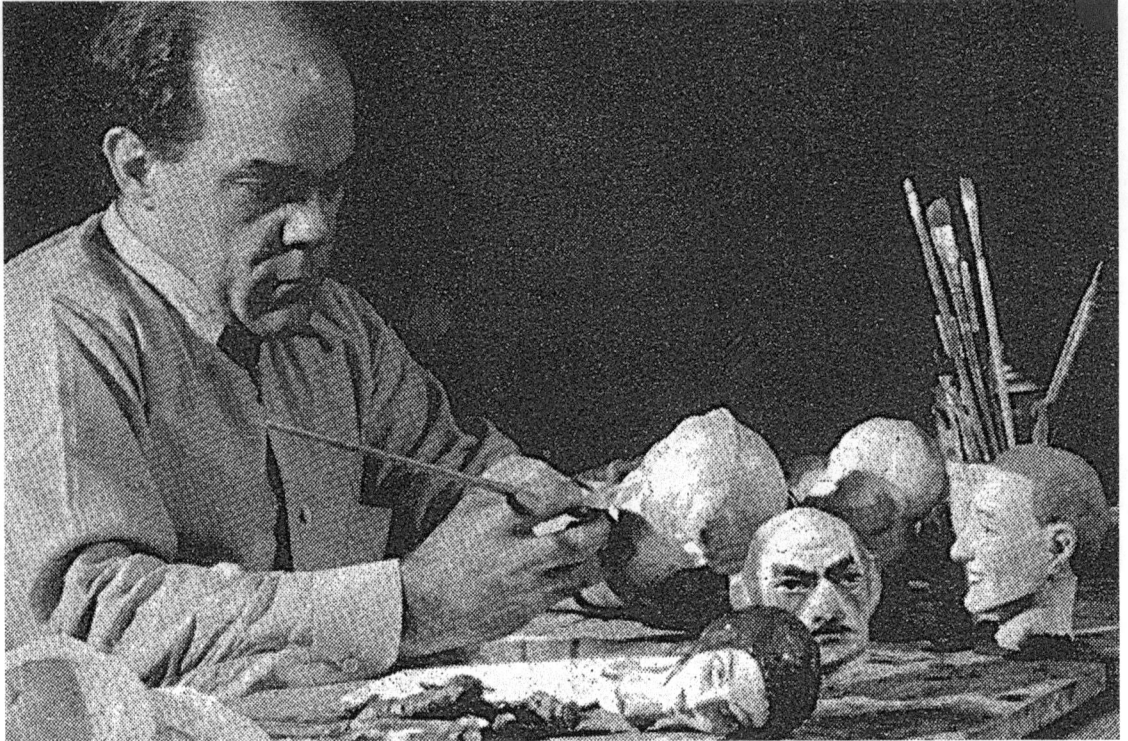

PERRY DILLEY
1937

Perry Dilley
1896–1968

Career: 1919–1968. Perry Jay Dilley, a commercial artist and puppeteer, turned the art world on its head with his classic and masterfully done puppet productions. While attending Manual Arts high school in Los Angeles, Perry studied jewelry making, served on stage crew and developed an interest in the French Guignol hand puppets. While his local contemporaries were using the marionettes, Perry's hand puppets, modeled in papier mâché or plastic wood, gave the puppeteer the ability to better control the puppet's movement, producing an elegantly, intimate performance.

Perry went on to study at the California School of Fine Arts and eventually the University of California in Berkeley. He gave his first public performance at the latter in 1922, and continued to give annual performances there for the next two decades. He became director of puppetry at the Cleveland Playhouse and for many years taught puppet theater at Mills College in Oakland.

Perry fine-tuned his craft by studying and collecting puppets and histories from the puppet masters of his time. He gave performances every Friday and Saturday night in his studio-theater in San Francisco, encompassing anything from cultural and original tales to classic novel adaptations and popular theater plays. Perry often played flute for the background music between scenes. Perry's wife, Grace Stearns-Dilley, both acted with him and also wrote and adapted many of the puppet playlets performed.

The Perry Dilley Puppet Theater revitalized the role of the hand puppet in modern puppetry in the United States. It's therefore ironic that one of his greatest achievements was creating a set of marionettes for Shakespeare's *"A Midsummer Night's Dream,"* produced by Ellen Van Volkenburg, founder of the Chicago Little Theater, for her 1924 San Francisco Bay Area performances.

BLANDING SLOAN
1947

Blanding Sloan
1886–1975

Career: 1919–1975. James Blanding Sloan, known as Blanding, made a name for himself both as a puppeteer and as an artist and theatrical designer. Blanding designed over a dozen Broadway productions, including the Ziegfeld Follies. While in New York, he was the lighting designer for well known puppeteer Remo Bufano's *"Orlando Furioso."*

In 1923, he and his wife settled in the San Francisco Bay Area and produced original puppet plays for children such as *"Rastus Plays Pirate,"* the story of a young black boy. In 1928, Blanding formed the Marionette Theatre for Adults, which became the Marionette Guild (1928–31). While mentoring a young artist/puppeteer named Ralph Chessé, the Guild presented classic works by Shakespeare and Eugene O'Neill for sophisticated adult puppet enthusiasts. One production, Charles Erskine Scott Wood's *"Heavenly Discourse,"* featured anatomically correct nude puppets. Blanding was arrested, but the show continued to sold-out audiences.

In 1931, Blanding moved to Los Angeles where he worked with Walt Disney and developed commercial theatrical projects. He also established the Blanding Sloan Puppet Club on Olvera Street, where for two years he presented his earlier San Francisco Marionette Guild productions.

Blanding was appointed as a Regional Theater Director for the Federal Theater Project of the Works Progress Administration (WPA). Later he created the East-West Film Company with his foster son/apprentice Wah Ming Chang and produced stop motion puppet films such as the 1947 controversial *"The Way of Peace."* In later years, he moved to Alameda County, where he continued to train and inspire younger puppeteers until his death in 1975.

Blanding is best known for his art exhibitions, which focused on controversial social and religious issues.

FORMAN BROWN
with Toscanni
1930s

Forman Brown
1901–1996

Career: 1920–1996. Forman George Brown and his cousin, Harry Burnett, attended the University of Michigan together. After seeing Tony Sarg's traveling marionette show *"The Rose & the Ring,"* the pair decided to become professional puppeteers. Harry made the puppets and Forman wrote the music and the scripts. Harry later met Richard "Roddy" Brandon at Yale (who became Forman's "life partner"), and together, the three formed the Yale Puppeteers. (For more on the Yale Puppeteers, please see the writeup for Harry Burnett, page 21.)

Forman composed plays and music which elevated the puppet's performance, leading to a stint on the Broadway stage from 1934–40. He wrote a segment in Leonard Sillman's *"New Faces"* at the Lyceum Theatre entitled *"It's A Small World,"* featuring Harry's puppet caricatures of popular entertainment stars. After that, it was on to the Barbizon Plaza Hotel with the puppet revue *"Sunday Nights at Nine."* Soon, Forman was composing songs and skits for such celebrities as Van Heflin, Elsa Lanchester and Shirley Temple. He also wrote music and prose for radio broadcasts. In 1940 the trio left New York and opened the Turnabout Theatre in Los Angeles, where Forman put to work all the lessons he had learned writing successful revues for both puppets and actors.

Although music and puppets were his first love, Forman also was a prolific writer. In *Punch's Progress* (1936) and *Small Wonder* (1980), he detailed the adventures of the Yale Puppeteers and the Turnabout Theatre. In 1933, under the pseudonym Richard Meeker, he published *Better Angel*, a fictional autobiography — which became one of the first acclaimed novels about gay life. The book was briefly republished as a paperback in 1951 with a new title: *Torment*. In the 1990 reprint he added an epilogue explaining why he used a pseudonym to protect his job and family.

Forman also published *The Pie-Eyed Piper and Other Impertinent Plays for Puppets* in 1933. At least three of his puppet plays have been produced at the Storybook Puppet Theater in Oakland, with Forman himself playing the accompanying piano on tape, and are still enjoyed by audiences of all ages.

HARRY BURNETT
1955

Harry Burnett
1901–1993

Career: 1920–1993. Harry and his cousin, Forman Brown, attended the University of Michigan together. While there, Forman took Harry to see Tony Sarg's traveling marionette show *"The Rose & the Ring."* Attracted to the novelty and mechanics of these miniature actors, Harry taught himself to build puppets and convinced Forman to put on shows with him to raise extra money. In 1927, Harry went on to pursue a post-graduate degree in dramatics from Yale. There, he met Richard "Roddy" Brandon, another accomplished performer. Together, Harry, Forman and Roddy founded the Yale Puppeteers. Forman wrote the plays and music, Roddy was the business manager and Harry made all the puppets.

After a brief educational tour of puppetry in Europe, Harry returned home, determined to show that puppets were not just for kids. He enlisted the talents of the great New York theatrical designer Norman Bel Geddes to create scenes for touring puppet productions of *"Bluebeard"* and *"Hansel & Gretel,"* and the Yale Puppeteers set off to tour the country. After many adventures, including abandoning Geddes's large scenery piece by piece across the American countryside, the trio decided to open a permanent puppet theater in Los Angeles. Their adventures are well chronicled in the book *Small Wonder* by Forman Brown. Before his career was through, Harry had opened three permanent adult puppet theaters: Club Guignol in 1929, the Teatro Torito (Theater of the Little Bull) on Olvera Street from 1930–31, and the famous Turnabout Theatre from 1941–1956. (For more on Turnabout, please see Chapter 11 about Puppet Theaters, page 297.)

The Yale Puppeteers received the very first Lifetime Achievement Award from the Los Angeles Drama Critics Circle in 1988. The 1933 film *"I Am Suzanne,"* about a puppeteer and an injured dancer, featured over 200 of Harry's unique creations. The puppets also appeared in the 1934 film *"Whom the Gods Destroy."* The Teatro Dei Piccoli Marionettes of Italy had been hired to build the puppets, but were not able to create all the needed characters in time.

In his final years, Harry taught puppetry to children, senior citizens and the handicapped, and was a mentor to many puppeteers throughout California and beyond.

PAULINE BENTON
1936

Pauline Benton
1898–1974

Career: 1921–1974. Pauline Benton is credited with being the first professional puppeteer to bring traditional Chinese shadow theater to audiences in North America, in the 1920's. In 1921, Pauline began her studies of Chinese shadows in the village of Luan Chow, near Peking. Heavily influenced by the magical shadows and performance, she collected and studied all available material. On her second visit to China, in 1936, she studied shadow manipulation with Master Li T'uo-ch'en. No woman had been trained before, due to an Asian taboo that forbade a man touching a woman's hand. Pauline had to learn by watching, and be corrected in sign language. This helped strengthen her puppet pantomime skills.

Pauline worked with American actor and musician William Russell, who loved Chinese instruments. Together they produced three adaptations and translations of Chinese plays, and became the Red Gate Players. Later, she worked with Lou Harrison, of the National Academy of Arts and Letters. Having collected an enormous range of shadow figures, musical instruments, and a theater, she translated and produced such Chinese classics as *"The Legend of the White Snake," "The Chinese Nightingale," "The Drum Dance," "The Fox Spirit," "The Temple of the Golden Mountain"* and many others. By 1932, she was booked on tours within 33 states. Based out of New York and California, Pauline performed in the Chinatowns of New York, San Francisco, Los Angeles and Seattle.

Pauline's work has been chronicled in the book *Shadow Woman, the Extraordinary Career of Pauline Benton,* by Grant Hayter-Menzies. An exhibition of her work, curated by Stephen Kaplin and Chinese Theatre Works, was presented in New York in 2017.

ELLEN GALPIN
1920s

Ellen Galpin
1892–1969

Career: 1922–1969. Ellen Galpin was a recognized puppet artist, elementary school teacher and an actress in London theater. She received degrees in Diagnostic Bacteriology from Stanford and Chicago University, although she never entered that field. The fine arts were her calling. To her credit, with the Majestic Stock Company, she is widely known as the first female stage manager/technical director in Los Angeles. In an age when women didn't, Ellen did!

Ellen studied acting in London and Europe, performed at the London Little Theatre and toured England and Scotland with the Benson Theatrical Company. Upon returning to California, she formed the Ellen Galpin Players and acted locally, before turning to puppetry. She also enjoyed a career working in film with director John Wray, of the Thomas Ince Studio, as his assistant director for the films *"Hail the Woman" (1921)* and *"Her Reputation" (1923)*.

In 1923, Ellen was hired by the Los Angeles Playground Department to organize a performing municipal marionette theater, as part of the Municipal Theatre Program. From 1923–1924 she created and directed puppet plays at the different city playgrounds, where performances were changed monthly. When there wasn't a building to perform in, a puppet stage was constructed on a semi truck, which allowed the puppets and stage equipment to be easily transported from playground to open park.

Ellen always had a love of children's drama. She was an actor in college, forming her own company and presenting fairy tales for children. After living in Alaska from 1925–1926, she returned to Los Angeles with a new puppet show, *"Cinderella,"* with puppets beautifully dressed by the native Alaskans. These puppets are now preserved in the collection of the historic Southwest Museum of Los Angeles. Ellen then toured her puppets in the United States from 1929–1931, presenting shows based on folk tales. She performed throughout California to Hawaii, and England, before settling in San Diego and establishing a studio in Spanish Village. Ellen semi-retired in 1958.

RALPH CHESSÉ
1950s

Ralph Chessé
1900–1991

Career: 1925–1991. Ralph Alexander Chessé was a true Renaissance man. In addition to being a puppeteer, he was also an actor, make up and stage designer, and prolific painter. In 1925, Ralph traveled to San Francisco and New York and became influenced by the works of Blanding Sloan and Remo Bufano. He settled in the San Francisco Bay Area and helped to found the Marionette Guild in 1928, which he kept running until the Depression finally closed the theater in 1931.

Ralph was heavily influenced by the theories of Edward Gordon Craig and his "uber-marionette." Ralph described his vision: "I wanted to make an instrument of theater, a surrogate which would serve my purposes as an actor." Through limited sets, imaginative lighting, and wooden marionettes, he breathed life into productions such as *"Hamlet,"* Eugene O'Neill's *"Emperor Jones," "Macbeth,"* and Moliere's *"The Miser."* Ralph also taught puppetry for adult education at San Francisco State College from 1949–1951.

In 1937, Ralph was appointed the State Director of the puppetry unit for the Works Progress Administration (WPA). He oversaw puppet productions in San Francisco and Los Angeles from 1936–40, including those shown at the Golden Gate Exposition.

With the creation of television, Ralph found himself involved with two ongoing series, *"Willie and the Baron"* (1951) and the long-running *"The Wonderful World of Brother Buzz"* (1952-65), which provided education on animals and nature. Brother Buzz, an elf turned into a bee, interviewed marionette animals created by Ralph.

After making puppets for *"Brother Buzz"* for fourteen years, Ralph turned once again to painting. In 1934, he was one of 25 artists selected under a Federal Grant to paint a fresco on the walls of Coit Tower in San Francisco. His final puppet performance was with his son Dion in 1985. They performed Moliere's *"The Doctor in Spite of Himself"* for Southern Oregon College. In 1987, Ralph published his autobiography, *The Marionette Actor* (available from the George Mason University Press).

HAROLD & ROBERT HESTWOOD
Disney Marionettes
1934

Harold & Robert Hestwood
1899–1966 & 1896–1962

Career: 1926–1966. Harold Keith and Robert William Hestwood both produced and performed in legitimate puppet theater while also publishing books. Harold was an author who wrote in verse, while Robert was the illustrator using linocuts (a variation of woodcut using linoleum sheets) as his preferred type of illustration.

The Hestwood Marionettes began their career working for the "Father of Modern American Puppetry," Tony Sarg. In 1926, Harold and Robert published the children's book *Gawpy, Book One*, which featured Harold's writing and Robert's illustrations. Eventually, the brothers and fellow Sarg puppeteers Jean Gros and Bil Baird left the Sarg troupe and ventured into the realm of adult puppet theater under the company name of the Drury Lane Players Ltd. Working in cooperation with Bill Baird in New York, in 1928 they produced a marionette extravaganza based on their book, titled *"The Gawpy Ballet, a Fantasy of Pelican Isle."* The music was composed by the Hestwoods. The show wasn't as well received as they'd hoped, and the puppets ended up in the storeroom collection of the Baird Theater. The pair returned to the tutelage of Sarg, and eventually to their homes in California.

The Hestwoods are best known for their work with Walt Disney Productions. From 1932–34 they produced puppet shows in L.A.'s Bullock's Wilshire Department Store from well-known Disney cartoons such as *"Mickey and Minnie in the Olympic Games."* They also mass produced a set of marionette collectibles which sold in the store and have become the holy grail for collectors of Mickey Mouse products. Their Mickey, Minnie and Pluto marionettes were in such demand that Bob Baker, in the '80s, reproduced them for sale within his line of "Disney Marionettes" which sold in Disney parks, stores and art galleries.

FRANK PARIS
1940s

Frank Paris
1914–1984

Career: 1927–1984. Frank Paris, of Native American heritage, lived on both coasts while pursuing his career. While in New York he performed twelve times at Radio City Music Hall and for an audience of 27,000 at Madison Square Garden. And while in Los Angeles he performed in the Olvera Street Puppet Theater and night clubs, also working in Hollywood films such as 1937's *"Artists and Models."* While laid up with asthma at age 13, Frank was leafing through the *Ladies Home Journal* and came across an article by Tony Sarg which inspired him to teach himself puppetry. A neighbor admired a marionette dancer Frank made, and soon he was performing for women's clubs at $5.00 a show! This led to night clubs, cruise ships and even Rio de Janeiro, where he presented his variety show *"Stars on Strings."*

Frank was also very prominent on early television with such shows as *"Pixie Playtime," "Magic Books," "The Adventures of Toby,"* and a show called *"Puppet Playhouse"* that featured Frank's puppets, including a freckle-faced boy named Howdy Doody. The show was a smash hit. Host "Buffalo" Bob Smith and NBC wanted to market the successful puppets and keep the merchandising profits. Frank figured he owned the puppets and was, in effect, renting them out. When he was told otherwise, he grabbed his puppets and stormed out. Meanwhile in the television show plot line, while Howdy was recovering from facial surgery, Bob got Velma Dawson to make a new Howdy puppet. When the bandages came off, the new *"Howdy Doody Show"* debuted, with the new Howdy puppet. Frank sued the studio and won, but as a condition, he had to destroy the original Howdy in the lawyer's office. But this didn't stop his successful career, which lasted for decades.

Frank taught puppetry at New York University and Columbia University Teacher's College. He was also the first member (and president) of the Puppetry Guild of Greater New York. He is credited with being one of the first puppeteers to create "Cabaret Style" puppetry, where the puppeteer is seen on stage performing with the puppet. In his waning years, Frank worked at Bob Baker's Marionettes, and performed by invitation in night clubs and at special events.

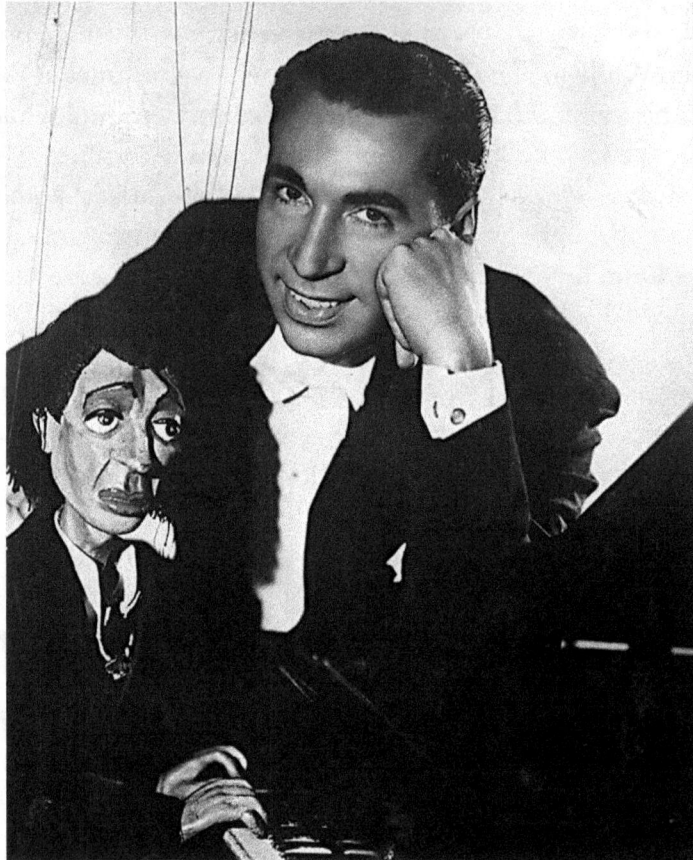

BOB BROMLEY
with Señor Disturbi
1930s

Bob Bromley
1907–1981

Career: 1928–1981. Bob Cressy graduated from Yale University with a B.A. in Theatre Techniques, which emphasizes direction, scenery and lighting in theatrical productions. In 1928 he began working with the Yale Puppeteers: Harry Burnett, Forman Brown and Richard Brandon. Acting as their main set carpenter, he built the scenery for their productions of *"Bluebeard"* and *"Hansel & Gretel"* created by legendary designer Norman Bel Geddes. When the Yale Puppeteers opened their second marionette theater on Olvera Street in 1930, Bob began his puppeteer apprenticeship with the group — and changed his surname to better fit with the alliterative Burnett, Brown and Brandon. Bob built many of the company's early Hollywood celebrity marionettes as well as other puppets. While watching a fizzing Bromo Seltzer tablet to settle his stomach, he thought…*"Bromo? No, Bromley!"* And so it remained for the rest of his life.

After the Yale Puppeteers left for New York, Bob and his partners C. Ray Smith and Wayne Barlow became the "Famous Olvera Puppeteers" from 1932–1935. Bob influenced and mentored the careers of Bob Baker, Virginia Austin Curtis and eventually Charles Taylor. In 1936, he created his own solo touring night club show which over the next 30 years led to the Bob Bromley Marionettes performing in such diverse countries as France, England, Australia, South America and even Africa. Although a lifetime resident of Los Angeles, his career was mostly international.

Bob's accomplishments include being the director of the Los Angeles marionette unit during the Works Progress Administration (WPA) in 1936, and helping to establish the performance concept of a marionette manipulator being seen on stage with his puppets; as well as a command performance for the Queen of England. He was also an avid columnist for the *Puppetry Journal*, the Puppeteers of America magazine, where he wrote many articles explaining how to get a job as a night club performer or begin a challenging career in puppetry.

WAH CHANG
1944

Wah Chang
1917–2003

Career: 1928 - 2003. Wah Ming Chang was born in Honolulu and settled in San Francisco with his family in the 1920s. When his mother passed away, his father asked Wah Ming's puppeteer/art teacher Blanding Sloan and his wife to become guardians for the young boy. Wah was mentored by Blanding as a puppeteer and watercolor artist, but is best known for his work in stop motion animation, as well as film making, set design, costuming and prop construction. In the early 1940s, Blanding and Wah partnered in the creation of the East West Film Company. Using miniature sets and stop motion puppets, in 1946–47 they produced the highly controversial anti-war film *"The Way of Peace."* Wah also made many shorts with animator George Pal, such as the famous *"Puppetoons,"* plus films like *"The Wonderful World of the Brothers Grimm"* and *"The Time Machine."* He shares an Oscar for the effects on *"The Time Machine"* under his company name of Project Unlimited, Inc.

Wah designed masks, puppets, costumes, sets and makeup for such series as *"The Outer Limits"* (the Zanti Misfits); *"Star Trek"* (most of the memorable props and creatures); *"Land of the Lost"* (dinosaur stop motion) and *"Planet of the Apes."* He created *"The Black Scorpion"* for Willis O'Brien, and designed the famous headdress for Elizabeth Taylor in *"Cleopatra."* Not bad for a young man who almost had his career stopped when he was stricken with polio at age 23.

Wah also designed sets for the Hollywood Bowl, as well as making the mechanical maquette models of Pinocchio and Bambi for Disney animators to follow. In 1994, he won the George Pal Memorial Award by the Science Fiction, Fantasy and Horror Film Association for all of his work in film and television. When he semi-retired, he spent his quiet years working on metal sculpture, water color painting and photography. He is famous for sculpting the delightful bronze characters and whimsical statues of Dennis the Menace that adorn the Hank Ketcham's Dennis the Menace Park in Monterey.

JOHNNY FAUST
Alice in Philcoland
1950

Johnny Faust
1920 - 1950

Career: 1928 - 1950. Born in Ripon, Wisconsin, John C. Faustman had a short but very impressive career in puppetry. At age eight he found a magazine article on how to build marionettes, and that year Johnny presented his first puppet show for his schoolmates as the Pixie Marionettes. When he was fourteen, he wrote and self-printed, on a small printing press he had at home, a book on puppets: *How to Make and Operate Marionettes.*

Johnny sought out the best puppet companies performing in the '30s and '40s, to learn more about the art. Working with these puppeteers, he fine-tuned his own craft while also practicing his skills as a cartoonist. He toured and performed with the Tony Sarg Marionettes and the Sue Hastings Marionettes, and worked with New York legend Bil Baird at the 1939-40 New York World's Fair. He eventually settled in the Los Angeles area and began working the night club circuit with his puppets.

In 1948-49, Johnny contracted with Philco Electronics, a radio and television maker, to promote their products with puppets in local appliance stores throughout the area. "*Alice in Philcoland*" was the name of the show he created, and after building two complete sets of puppets, he was able to cover several stores per day. Needing help with these performances, Johnny gave Alan Cook, who would in the future become a noted puppet historian, his first professional puppeteering job.

Several of Johnny's "*Alice*" marionettes are preserved in the Alan Cook Puppet Collection. Johnny also donated time to perform for ailing youngsters at local Children's Hospitals.

Ellen Van Volkenburg

Career: 1914–1978. Ellen and her husband Maurice Browne ran the famous Chicago Little Theater. They produced live actor and puppet plays. In 1916, her first puppet play *"A Midsummer Night's Dream"* was produced. She brought the play to San Francisco in 1924 with new marionettes created by Perry Dilley. Ellen directed *"The Rose and the Ring"* puppet play for Tony Sarg. She created the word "puppeteer" which found its way into standard dictionaries. If men who wrangled mules were called "muleteers" - why not call people who wrangled puppets "puppeteers"? Ellen also taught puppetry at Cornish College of Art in Seattle, Washington.

R. Bruce Inverarity

Career: 1928–1999. While living in San Francisco in 1927, Robert Bruce Inverarity apprenticed with Blanding Sloan who introduced him to puppetry. From 1934 - 36, Bruce was the first puppetry instructor at the University of Washington in Seattle, where he produced many puppet plays. He wrote *Playable Puppet Plays* and *A Manual of Puppetry* to use in his classes. Bruce was director of the Northwest WPA (Federal Arts Project) Puppetry Theater, 1936–1939, and Director of the Washington Arts Project, 1939–1941. He also taught art at Cornish School where he worked with Ellen Van Volkenburg.

3

1930–1939

THE GREAT DEPRESSION, which started on October 29, 1929, ended officially in 1939. By the time it was finished, personal income, tax revenues, profits and prices had dropped dramatically. International trade plunged by more than 50% and unemployment rose to 25%. Before signs of recovery become evident in 1933, many countries in addition to the United States suffered. Newly elected President Franklin D. Roosevelt was quick to legislate the"New Deal" policies. But it wasn't until the "Second New Deal," on May 6, 1935, that the Works Progress Administration (WPA) was formed and later Social Security was implemented.

The WPA was dissolved on June 30, 1943, but for eight years it provided millions of Americans with jobs. Jobs for everyone, which led to federal offices in major cities for all types of workers. As a result, the United States built a massive infrastructure with dams and freeways, and federal lands became beautiful with parks, majestic buildings and improvements.

It was also a golden age for the arts. New performances and works of public art were constantly being produced — all paid for by the government. In 1936, Bob Bromley was appointed director of the Los Angeles Puppetry Unit, and Ralph Chessé was the director of the San Francisco-based unit. In 1937, Ralph became the state director and supervised both units until 1940, when the WPA changed its focus to wartime efforts. Yet before it all ended, American puppet programs created beautiful shows which were performed at schools, festivals and at least nine world fairs.

With so many wonderful things being produced in the world-wide arts scene, it's no wonder film and literature expanded into new areas of imagination. As the country sought to forget its daily troubles, science fiction and fantasy genres began to find their rightful places in the publishing empire with such favorites as T. H. White's *The Sword in the Stone (Once and Future King)* and J. R. R. Tolkien's *The Hobbit*. Comic book literature blooms with the adventures of Superman in Action Comics, 1938. And all of this spilled over to radio, which was fast becoming the dominant form of mass media in industrial nations. Where were you when Orson Welles and his Mercury Theater broadcast H. G. Wells' *"The War of the Worlds"*?

And let's not forget Hollywood and the film industry. Charlie Chaplin kept us laughing with *"Modern Times"* (1936) while Metro-Goldwyn-Mayer spellbound us with *"The Wizard of Oz"* (1939) and Walt Disney breathed life into cartoons with *"Snow White"* (1937). All escapism at its best. And escaping was exactly what the general public wished to do. Soon, the puppet theater offered many chances for people to do just that.

Hand puppets and ventriloquists were becoming popular entertainments for audiences, all thanks to the WPA and vaudeville. Marionettes also remained crowd-pleasers. Los Angeles became home to four long-running puppet theater enterprises. Olvera Street featured three different marionette companies, while Catalina Island was home base to a fourth. The Yale Puppeteers, Bob Bromley, Walton and O'Rourke, and the Nickabob Puppeteers entertained nightly to standing room only crowds throughout the 1930s. These Californian puppeteers even left the state for a while and tried their luck on the Broadway stages of New York. The chief employment for puppeteers in the Golden State remained performances of cabaret puppetry in night clubs, classic fairy tales and literature at school assemblies, and tried and true vaudeville. And yet, by the end of the decade, vaudeville had passed.

Although the WPA helped keep the puppet arts alive, another important puppetry institution was founded in 1937: the Puppeteers of America. Starting in 1930, Detroit puppeteer Paul McPharlin religiously kept records of the history of puppetry in the United States in his self-published *Puppetry Yearbooks*. In 1936, he organized the first American Puppetry Conference in Detroit, Michigan, to bring together the nation of puppeteers. The festival welcomed college professors, elementary school teachers, museum curators, therapists, recreation leaders, authors, hobbyists and puppet builders — anyone who saw the benefit of puppeteers sharing skills and ideas. A full accounting of this event can be found in McPharlin's 1936 book, *Puppets in America A History 1739 to Today* by Puppetry Imprints. As a result of the festival, the Puppeteers of America was born, and McPharlin was the association's first "honorary" president.

So as history has shown us, from the darkest pits of despair, bright ideas flared up and lit the way to better times. The 30s gave us the Depression, but also gave us science fiction, fantasy, and a new way to unite and excel at the puppet arts. All signs pointed to a bright new future for California and the rest of the country. But on Sept 1, 1939, almost a complete decade after the "Black Tuesday" stock market crash, World War II raised its ugly head in Europe and changed the face of puppetry once again.

MITCHELL MARIONETTES SHOWBOAT
1965

Howard Mitchell & the Mitchell Marionettes
1918–2012

Career: 1930–present. Howard Mitchell found his love of puppetry in seventh grade, when he joined a puppet club in school. His second love was magic. And in 1936 he met third love, Marjorie Singleton, who became his magic, puppetry partner and his wife. After World War II, the two formed the Mitchell Marionettes, along with their daughters Susan and Nancy.

The Mitchell Marionettes performed on TV, at Disneyland, Six Flags Magic Mountain, and at state, regional and national fairs and many smaller venues across the U.S. They've also appeared at a number of the largest fairs and expositions in Canada. The Mitchells are best known for their iconic Mississippi River Showboat Stage which rolled in for their comedy marionette performances. Howard was also known for his highly innovative "Grand Turk Illusion" marionette that would explode in an instant into six smaller puppets. In the 1950s, Howard led the way in latex rubber technology with his line of ventriloquist figures marketed under the name of "Flex-O-Flesh." During this time he taught his young daughters the art of ventriloquism and their act became part of the Mitchell shows. His skills as a magician and puppeteer created a relationship with Ringling Bros. and Barnum & Bailey Circus, where he created massive latex illusions during the 1960s. He was inducted into the Society of American Magicians Hall of Fame in 1971. The Mitchells also helped found the Los Angeles Guild of Puppetry.

Howard and Marjorie were on the cutting edge of puppetry robotics in the early '80s. Life size "Happy Harry the Chimpanzee," with fully articulated facial animation, was one of the most sophisticated robotic puppets of that era. Harry rode his bike through the fairgrounds, singing and telling jokes. He was later followed by "Millie the Monkey," these unique puppet creations amazed audiences for 35 years!

Daughter Nancy became a professional solo puppeteer and ventriloquist, and in 1969 established Minikin Puppet Productions. When Howard and Marjorie retired in 1998, Nancy and husband Jack Gebhardt continued Minikin Puppets and the Mitchell Showboat Marionettes with their own special brand of magic.

WOLO VON TRUTZSCHLER
Princess Trundlebumps & Aloysius Mouse
1950s

Wolo von Trutzschler
1902–1989

Career: 1930s–1989. Wolo von Trutzschler was born Baron Wolff Erhardt Anton George Trutzschler von Falkenstein. His younger sister had difficulty pronouncing his proper name and gave him the nickname "Wolo."

Wolo came to America as a young man to study agriculture, but quickly switched to drawing caricatures of people in night clubs. While drawing on Los Angeles' Olvera Street, he was approached by an admirer, ventriloquist Edgar Bergen. Edgar asked Wolo to draw an illustration for a "hayseed" character — which became Bergen's famous dummy Mortimer Snerd.

Wolo moved to San Francisco, where he illustrated a column for the *San Francisco Chronicle*. He also wrote and illustrated five popular children's books based on fictional animals in the imaginary forests of "Friendship Valley." While talking to 500 librarians about his book, he experienced a bout of stage fright. To help get past it, he placed a handkerchief on his hand and made it into one of the girl squirrels from his story. Soon he was staging puppet shows in Golden Gate Park and up and down the West Coast. This led to television appearances on a short-lived show sponsored by Red Goose Shoes and then on KPIX channel 5's *The Morning Show*," featuring his own puppet character, Aloysius Mouse.

After the television show was cancelled, Wolo opened a toy shop in San Francisco called Happy Things. He and a young puppeteer by the name of Lettie Connell gave puppet performances in the front windows of the shop.

Wolo manipulated the Walton & O'Rourke puppet "Golo the Giant" in the 1953 movie *"Lili"* starring Leslie Caron. He also designed a play set at Children's Fairyland in Oakland featuring murals from his books. As well he designed a puppet show for the park about the fictional history of its famous Talking Storybook Magic Key. Another of his many public murals graces the walls of the Children's Hospital in Palo Alto.

GEORGE PAL
The Wonderful World of the Brothers Grimm
1962

George Pal
1908–1980

Career: 1931–1980. Hungarian-born György Pál Marczincsak worked as an animator in Germany, Prague and Holland and finally settled in California. He had planned to study architecture at the Budapest Academy of Art, but a clerical error placed him in illustration classes — and the rest is history.

George started filming puppets in 1931 when he founded the Trickfilm-Studio GmbH Pal und Wittke in Germany. He there created and patented the "Pal-Doll technique style," which later became known in the U.S. as "Puppetoons."

His technique was replacement animation: the use of a series of different hand-carved wooden puppet heads or limbs for each frame as the puppet moves or changes expression, rather than moving a single puppet as is the case with stop motion animation. A typical Puppetoon required 9,000 individually carved and machined wooden figures or parts.

Fleeing war-torn Europe, George started work in Hollywood in 1939. Cartoon animator Walter Lantz helped him gain citizenship. The Hungarian-American animator, film director and producer immediately began creating Puppetoons animated puppet film shorts. The series, which ran from 1940-1948, numbered over 40 shorts and received seven Academy Award nominations. Working alongside George were legendary puppeteers Wah Chang, Bob Baker, Don Sahlin and a very young Ray Harryhausen. In 1944, George was presented a special Oscar for his work.

After "Puppetoons", George went on to produce and direct fantasy films such as *"Tom Thumb," "7 Faces of Dr. Lao,"* and *"The Wonderful World of the Brothers Grimm."* His science fiction films include *"Destination Moon," "When Worlds Collide," "The War of the Worlds"* and *"The Time Machine."* In 1960, he was presented with a star on the Hollywood Walk of Fame. In 1987, filmmaker Arnold Leibovit reintroduced a generation of filmgoers to George's work with a compilation of shorts titled *"The Puppetoon Movie."*

PAUL WALTON & MICHAEL O'ROURKE
Stripsey Rosale
1930s

Paul Walton & Michael O'Rourke
1906–1983 & 1908–1981

Career: 1931–1966. In 1931, while pursuing a Navy career, Michael O'Rourke saw a puppet show in Tokyo and realized puppeteering was his destiny. He and long-time friend Paul Walton settled in Hollywood, where the duo opened their Olvera Street theater, known as the "Olvera Street Puppets," at #21 Olvera Street. From 1935 to 1939 they performed nightly to celebrity crowds, filling a "puppet void" that occurred when the Yale Puppeteers had closed down operations in L.A.

Natural artists, sculptors, designers, writers, choreographers and actors, life destined these men to form their own unique theater specializing in fast moving puppet revues for adults. And after five successful years, they were captivated by the lights of Broadway. They played the Rainbow Room, the Cotillion Room, the Park Plaza and had a two-year gig at the Winter Garden Theater. During World War II, Paul and Michael traveled with the USO, entertaining the troops on foreign soil. Then it was back to the lure of Hollywood.

Walton & O'Rourke were constantly in demand in night clubs, theaters and film. They performed their puppets in over 12 motion pictures, and were regulars on the Ed Sullivan, Johnny Carson, Steve Allen and Ernie Kovacs television shows. In 1953 they built and manipulated the puppets for the movie "*Lili*," starring Leslie Caron. With such a colorful legacy, it's no wonder they influenced the careers of Bob Baker, Tony Urbano, René Zendejas and more.

The Walton & O'Rourke Marionettes performed from L.A. to New York and on to Europe, Australia and the Far East. After Paul's stroke in 1966 the theater disbanded and Michael, who couldn't fathom performing without Paul, put the puppets away. Years later Michael's granddaughter Valerie Rock, with her daughter Tapatha, found and restored the puppets and used them to make videotapes to teach and entertain. This seems fitting, given that Paul and Michael carved lifelines into the hands of their creations in the hopes they would have long and useful lives.

ALTON WOOD & BOB BAKER
1950s

Bob Baker
1924–2014

Career: 1932–2014. Robert Allison Baker III saw his first puppet show at the Barker Brothers Department Store when he was seven. Henrietta Gordon, the head exhibitor of puppets for Bullocks Wilshire Department Store, began coaching him. After the two performed a puppet show for film studio producer Mervyn LeRoy, Bob became known as "The Puppeteer to the Stars!"

As a teenager, Bob worked with puppeteer Bob Bromley and the Federal Theater Puppet Project, and helped Harry Burnett at the Turnabout Theatre. He went on to attend UCLA and the Art Center College of Design. Bob also worked with puppet film director George Pal on movies. Simultaneously, he started his own business, manufacturing toy marionettes which sold from 1942–1949 in more than 50 department stores including Saks Fifth Avenue and Neiman Marcus.

In 1949, Bob launched *"The Adventures of Bobo,"* a televised marionette show, and met his lifelong partner Alton Wood, an accomplished pianist and business manager. In 1963, the two created the now legendary Bob Baker Marionette Theater. Declared a Historic Cultural Monument of Los Angeles in 2009. Bob also worked closely with Walt Disney, creating the mechanical puppet windows that adorned Main Street in Disneyland Park. He created an extensive line of "Disney Marionette" characters, sold exclusively in Disney parks and art galleries.

Bob has over 400 movie and TV credits, creating puppets for such films as *"G. I. Blues,"* *"A Star is Born,"* *"Close Encounters of the Third Kind,"* *"Bedknobs and Broomsticks"* and *"Escape to Witch Mountain."* Bob's television appearances include *"The Wild, Wild, West,"* *"Voyage to the Bottom of the Sea,"* *"Land of the Giants"* and *"The Magician."*

An active member of the Screen Actors Guild until his death, Bob worked alongside Tony Urbano to create a puppeteers' caucus in the film industry. He served as a governor in the animation division for the Academy of Motion Picture Arts and Sciences and the Television Academy of Arts and Sciences. In 1987, Bob received the President's Award from the Puppeteers of America.

Virginia Austin Curtis
and Clippo
1970s

Virginia Austin Curtis
1903–1986

Career: 1933–1986. Virginia Austin Curtis graduated with a degree in music from a music school in Chicago. She moved to Los Angeles, where she worked in a tea room by day and sold music related items on Olvera Street at night. She found Bob Bromley's "Famous Olvera Puppeteers" fascinating, and when the 1933 earthquake closed the tea room, she sought employment with the puppeteers. Soon, Virginia was touring with the company, doing women's voices, manipulating, and singing for the opera star marionette "Madame Obligato," while Bob mentored her in the art of puppetry.

In 1936, Virginia designed a small clown marionette she named "Clippo." Chicago-based Marshall Field's department store approached her about making exclusive Clippos for them. They then connected her with the Effanbee Doll Company, which for the next eight years produced Clippo marionettes for sale all over the country. Virginia traveled the United States demonstrating her puppets in stores. She also sculpted W. C. Fields and Charlie McCarthy dolls for Effanbee after ventriloquist Edgar Bergen asked her to sculpt the head of his new vent figure Mortimer Snerd, Charlie McCarthy's best friend.

Virginia began singing and performing professionally with Clippo and friends at the Paramount Theater and the Palace Theater. From 1939–1953 she performed on the theater circuit in New York, and in supper clubs. She appeared on *The Ed Sullivan Show,"* and did a special performance at the White House for President Franklin D. Roosevelt. During the war, Virginia performed in hospitals and camps supporting the troops. After the war ended, she took over the manufacturing of Clippo, under the name Curtis Crafts, and expanded the puppet line to include stages, scripts and the "Clippo Club" for children. Clippo marionettes are still a sought after, highly-prized collectible today.

In her golden years, Virginia opened the Puppet Theatre Workshop in Sierra Madre. The Workshop taught puppetry to young students and acted as a space for traveling puppeteer performances and meetings of guilds and artists. Puppeteer Jack Aiken produced an award-winning film on Virginia's life and accomplishments titled *"A Place to Pretend."*

RAY HARRYHAUSEN
1958

Ray Harryhausen
1920–2013

Career: 1933–2013.Raymond Frederick Harryhausen is one of the greatest stop motion puppet animators of the 20th Century. He was an American-British artist, designer, painter, illustrator and sculptor. Ray's first attempt at puppetry was creating marionettes. But after seeing *"King Kong"* (1933) numerous times, he began experimenting with using stop motion puppets (particularly dinosaurs).

Ray was mentored by stop motion greats Willis O'Brien and George Pal. Inspired by their work, he created the process of "Dynamation," later "SuperDynaMation" and "Dynarama," combining rear film projection and stop motion puppetry. He did all of his own animation and his puppet metal armatures were made by his father Frederick.

After the war, working in the United States Army Special Services Division, Ray produced his first *"Fairy Tales"* puppet films (1946–53) using surplus 16 mm film. From 1953 to 1981 Ray and his film partner, producer Charles H. Schneer, created many of the best loved fantasy and science fiction films to grace the silver screen. Highlights include *"Mighty Joe Young"* (1949), *"The Beast from 20,000 Fathoms—* (1953), *"It Came From Beneath the Sea"* (1955), *"Earth vs. the Flying Saucers"* (1956), *"20 Million Miles to Earth"* (1957), *"7th Voyage of Sinbad"* (1958), *"The Three Worlds of Gulliver"* (1960), *"Mysterious Island"* (1961), *"Jason and the Argonauts"* (1963), *"First Men in the Moon"* (1964), *"One Million Years B.C"* (1966), *"The Valley of the Gwangi"* (1969), *"The Golden Voyage of Sinbad"* (1973), *"Sinbad and the Eye of the Tiger"* (1977) and *"Clash of the Titans"* (1981).

Ray is credited with influencing the future careers of Phil Tippett, Henry Selick, and Nick Park as well as Steven Spielberg, George Lucas, Peter Jackson, John Landis and James Cameron. He has a Hollywood star on the walk of fame, and was inducted into the Science Fiction Hall of Fame in 2005. In 1992 he was awarded the Gordon E. Sawyer Award for technological contributions (effectively a lifetime achievement Oscar) by the Academy of Motion Picture Arts and Sciences.

MIKE & FRANCES OZNOWICZ
1956

Mike & Frances Oznowicz
1916–1998 & 1910–1989

Career: 1933–1998. As a young boy in Belgium, Isadore Oznowicz strayed into a puppet performance of the Teatro Dei Piccoli, and was entranced by puppets and the theater. Enlisting the aid of his father, a wood carver, Mike created his first puppet show. Later, with a degree in commercial art, Mike ventured into the world of avant-garde and political puppetry. He began performing on the street with Punch and Judy as the political crisis in Europe developed.

Frances Ghevaert, a Catholic, fell in love with the Jewish puppeteer and they soon married. Frances' degree in haute couture, the creation of exclusive custom-fitted clothing constructed by hand from start to finish with high-quality fabric and great detail, made her popular with fashionable women as well as giving her the ability to clothe Mike's puppets. However, the Oznowiczs were not popular with the German Nazis, and had to flee the country twice. Burying their puppets with Frances's mother, they finally arrived in America, where they landed in Oakland and raised a family.

Both Mike and Frances felt that puppetry in America was a step-child of the arts, unsupported by the funds that ballet, opera, dance and music received. So besides performing with their puppets at Yosemite each summer, the pair turned to the political business of puppetry. Mike was twice president of the Puppeteers of America, helped found the San Francisco Bay Area Puppet Guild, was Regional Director of puppets in California, and served on many theatrical boards in the San Francisco Bay Area. Frances, well known for her exquisite puppet costumes, clothed many puppets for Tony Urbano of Hollywood and Lewis Mahlmann at Children's Fairyland in Oakland.

In addition to keeping puppetry as an art form alive and controversial, the couple also raised an artistic family: Ron, a business advisor; Jenny, who worked at Lucasfilms and of course Frank, who became Jim Henson's second-in-command of the Muppets, and one of America's finest puppeteers. The Oznowiczs also supported the careers of many young California puppeteers.

BILL SOUSA & BETSY BROWN
1970s

Betsy Brown
1918–2001

Career: 1934–2001. Betsy Brown grew up on the plains of Texas. As a child, her father treated her to special trips to see live vaudeville. The puppets and the circus atmosphere spoke to her, and when she saw Tony Sarg's *"The Adventures of Christopher Columbus"* she knew she wanted to be a puppeteer. Working from an article by Tony Sarg and through sheer perseverance, she learned the craft. Along the way, Betsy also became a clown, using mime and costumes as well as puppets. She held an M. A. in Children's Theater from Cal State Northridge and a B. A. in Fine Arts from Immaculate Heart College.

In the 1970s, Betsy directed one of the first puppet companies to feature bilingual and bicultural presentations. Billed as Teatro De Los Puppets, she and her fellow teacher, Bill Sousa, entertained in their community and on the streets of East Los Angeles. Betsy loved to experiment with color, scale, movement and audience participation. Roaming through urban schools and communities, she helped children awaken to their cultural heritage with her large costumes, masks and rod puppets. Shows like *"Father Serra and His Missions"* and *"Señor Chatito and the Ancient Gods of Mexico"* enchanted audiences not used to seeing shows about their cultures.

Betsy was an instructor of puppetry and clownology at Los Angeles Valley College and Cal State L.A. She also taught at the University of California Santa Barbara and the University of California Irvine, and received recognitions from several Los Angeles mayors and libraries for her artistic teaching methods.

Over the course of her career, Betsy trained many puppeteers, teachers and librarians in the puppet arts and bilingual performing. Forman Brown of the Yale Puppeteers often wrote her personal plays, poems and musicals based on Betsy's stories about saints and children's literature. Betsy also performed puppet concerts with symphonies at the Hollywood Bowl and the Los Angeles Music Center.

OLGA STEVENS
1950s

Olga Stevens
1899–1983

Career: 1934–1983. Olga Louise Stevens was a woman of many talents: a dance instructor, theatrical tour/stage manager, actress, costumer and businesswoman. She was an opinionated, forceful and "let's get this done right" type of individual and played an important role in the founding and growth of the Puppeteers of America. She and her husband Martin organized the first festival in Cincinnati in 1937, and Martin served as the organization's first elected president. Their legendary studio-home-theater, called "The Mousetrap," became a home and gathering place for many national and international puppeteers.

In the early '30s, Olga Seegmueller married Martin Stevens and began her legendary career. Olga was charged with running the business, costuming the marionettes and performing as a lead puppeteer. Soon, known as the Figure Theatre of Martin & Olga Stevens, or the Stevens Marionette Theatre, their shows favored serious adult drama. Notable Stevens Marionette performances included *"The Nativity," "The Passion Play," "Cleopatra"* and *"Joan of Arc."* Their final touring productions were *"Macbeth"* and *"The Taming of the Shrew."* Olga also worked on productions with puppeteers George Latshaw and Jim Henson. She performed with Rufus and Margo Rose on *"Jerry Pulls the Strings"* and in their other puppet films *"Rip Van Winkle," "Treasure Island"* and *"Aladdin."* Martin and Olga divorced in 1957. She then moved to Ojai, California, and dedicated her talents to the advancement of the Puppeteers of America and puppetry in the United States.

In 1966, Olga was appointed the Secretary of the Puppeteers of America, a post which she held for the next eleven years. In 1972, she was presented with the President's Award for all her accomplishments. Olga was the right hand of the president and the right arm of the Puppeteers of America. George Latshaw, Dick Myers and Don Sahlin were just a few of the individuals she helped mentor in the art of the puppet.

LESLIE & ELEANOR HEATH
Leselli Marionettes
1950s

Leslie & Eleanor Heath
1910–2002 & 1909–2002

Career: 1935–2002. Leslie and Eleanor Heath were a husband and wife team who worked together as the Lesselli Marionettes. Both Les and Ellie studied theater in college. They graduated with teaching credentials, which they used later to teach puppetry in schools and colleges. They toured up and down California bringing their puppets to many fairs and events in the state.

Except for a brief period during World War II, where Les was awarded the Bronze Star, the couple continually turned out quality puppet theater. As a team they worked so well together, they could guess each other's timing and manipulation during their live performances. They always carried a recorded tape of the show to have a backup for any vocal issues, but they preferred live voice work to better sync the show to the dynamic of their varied audiences.

During the school year, Les and Ellie traveled the state and across the country performing fairy tales such as *"Snow White," "Pinocchio"* and *"Hansel & Gretel."* And during the summer they were at all the county fairs presenting variety and advertising shows for clients such as the Dairy Council. They even had an adult show based on the classic melodramas.

The Heaths were trained in puppetry by American puppeteer Martin Stevens. In the workshop Les would sculpt and paint the puppets, while Ellie wrote the scripts, costumed the figures and painted the scenery. Over the course of their career the Heaths, who styled their shows as if on the theater stage, performed on television, in film, night clubs and for advertising campaigns — and inspired puppeteers Luman Coad and Jim Menke. In his later years, Les also acted as the Entertainment Director for several state fairs.

DANIEL LLORDS
1950s

Daniel Llords
1926–2009

Career: 1935–2009. Daniel Llords, a child prodigy, was born Daniel Linus Hornafius. Music and theater were his passion. Daniel was a concert pianist, singer, dancer, film actor, radio voice, playwright and of course...puppeteer. By the time he was through with education, he had earned two Master of Theater Arts degrees with extended studies in London, Paris and Edinburgh.

In 1959, Daniel opened a small marionette theater on Cannery Row in Monterey. By 1962, when the theater closed, he embarked on his first world tour, billed as "Llord's International" - a marionette concert theatre for adults. Mixing puppetry with all his other art forms, he began performing with symphony orchestras presenting such classics as *"The Firebird Suite," "Petrushka," "Don Quixote,"* and *"The Emperor Waltz."* His slogan was "Music, Marionettes, Two Hands and One Man."

Daniel performed five world tours in one decade alone. Although he spoke some lines in the languages of the countries he visited, his program was designed to be language-independent, understood by audiences around the world.

Daniel met his life partner known only as "Jones," in 1959. Jones acted as Daniel's personal and stage manager throughout his career. In 1997, when Jones passed, Daniel retired his company and enjoyed a casual, quiet life, directing numerous theatrical productions for the Actor's Community Theater of Hillsboro, Ohio, and authoring a handful of plays and musicals under the name David Horn.

Daniel was president of the Puppeteers of America from 1967 - 1969. His bi-monthly *Puppetry Journal* column "International Notebook," was published from 1969–1981. In Prague, he was elected to the Praesidium of Union International de la Marionette, an international organization of scholars, teachers, directors and artists working in the various related fields of puppetry. In a very Wagnerian, operatic request, Daniel's last Will and Testament instructed that all of his puppets, staging, and props be destroyed upon his death.

SID & MARTY KROFFT
& *Les Poupées de Paris* dancers
1960s

Sid & Marty Krofft
1929–present & 1937–present

Career: 1939–present. At age 10 Sid Krofft saw his first puppet act in vaudeville, then saw an ad in the first Superman comic for a Hazelle marionette, which his parents purchased for him. Self-taught, he became a street performer with his marionettes and wind-up Victrola. He was soon playing in night clubs and vaudeville. As a teen he was billed as "the world's youngest puppeteer" in the Ringling Bros Circus sideshow. One of Sid's trademarks was to build a small ice rink in the night club and perform the marionettes on ice while he skated. Sid toured the world in 1957 and was opening act in a national tour for Judy Garland.

In 1958, Marty joined his brother as his assistant on the road, acting as his second puppeteer. In 1961 they became partners, and at their first meeting with Walt Disney he gave them some advice, "Always put your name on everything you create, because some day it will become worth something." Their first successful venture was the adult marionette revue called *"Les Poupées de Paris."* Fashioned after the French *"Follies Bergere," "Les Poupées"* was soon playing Los Angeles, San Francisco, and the Seattle and New York World's Fairs, with two troupes performing simultaneously. Through the 1960s they operated puppet theaters in all Six Flags amusement parks.

The Kroffts' next feat was to become producers. When Hanna-Barbera hired them to build the costumes and sets for *"The Banana Splits Hour,"* they found their niche. Their successes include *"H. R. Pufnstuf," "Lidsville," "Sigmund and the Sea Monsters"* and *"The Land of the Lost."* The brothers produced twenty additional television series, as well as variety shows on evening television with Donny & Marie Osmond, Barbara Mandrell and *"The Brady Bunch Hour."*

In 1976 they opened up the first indoor amusement park, The World of Sid & Marty Krofft. They returned to television in 1987 with a puppet political comedy show called *"D.C. Follies."* It is rumored that at their peak in the 1970s, the Kroffts employed 250 plus puppet builders and 130 puppeteers presenting ten shows a day.

The brothers have recently been honored with their own star on the Hollywood Walk of Fame.

John Ralph Geddis & François Martin

Career: 1924–1978. John, scenic art assistant turned actor and dancer, and François, actor and painter of sets in silent films, together created the Tantamount Theater in Santa Barbara and Carmel Valley. In the early years the theater presented puppet plays, followed by dance recitals, poetry readings and occasional film presentations. John and François specialized in puppet adaptations of plays by Shakespeare, Moliere and American theater classics. They also worked with Ellen Van Volkenburg in her San Francisco production of *"A Midsummer Night's Dream."* In 1978, the Tantamount Theater burned to the ground with over 600 puppets inside.

Wayne Barlow

Career: Early 1930s–Mid 1940s. Wayne produced puppet shows for J. W. Robinson's Department Store in Los Angeles from 1934–1942, based on classical stories and Disney themes like *"Three Little Pigs," "Dumbo,"* and *"Snow White."* He worked with a revolving marionette stage that allowed puppets to cross from scene to scene. Barlow also ran puppet making workshops in conjunction with the store's basement theater. After the Yale Puppeteers moved to New York, Wayne co-founded the Famous Olvera Puppeteers (1931–1935) with Bob Bromley and C. Ray Smith. He also inspired and mentored the career of Bob Baker.

Velma Dawson

Career: Early 1930s–2007. Velma had a career in puppetry, film and dance. She appeared, ballroom dancing, in many musical films and in vaudeville. At one time she was also assistant to Edgar Bergen in his vaudeville variety and ventriloquist show. In 1948 Velma carved and created the second, and most well known, marionette of Howdy for the *"Howdy Doody Show."* In 1998 she helped re-make Howdy for the Jim Carey film *"Man on the Moon."* She also sculpted and sold lovely porcelain figurines. Velma was mentored by Wayne Barlow, Jack Shafton, and influenced by Walton and O'Rourke.

Jack Shafton

Career: Early 1930s–1981. Jack started his career in high school and with two friends was known as the Colonial Marionettes. They had a show on the Venice Pier for several years which was put on hold during World War II. After the war, Jack designed marionettes for commercial characters on television such as the Chicken of the Sea Mermaid and "Speedy" the Alka Seltzer man. He is best known for creating the marionettes for the Kroffts' *"Les Poupées de Paris."* Jack created puppets for countless children's television programs. In 1975 he opened the famous costume shop Shafton Inc. of Hollywood.

Roy & Harry Patton

Career: 1934–late 1940s. Roy Patton, and his brother Harry, were well known carvers of fine marionettes. They were influenced by the Bible puppet shows they grew up with in their Quaker community. In 1934 the brothers joined William Duncan and Edward Mabley's Tatterman Marionette Theater as carvers. Roy later became a puppeteer and set designer. As a wood crafter, Roy carved all of the puppet heads for the Tatterman's most famous show, *"Peer Gynt,"* in 1937. The Pattons also worked on other Tatterman shows, both theatrical and industrial, until the company closed around 1941.

Stan Kramer

Career: 1939–2001. When Stan was a teen, he toured the United States and Europe professionally, working with his parents on the vaudeville stage. In the late '50s to '60s, he was head puppeteer for Sid & Marty Krofft and *"Les Poupées de Paris,"* Stan specialized in elaborate trick marionettes. He quickly put on his own takeoff of *"Les Poupées"* from 1960–67 called *"Les Jolie Poupettes."* His puppetry partner, Ted Soares, also worked the Krofft shows. Stan was one of very few marionette entertainers who successfully performed on the vaudeville stage, cabaret stage and television.

ᔈ 4 ᔈ

1940–1949

WORLD WAR II, which lasted from 1939 to 1945, helped to unify our country after the Great Depression. That said, it also sent many of our artists to war. But…what could an artist do for the war effort, you ask? Plenty! Walt Disney stopped his current projects, and turned his whole studio into a propaganda factory producing cartoons and short films to bolster the country's spirits. George Pal created one of his most famous Puppetoons, "Tulips Shall Grow," in 1942. The images of the Nazi war machines tearing up Holland and its windmills, only to be destroyed by a thunderstorm, was an effective use of the puppet's pizzazz. And many puppeteers traveled overseas to bring joy to the troops while performing in U.S.O. shows or in the wards of army hospitals. Even Ray Harryhausen put his puppet talents to work. His superior officer in the Special Services Division, none other than film director Frank Capra, had Ray animating short films about the use and development of military equipment. The stop motion classics included titles such as *"How to Bridge a Gorge"* and *"Guadalcanal."* When the war was over, the puppeteers returned home again and picked up the strings of their lives.

Films and television were quick to put puppets back to work. Studios were hiring puppeteers to bring a new life to scenes in movies, while stop motion animation was at its peak. George Pal and his apprentices were producing Puppetoon shorts from 1940–1948, and Walt Disney hired puppeteers like Bob Jones and Wah Chang to create in three dimensions the objects his animators conceived. They also built many of Disney's cartoon concepts into moveable models which the animators could pose and study while drawing. Ventriloquists such as Edgar Bergen, Paul Winchell, Jimmy Nelson and Señor Wences were finding "their voices" as they left radio and turned to the new invention of television by the end of the decade. Puppeteer Burr Tillstrom of "Kukla, Fran & Ollie," pre-"Mr. Rogers' Neighborhood," began to win the hearts of thousands of viewers.

Americans wanted to "believe" again, and puppets were the perfect vehicle for rediscovering childhood hopes and dreams.

Now, puppetry was found not only on the silver screen — it also began to appear frequently on the written page. As more people started to have their own home workshops, magazines such as Popular Mechanics, Popular Science, and even Minicam Photography began publishing "how to" articles on making marionettes, scenery and puppet theaters. The Ladies' Home Journal and craft publications even got into the act. Walton & O'Rourke, Bil Baird, Rufus Rose, George Cole and Frank Paris were becoming national celebrities, doling out secrets of the trade or posing for product advertisements. The age of learning puppetry as an apprentice was fast disappearing, as it was discovered you could become a master by just opening the pages of a "popular" magazine (pun intended)!

The Puppeteers of America revived after the war. Paul McPharlin had enlisted and while serving, had entertained troops. When discharged, he and other puppeteers began to re-kindle what they had started in 1937. And like the magazines mentioned in the previous paragraph, Paul's self-published books on puppetry were just as important (although not as accessible) for generating new puppeteers. He started in 1930 with the Puppetry Yearbooks (16 volumes), and before his death in 1948 also produced 12 instructional puppet handbooks. Today, those books, most of which were limited editions with 1,000 or fewer copies, are highly collectible. After his passing, his wife Marjorie Batchelder McPharlin published his definitive book on American puppetry: The Puppet Theatre in America: A History - 1524 to Now, In the interim, another noteworthy member of the puppeteers' organization, George Latshaw, became the editor of the P. of A.'s newsletter, The Grapevine. In 1949 he changed the format and the Puppetry Journal was born. With that, puppeteers once again could congregate, read about and easily share new ideas across the states.

In California the puppet arts excelled. Mike and Frances Oznowicz brought their efforts to build a stronger puppet community to the Bay Area, where the puppets abandoned by the WPA project found a new home in Oakland and began one of the longest running recreational puppet programs: the Vagabond Puppets! In Los Angeles, the Yale Puppeteers opened their famous Turnabout Theatre, revolutionizing revue puppet shows, as Marie Hitchcock and her sister Genevieve laid the groundwork for the future of puppetry in San Diego. The '40s were booming for puppeteers as families begin to reunite after the war. The upcoming "Baby Boom" only helped to make the puppet a bigger part of American life. And say kids! Do you know what time it is? That's right, it's Howdy Doody Time! In the next chapter we'll learn how this odd little puppet appeared in our lives in 1947, helping to usher in a golden age of television and puppetry.

ALAN COOK
2011

Alan Cook
1932–2019

Career: 1940–2019. Alan Gregory Cook was a recognized puppet authority and collector. Preserving the history of puppetry in the United States had become a mission for Alan — his curated collection, now at the Northwest Puppet Center in Seattle, encompasses more than 5,000 puppets. Alan started his puppetry career at age 8 when he joined a WPA organized puppet class at his grammar school, taught by Lora Knight Pattison, then formed the Cookie Box Puppet Theater. After that, Alan saw any puppet show he could. He first attended a puppet festival in Oklahoma in 1948, where he met half of America's leading puppeteers. The Puppeteers of America membership was around 300 at that time, with very few members in California.

Alan's first job was with Johnny Faust, presenting *"Alice in Philcoland"* in 1948–49. He replaced a puppeteer who ran afoul of the law, and was quickly trained by Don Sahlin. Alan next worked for Art Clokey Productions animating the stop motion show *"Davey and Goliath."* Next, he left Gumby's world to work for George Pal when Wah Chang got him a job on *"The Wonderful World of the Brothers Grimm."* After that, he toured with Sid and Marty Krofft's *"Les Poupées de Paris,"* in Vegas, and at the New York World's Fair. He also worked for René Zendejas and his Artists.

Alan drew upon his degree in Art History from University of Southern California for his first love — curating puppet exhibits. Of the many exhibits he helped curate, *"Puppets - Art & Entertainment"* in 1980 was the largest. Eleven major U.S. venues sponsored the display, including the Oakland Museum. Alan's vast collection of puppet arts was first displayed in Los Angeles as COPA, the Conservatory of Puppetry Arts, in 1999. Later, the collection outgrew the space and moved to Seattle. Alan was named an UNIMA (Union Internationale de la Marionnette) "Member of Honor," and attended as many P. of A. festivals as he could. He considered these events an essential means to maintaining the sense of community between artists and the art they share.

TONY URBANO
1960s

Tony Urbano
1935–present

Career: 1940–present. In 1939, at age four and a half, Tony Urbano saw his first puppet show at the Golden Gate Exposition on Treasure Island in San Francisco. The show, sponsored by the Roma Wine Company, launched one of the most successful puppet careers in history. Not long after, Tony was using Hazelle and Clippo marionettes to entertain local kids. He built his first puppet at age eight, leading to him taking classes from Ralph Chessé , and later working under puppet legends Bob Baker, Bob Kelly and the Yale Puppeteers.

By the time he became director of the Storybook Puppet Theater at Children's Fairyland (1958–62), he had completed a stint in the U. S. Army and toured the United States with Turnabout Theatre. After Fairyland, he settled in Los Angeles and built hundreds of marionettes for Sid and Marty Krofft's *"Les Poupées de Paris,"* as well as puppets for Shari Lewis and toured the Soviet Union with the Bil Baird Marionettes. Tony studied design at the Chouinard Art Institute, and went on to produce puppet shows for Disneyland and Universal Studios (where he had his own theater) as well as productions at the Laguna Beach Festival of Arts. Besides being the major force behind the multi-Emmy award winning CBS television show *"Dusty's Treehouse"* (1968–80), his companies work has been seen in more than 350 commercials, including such icons as the McDonald's Chicken McNuggets, Parkay ("Butter"), and the Snuggle Fabric Softener Bear. His film highlights include *"Short Circuit," "The Flight of the Navigator," "Team America: World Police"* and the *"Men In Black""* films. In 1990 Tony was officially profiled in *Who's Who in Entertainment.*

Tony was co-chair for the steering committee that helped create the Puppeteers' Caucus for the Screen Actors Guild. This talented artist has also performed as lead baritone for the Lamplighters of San Francisco, which produces Gilbert and Sullivan operettas. He has taught at various colleges and universities and entertained on cruise ships around the world. Among his many successful endeavors, Tony has mentored the careers of Tim Blaney and Kevin Menegus, along with many other professional puppeteers. Tony received the President's Award from the Puppeteers of America in 2003. He credits his Aunt Sam (Elvira Kienitz) for his success and beautiful marionettes.

RENÉ ZENDEJAS
1948

René Zendejas
1927–2014

Career: 1940–2014. René Gerardo Zendejas was born in San Salvador, El Salvador, and emigrated to California when he was three. As a child actor and dancer, he appeared with Shirley Temple and was in the *"Our Gang"* comedies. At age nine, he left film to study violin, Spanish dancing and singing. But what interested him most was puppets. One day he witnessed a display of Clippo puppets in a department store and was so impressed that he bought a whole set. This led to him meeting Bob Baker, also in high school, who began mentoring René for $1.00 a lesson. He also studied the puppet artistry of Jack Shafton, Walton & O'Rourke and the Turnabout Theatre. By age 14, René was performing his shows at the Broadway Department Store in L.A. He claimed, "At 13, my mother bought me a puppet because I was ill and needed a sickbed hobby, and I've been sick ever since."

Billed as René & His Artists, René played Las Vegas, fairs and theaters with his skillful marionettes, as well as major hotels and night clubs across the United States. He created puppet shows for Six Flags Magic Mountain, Knott's Berry Farm, the San Diego Zoo and Universal Studios. He also built and performed marionettes for Sid and Marty Krofft. Popular television shows such as *"The Ed Sullivan Show," "Bozo's Circus," "Murder She Wrote," "Fantasy Island," "Columbo"* and *"Tales from the Crypt"* have all featured his artistry. From 1971–1978 he had a hit bilingual puppet show, *"Domingo,"* on ABC channel 7. And if that wasn't enough, he made puppets for McDonald's commercials for 17 years! In 1999, René and Velma Dawson made a duplicate marionette of Howdy Doody for the Jim Carrey film *"Man on the Moon."*

René established Venterprise, a company that built personalized ventriloquist dummies for ventriloquists. He often helped Jay Johnson figure out complicated actions for his popular vent figure *"Bob"* for the television series *"Soap."* René personally influenced the careers of Thom Fountain, Jay Johnson and Joe Selph. "I love what I'm doing and I'm doing it because I love it," he said.

PAT PLATT
1960s

Pat Platt
1923–2018

Career: 1941–2018. When Patricia Platt finished reading, cover to cover, Winifred H. Mills & Louise M. Dunne's *Marionettes, Masks & Shadows*, she had no idea it would change her life. She always claimed she was a hobbyist turned professional, and it wasn't until much later that she first saw Harry Burnett's Turnabout Theatre and seriously considered creating a puppet business. In an effort to build a puppeteer community, she gathered twelve other enthusiasts, and founded the San Diego Guild of Puppetry in 1957. Under Pat's leadership, in 1964, they joined forces with Marie Hitchcock to convince the San Diego Recreation Department to allow puppet shows to be performed on a routine basis in the theater building in Balboa Park. The space eventually was renamed the "Marie Hitchcock Puppet Theater."

Pat's first professional show was *"The Dragon Snee Zee,"* a puppet play by Carl Glick, originally written for Remo Bufano during the WPA era. The puppets were created with heads made from the gourd plant. Pat would let the shape of the gourd influence the character, adding facial features as needed. These natural wood/fiber shapes that grew on vines became a popular puppet form and Pat led the way with many articles and classes on construction. Her gourd puppets were a popular feature during the summers at Yosemite State Park. In 1965, through the Puppeteers of America, she traveled with other peers to Europe and visited specific artists and companies in the puppet arts. With her batteries recharged, she figured it was a good time to open her own permanent puppet theater.

In 1965, the Puppet Playhouse opened its doors in San Diego and continued to provide quality puppet entertainment and birthday party venues until 1981 when Pat semi-retired. Lewis Mahlmann of Children's Fairyland and Pat continued to exchange shows between the park and the Puppet Playhouse during this time. Pat's puppets are still in repertoire in Fairyland. She is a featured artist in Marjorie Batchelder McPharlin's book *Puppets in America Since 1948.*

Don Sahlin
with Rowlf
1960s

Don Sahlin
1928–1978

Career: 1942–1978. Don Sahlin's career reads like the "Who's Who" of puppetry. For 36 years he worked for almost all of the top names in the profession. Born in Stratford, Connecticut, Don was bitten by the puppet bug at age 11 when he saw the New York Marionette Guild perform *"Hans Brinker and the Silver Skates."* By 16 he was earning his first money, $15.00 a show, as a puppeteer presenting *"Hansel & Gretel."* After that, he spent the rest of his life jumping from California to New York, working wherever he could.

Don was apprenticed by Tony Sarg puppeteers Rufus & Margo Rose and by Martin and Olga Stevens. He toured with the Stevens company, and was a puppeteer and builder for the Roses on their television show *"Howdy Doody."* In Los Angeles, he worked with George Pal on a number of stop motion films. He then returned to New York where he spent many years working with Burr Tillstrom on *"Kukla, Fran & Ollie,"* where his main job was building new copies of these famous puppets, including those used by Burr on Broadway in his show *"Kukla, Burr & Ollie."* Don also worked with Remo Bufano on his New York stage shows, as well as on the stop motion film *"Hansel & Gretel"* by Michael Myerberg in 1954. He then spent many years building puppets at Bob Baker's Los Angeles studio. Don performed the puppets he and Bob made in the 1960 film *"G.I. Blues"* with Elvis Presley. He even spent time performing Chinese shadows with Pauline Benton.

Don is most well known for his work with Jim Henson and the Muppets, from 1962–1978. Jim credits Don's playfulness and creativity as being a vital element in the success and design of the Muppets. The first puppet Don made for Jim was Rowlf the Dog. He also built all of the original Sesame Street Muppets. And in Jim's Oscar nominated short film *"Time Piece,"* in 1965, he did all the special effects. Don's passions were opera, kites and rockets.

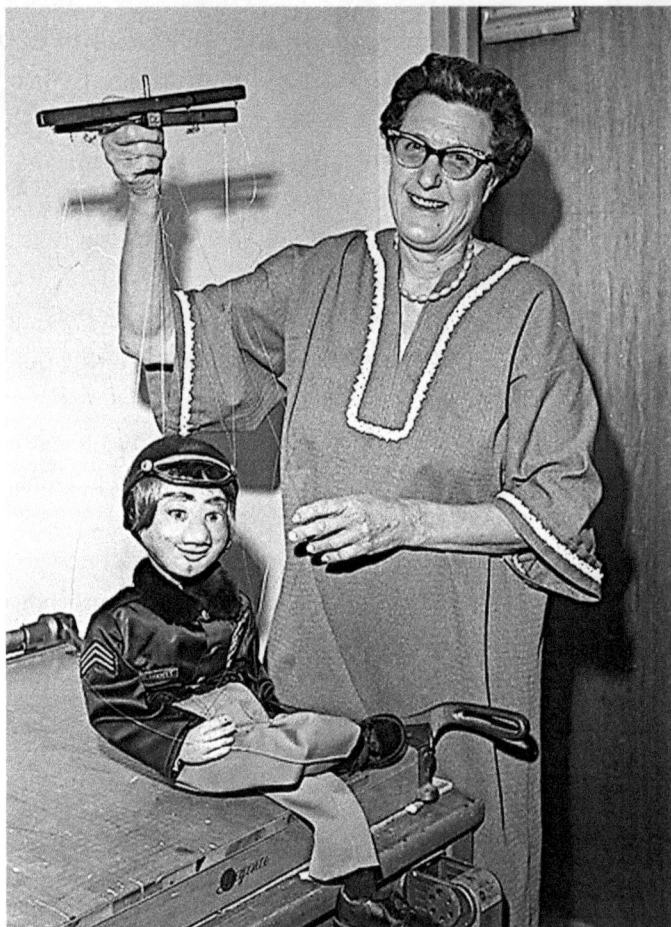

MARIE HITCHCOCK
with Sgt. Friendly
1976

Marie Hitchcock
1911–1994

Career: 1944–1994. Marie Angela Hitchcock's early life and successes remain a mystery, even to the ever-widening eyes of the internet. We do know she and her sister, Genevieve Engman, had a burning passion for puppetry and animal programs in the San Diego area. The sisters were in their thirties when they began performing as the Padré Puppeteers. Genevieve would build the puppets, while Marie was the onstage performer. In 1963, Genevieve was injured and Marie continued the tradition alone.

In 1947, the sisters began performing at the Palisades Building, part of the California Pacific International Exposition, in Balboa Park. Sponsored by the San Diego Park and Recreation Department, they began presenting shows there often, as well as at shopping centers, clubs and festivals in the San Diego area. Marie's marionettes of Sergeant Friendly (Badge 164, San Diego Police), Captain Safety and Uncle Sam were soon presenting educational programs in San Diego schools, reaching some 60,000 children a year.

Marie also had a deep love for safety and humane care for animals. Her public presence was so well known, she was named San Diego's official Puppet Lady by the City Council, as well as being the Ambassador of Kindness for the San Diego Humane Society. When the California condor population was in danger of becoming extinct, and had dwindled to just two dozen left in the wild, Marie and Genevieve created a mother condor puppet who helped feed newly hatched saved babies at the San Diego Zoo as the newly hatched birds would not allow humans to feed them. This led to the creation of a new puppet-based tool that keepers could use to feed animals born in captivity, and Marie received a letter of commendation from Governor Ronald Reagan.

In 1986, after campaigning for years to save the Palisades Building in Balboa Park as a "puppet only" venue, the historic structure was refurbished and on Marie's 75th birthday officially became the Marie Hitchcock Puppet Theater.

LETTIE CONNELL SCHUBERT
1984

Lettie Connell Schubert
1929–2006

Career: 1945–2006. A 3rd generation San Franciscan, born Frances Electa Orton Connell, "Lettie" became immersed in the puppet arts. Inspired as a child by Ralph Chessé's production of *"Alice in Wonderland,"* she was delighted to be going to the same school as Ralph's son, Dion. Her career took off when she enrolled in a class taught by Ralph at her alma mater, San Francisco State College, in 1949. With new knowledge, she left her job in a mannequin factory to become a working puppeteer.

Ralph saw unique talent in Lettie, and they joined forces on television and stage projects. In 1951 they worked together on the television show *"Willie and the Baron."* A year later she became entangled in Ralph's finest show, *"The Wonderful World of Brother Buzz."* Produced by the Latham Foundation for the promotion of humane education, this early kid's show about the behavior of animals ran for 14 years on KPIX-TV. Segments of actual wildlife footage was narrated and entwined with marionettes built by Chessé. Until 1961 Lettie played the role of Miss Busy Bee, while Dion Chessé played Brother Buzz. This led to a show on KRON-TV in 1953 called *"The Looking Glass Lady."* From 1957–58 on KPIX-TV, Lettie had an ongoing popular segment on *"The Morning Show"* called *"Twinkle & George."* Twinkle was a fairy and George was her dog. From 1954–1960, Lettie was director of the Oakland Recreation Department's Vagabond Puppets, touring the local parks in the summer. During this time, she mentored future teen puppeteers including Frank Oz and Jerry Juhl.

Inspired by Perry Dilley, Wolo, Burr Tilstrom and Marcel Marceau, Lettie was known for her sensitive puppet manipulation and storytelling. Her iconic book *A Manual of Hand Puppet Manipulation* is a classic. Lettie was Regional Puppet Director and on the boards of the Puppeteers of America and UNIMA-USA. Labeled as the "Godmother of Puppetry," she nurtured and mentored the careers of Lewis Mahlmann, Randal Metz, Michael and Valerie Nelson and countless members of the Puppeteers of America.

SKY HIGHCHIEF
1979

Sky Highchief
1929–1990

Career: 1945–1990. Ralph Emory, better known by his professional moniker of Sky Highchief, decided he wanted to be a puppeteer after seeing the Tony Sarg Marionettes. While working as a dancer and skater in the Ice Follies, Ralph became an interim puppeteer on the original *"Howdy Doody"* show. This led to him joining the famous Suzari Marionette troupe of New York City. While working on such shows as *"Holiday on Ice"* and *"Ice Vogues,"* he became an expert on creating costumes, wigs and headpieces. Under the name of Ralph Emory, he worked on Michael Myerberg's 1954 stop motion animation classic, *"Hansel & Gretel."* After the film was completed, Myerberg asked Ralph to create marionettes of the stop motion puppets and mount a touring production utilizing the famous film soundtrack.

In 1960, the quest for puppetry led Ralph to Los Angeles and to his beloved Hollywood. Now known as Sky Highchief, he created the wigs for Sid and Marty Krofft's *"Les Poupées de Paris"* puppet extravaganza. Sky had a passion for creating sculpted marionettes of Hollywood stars. Soon he found himself designing scores of wax sculptures for the Movieland Wax Museum and other well known waxworks, including figures of Johnny Carson, Mae West, Elizabeth Taylor and Liberace. Like most marionette artists in Southern California, Sky created a spectacular Las Vegas night club revue act — his was titled *"Hooray for Hollywood."* After that came the inevitable cruise ship productions and shorter versions of his revue show.

The Sky Highchief Marionettes performed at Magic Mountain and many of the Six Flags amusement parks. Fate eventually reunited Sky with his old friend Howdy Doody, when he manipulated the marionette for a special appearance on the *"Happy Days"* television show. Sky was known for taking the proceeds from his appearances and using them to create more and more dazzling costumes for each puppet likeness he created. Many of them were never performed or seen by the public.

FRANK & DOROTHY HAYWARD
1953

Frank & Dorothy Hayward
Unknown–1956 & 1927–2019

Career: 1945–1959. Frank and Dorothy Hayward were appointed the first directors of the Storybook Puppet Theater at Children's Fairyland in 1956. The Oakland couple were popular entertainers who used both puppetry and magic in their Hayward Marionettes shows. They had just started running the theater, and were in their 3rd month, when Frank suffered a heart attack and died. At that time Dorothy had just given birth to their first child, while Frank was in the process of building *"Wizard of Oz"* for the Hayward troupe. Not knowing much about building puppets, Dorothy turned to the fledgling San Francisco Puppet Guild and asked for their help in fulfilling the theater contract until she could find other means. Roberta Mack, Marian Derby and Lewis Mahlmann supplied productions that she ran at the attraction in 1956.

In 1957, Dorothy hired Bob Mills, who had just arrived from Hawaii, to build new shows. Dorothy was then offered the position of Programs Director at Fairyland while overseeing the puppet theater and teaching puppet classes to young children. By year's end Bob was hired away by Walt Disney to perform at Disneyland, and Dorothy was looking for help once again. Tony Urbano was just out of the army at the time, and settled into the theater. After a year, Dorothy retired and Tony became the second official Puppet Theater Director in 1959.

After retiring, Dorothy moved to Detroit. She married Gil Oden, the puppetry curator of the Detroit Institute of Art, where for many summers Fairyland puppet shows had performed.

During her tenure at Fairyland, Dorothy created the annual "Puppet Fair." The first fair was established to honor Frank and the newly opened theater. Since 1956, the park and members of the San Francisco Puppet Guild have hosted puppet weekends every August.

SHARI LEWIS
with Lamb Chop & Charlie Horse
1960

Shari Lewis
1933–1998

Career: 1946–1998. Shari Lewis (Phyllis Naomi Hurwitz) has been described as the "first lady of American ventriloquism." Her puppets and work have been seen and loved by millions of Americans through the venue of television. Teaching children good values was at the core of her philosophy. It has been said she experimented with child psychology through television.

Shari was a professional magician, dancer, singer, acrobat, juggler, pianist, violinist, and of course, a ventriloquist. Her mother and her father, a professional magician, schooled her in many entertainments. Famed New York marionettist Ascanio Spolidoro taught her puppetry, while ventriloquists John W. Cooper, Dick Bruno, Roy Douglas and Stanley Burns shared the secrets of ventriloquism.

In 1952, on Arthur Godfrey's "*Talent Scouts*" show, Shari won 1st place for her ventriloquism. Inspired by Paul Winchell, Shari used large cumbersome wood puppets such as Sampson, Randy Rocket and Taffy Twinkle in her early work. In 1956, her first soft puppet, Lamb Chop, debuted on "*Captain Kangaroo*." Soon, Charlie Horse and Hush Puppy joined her on shows such as "*Shariland*" (1956–58), "*The Shari Lewis Show*" (1960–63), and "*The Shari Show*" (1975–76). She then returned to public television with "*Lamb Chop's Play-along*" (1992–97) and "*The Charlie Horse Music Pizza*" (1998–99). Shari, the winner of 12 Emmys for television broadcasting, made 19 home videos such as "*Lamb Chop's Chanukah*," "*Lamb Chop in the Haunted Studio*," "*Shari's Passover Surprise*"; and wrote over 60 children's books. She even had her own series on BBC1 in England on Sunday nights.

Other highlights include performances at the White House, for Queen Elizabeth, and at many casinos in Las Vegas. Shari also conducted over 100 symphony orchestras. Her daughter Mallory Lewis, who was a creative consultant and writer for her mother, now performs Lamb Chop. Tony Urbano, one of Lewis' puppet makers, once recalled advice Shari gave him: "One laugh is worth a thousand sequins!"

BRUCE CHESSÉ
Urashima Taro
1993

Bruce Chessé
1935–present

Career: 1948–present. Bruce Kemble Chessé is the son of famed marionette artist Ralph Chessé, and brother to Dion. His career began at 13 when he took an active interest in his father's art. Bruce, a graduate of San Francisco State, holds a Bachelor's degree in Anthropology, and a Master's degree in the Creative Arts. He is known as an international puppet designer, manipulator, actor, director, teacher and author. Throughout his puppet history, he has traveled the world teaching and performing. Bruce is also a member of SAG-AFTRA (Screen Actors Guild & American Federation of Television and Radio Artists).

Bruce calls himself a resource specialist in educational puppetry, with an uncanny gift for sculptural shapes and an ability to use puppets for communication and problem solving. Bruce had his hands (pardon the pun) in many aspects of puppetry in the San Francisco Bay Area from 1948–1983. He was a popular director of Oakland's Vagabond Puppets from 1970–1972, has worked with many police departments teaching kids relevant issues and safety with puppets, taught puppetry with handicapped children and the Mentally Gifted Minor Program, taught nutritional education with puppets in the schools, and wrote the popular 1975 "how to" book: *Puppets From Polyfoam: Sponge-ees!* with Beverly Armstrong illustrating. He also served as a consultant in the field of puppetry in education, with the Puppeteers of America.

In 1982, Bruce moved to Oregon and became the Artistic Director of the Oregon Puppet Theatre with partner Susan Barthel. They have been featured in the Price Stern Sloan's famous *"Wee Sing"* videos. Since then, Bruce has published more books and articles on advancing the art of puppetry such as *Making and Using Puppets in the Primary Grades,* and *Puppets for Dreaming and Scheming* with Judy Sims. He is now semi-retired and has taken on the exhaustive job of running Chessé Arts Ltd., which is dedicated to the preservation and exhibition of his father's works.

Above
BOB CLAMPETT
1950s

Right
DAWS BUTLER
1949

Bob Clampett, Daws Butler & Stan Freberg
1913–1984, 1916–1988 & 1926–2015

Career: 1949–1955. What happens when three of the most imaginative minds in California get together? *"Time for Beany"!* This brainchild of animator Robert Emerson Clampett and vocal artists Daws Butler and Stan Freberg took the fledgling television airwaves by storm. Bob Clampett, a graduate of the Otis Art Institute, was the creator of the show. Bob's cartoon/puppet legacy is impressive. As an animator and director at Warner Bros. Cartoon Studio, as well as Disney, Bob was responsible for the creation of many of our cartoon character favorites and the *Looney Tunes* and *Merrie Melodies* cartoons.

Charles Dawson Butler also left quite a legacy. Besides being a puppeteer, Daws voiced Yogi Bear, Huckleberry Hound, Quick Draw McGraw, Snagglepuss, Captain Crunch and countless others. His work with Hanna-Barbera Studios and advertising companies has inspired the careers of many future voiceover artists.

And Stanley Freberg is legendary for his comedy records and song stylings. Who could ever forget *"St George and the Dragonet,"* that great comic routine he and Butler recorded lampooning television's crime classic *"Dragnet"*?

"Time for Beany," which first aired on KTLA Los Angeles in 1949, is the puppet adventure story of Beany and his uncle Captain Horatio Huffenpuff, who spoil the evil plans of dastardly Dishonest John. Luckily, Cecil the Seasick Sea Serpent is on their side. The show was puppeteered by Butler and Freberg, who also supplied all the voices. Much in the style of Jay Ward's *"Fractured Fairytales,"* the pun-filled 15-minute adventures appealed to an audience of all ages. Due to its almost instant popularity, the show was elongated to 30 minutes and, via kinescope, was distributed on KTTV nationally by the Paramount Television Network. During its seven-year run, the show won three distinguished Emmy Awards. Cecil's catchphrase, "I'm coming Beanyboy!" was long a popular cry on playgrounds by youngsters wearing stylish beanie hats.

Mel Helstein

Career: 1948–1990. Melyn Helstein was a Professor Emeritus in the Department of Theatre Arts at UCLA where he taught from 1948–1986. Mel was widely respected for his support of new play programs, his development of one of the nation's leading puppet theater programs (which he started teaching in 1954), and his wide publication of research on puppet theater. Mel designed, produced, directed or performed in over 80 puppet productions. In 1976 Mel curated, at the Museum of Cultural History, UCLA, the exhibit: Asian Puppets: Wall of the World. He served two terms as president of UNIMA-USA.

Alton Wood

Career: 1949–2001. Alton was partner and co-founder of Bob Baker Marionette Productions, the longest running puppet theater in Los Angeles. He was a performer in, as well as the business manager of, this unique marionette organization, developing the idea of performing marionettes in the round with an audience seated on the floor. Alton was an accomplished pianist with a B.A. in music from the University of Texas. He studied piano in New York City before relocating to Los Angeles, where he performed Bob's puppets in countless films, commercials and television productions.

ᔐ 5 ᔑ

1950–1959

THE BEGINNING of the '50s found us once again involved in a foreign war. The Korean War, which lasted from 1950–53, frequently sent our youth to battle and upset the framework of family life anew. America once again sought solace in a remembered childhood. When the war was over, soldiers returned to the comfort of family strength… and television. The first color TV was sold in 1953. '50s television brought us fear of communism and the black listings from the McCarthy hearings, the beginning of the Cold War with Russia, and a terror of atomic bombs and mutant alien life forms found in U.F.O.s. Popular at the movie theaters were films like the puppet movie *"Lili"* based on Paul Gallico's *The Love of Seven Dolls*, the science fiction monster *"Godzilla,"* and heroic-fantasy adventures such as *"20,000 Leagues Under The Sea."* Another favorite film genre during this time period was mystery, such as Alfred Hitchcock's repertoire, and countless American cowboy films and tales. Science fiction and fantasy novels also found a willing hold in the American imagination. *The Chronicles of Narnia, The Martian Chronicles, Fahrenheit 451*, and anything about aliens and robots were a must read. And Hollywood and the Californian puppeteers were ready to stoke these smoldering flames of imagination.

Television was a hit! And people loved to watch puppets. *Howdy Doody* had an audience of over 15 million viewers. And as television searched desperately for shows to fill their open time slots, puppeteers and "kiddie" hosts flourished. There were spacemen, cowboys, clowns and fatherly puppeteers who traveled to cartoon kingdoms and other film worlds with their trusty puppet companions by their side. Hosts included Bruce Sedley and King Fuddle, Buffalo Bob and Howdy Doody, Captain Kangaroo and Mr. Moose, as well as Shari Lewis, Paul Winchell, Paul Ashley and all their friends. On television, puppets and their puppeteer hosts taught us about lands based on fairytale and literature, about animal care and safety, and acted as our second family. They allowed people to escape from the everyday problems, even if only for a little while. Vaudeville had slowly come to an end in the '30s due to the introduction of moving pictures. And it's ironic that most vaudevillians left the stage proscenium with their acts, to reappear with them on the television proscenium. A popular comedian once joked, "When vaudeville died, television was the box they buried it in."

The '50s was also the age of amusement parks. Boardwalks, playgrounds and amusement lands opened up their gates to fun-seeking families — and to puppets! In 1950, Oakland created Children's Fairyland, a playground based on children's literature and nursery rhymes. Puppet shows were so popular at the park, in 1956 the Storybook Puppet Theater — now the oldest continuously operating puppet theater in the U.S. — was founded. And Fairyland helped inspire Walt Disney, who opened Disneyland in 1955. In fact, Walt hired away puppeteer Bob Mills from Fairyland to run his own puppet theater in Disneyland. Soon, California puppeteers found themselves working at playgrounds, piers and amusement parks all over the state.

But besides the pop culture and amusement venues that began the careers of many puppeteers, what was influencing the world of puppetry at that time? Puppeteers of America guilds were forming across the nation, and that certainly created a sharing of ideas with like-minded individuals. The San Francisco Guild was founded in 1954 but did not become an official guild until 1961. The Los Angeles guild, founded in 1956, was chartered in 1957. The San Diego Guild was founded in 1957 and chartered in 1961. Also in 1957, California hosted the first Puppeteers of America National Festival to come to the West Coast. But those weren't the only opportunities producing puppet careers. There were two important puppetry writings inspiring puppet enthusiasts. The most important was the publication of *Marionettes, a Hobby for Everyone* by Les and Mabel Beaton in 1948. This book showed hobbyists how to make puppets and produce their own shows. It even had patterns! The puppeteers who were inspired by this tome, of which there are many, called themselves "The Beaton Babies," and the book "The Beaton Bible." And equally important was the *Stevens Correspondence Course of Puppetry*, launched in 1957 by Martin Stevens. This 20-session, by-mail course included blueprints for creating marionettes both simple and complex. And of course, Martin answered all questions by mail.

Not since the 1930s had puppetry seen such an influx of new visionaries of the puppet theater. In Los Angeles, Bob Baker, who always wanted to open a school for puppetry, was quickly gathering this new talent to work for his company, while Jean Cease was getting ready to open the first of her three Geniiland Puppet Theaters to perform for parties and events. And a new form of stop motion by Art Clokey, called claymation, was supplying jobs and know-how for the hungry television puppeteers. In the San Francisco Bay Area Lettie Connell Schubert was re-inventing playground performances with her Oakland's Vagabond Puppets while Ralph Chessé was creating hundreds of marionettes for his local television productions. Through the magic of television, and the ready exposure of puppetry in the parks and schools, the puppet was becoming our childhood friend. In fact, toy companies were making replicas of many of these puppets and selling them to happy children. By the end of the next decade we would marvel at how the puppet transformed from being our friend to our teacher as *"Sesame Street"* entered our homes.

BENJAMIN BLAKE
with Wizard
1961

Benjamin Blake
circa 1933–present

Career: 1950–1969. Benjamin Blake was a puppet artist, painter, sculptor and teacher of creative arts. He started building puppets as a hobby in high school and took the Bay Area by storm in the early 1960s. Benjamin studied art at the Phoenix School in New York, the Rhode Island School of Design and the Boston Museum School of Fine Arts. He went on to teach art at the Boston Museum of Fine Arts before moving to California. His beautifully sculpted puppets were defined by the elegant angles he designed into his puppet heads. While living in Massachusetts he was employed by the Whiting Milk Company, which paid to have his Concert Puppet Theater traveling wagon present shows at schools and events. Benjamin also performed many puppet concert pieces with the Boston Symphony Orchestra, under the company name Studio 9 Marionette Theater.

Benjamin's finest work was for a television special. In 1962, he performed Benjamin Britten's children's opera *"The Little Sweep"* with puppets on KPIX, channel 5. The special was hosted by Ray Bolger, one of the stars of *"The Wizard of Oz."* Using local San Francisco puppeteers Lewis Mahlmann, Luman Coad and Marian Derby, his original creations performed to a recording of the London opera by Britten's original child cast.

Benjamin taught painting to adults at the Creative Workshop of Los Altos, and was an inspiration for puppeteer Elizabeth Luce, who as a young child attended his puppet classes at the Los Altos school where he taught dramatics.

In the early 1970s, Benjamin sold many of his puppets along with his portfolio to Lewis Mahlmann at Fairyland, and quietly vanished. It's rumored that he took up a simpler, less object driven life and gave up his possessions to focus on art. His puppets are still used in performances at the Storybook Puppet Theater in Oakland.

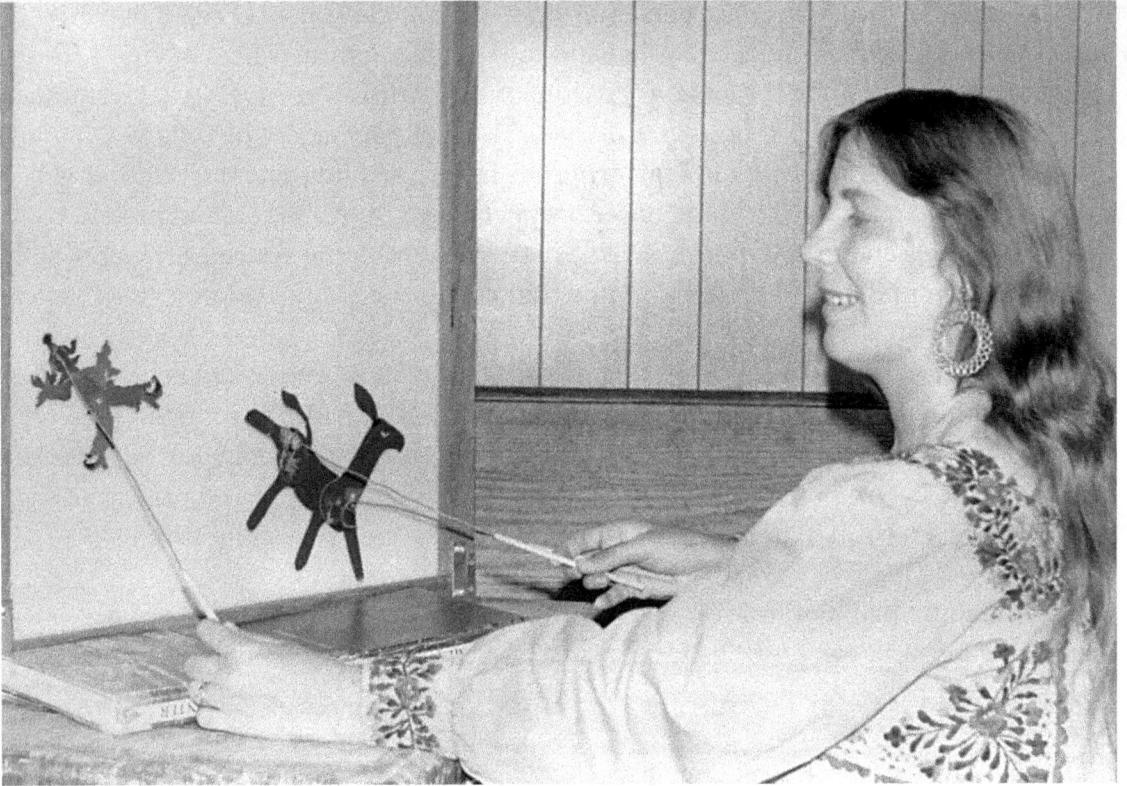

ELISHEVA HART
1977

Elisheva Hart
1939–present

Career: 1950–present. Elizabeth Hart (Polus), known as Elisheva, began her puppet career when she was eleven. During childhood she often suffered from asthma and made up stories while puppeteering her teddy bear in protective isolation. In 1950 she attended a puppet class in San Diego. Her teachers, Mr. and Mrs. Ed Churchman, quickly recruited her as a Junior Member of the Puppeteers of America. During her career she has progressed from hand puppets, to shadow puppets, to table top puppetry, and finally storytelling with puppet friends.

Elisheva has an A.S. degree in Theater Technology and has written many articles on various forms of puppetry. Her favorite style is shadow puppets. She has studied Indonesian Wayang Kulit with Javanese master dhalang Pak Oemartopo, and taken classes from shadow legend Lotte Reiniger in Canada. Elisheva has been the Shadow Consultant for the Puppeteers of America, and has written several booklets on lighting, shadows and bilingual puppetry.

In her early career, Elisheva did one-woman shows as the Folk Puppet Theater. She would tell puppet stories dressed as Mary Poppins or perform her popular *"The Dinosaur Show"* and shadow puppetry. In the 1970s she partnered with storyteller Ruthmarie Sheehan to form Story Wagon Puppets. Their theater, shaped like a stagecoach wagon, toured Santa Cruz libraries performing shows such as *"Tinderbox"* and their most famous *"Look What I Can Do!,"* an original tale funded by a government grant teaching students about children with disabilities being mainstreamed into their neighborhood schools. The 1980s found her partnered with musician David Whitaker, presenting tabletop puppetry as the Dragonfly Puppets. Shows such as *"Chakra Tales," "Groovy Alice in Wonderland"* and *"Brer Rabbit Tales"* were musical, fun and toylike.

Elisheva is still active with the San Francisco Puppet Guild. She hopes her articles help inspire a future generation of puppeteers in California.

BOB MILLS
Tinkerbell's Toy Shoppe, Disneyland
1958

Bob Mills
1936–present

Career: 1950–1961. Robert J. Mills was born in Los Angeles to a military family, moving around to wherever his father was stationed. While a high school student he found a hobby and a future in puppetry. A natural sculptor, he continued to improve his marionettes, and went from the school talent show to touring professionally. When his dad was stationed in Hawaii, Bob auditioned for a children's show on Kona television called *"Just Kids"* and won the role of puppeteer, alongside kiddie host Chubby Rowland. To make extra money for college he took on another role, doubling as the show's resident clown "Kola." In 1957, Bob left the show and settled in the San Francisco Bay Area. He was quickly hired by Dorothy Hayward, director of the newly opened Children's Fairyland's Storybook Puppet Theater, to be her puppet assistant and fabricator. After a year on the job, Walt Disney visited Fairyland and, impressed by Bob, hired the Bob Mills Marionettes to create the puppet theater at the Tinkerbell Toy Shoppe in Disneyland.

 For the next four and a half years Bob produced puppet shows in Fantasyland. His duties included performing eight shows a day, six days a week, as well as demonstrating puppets for sale. He finally decided to put away the puppets in 1961 and apply for an apprenticeship in makeup design with William Tuttle at M.G.M. Studios. Since then, Bob has worked for many studios and films, including doing makeup for fantasy classics like *"Planet of the Apes," "The Seven Faces of Doctor Lao"* and *"Batman."* Today he is the personal makeup artist for such stars as Michael Keaton, Bette Midler, Richard Gere and Julia Roberts.

On special occasions Bob still pulls out the puppets to perform for charities (and his grandchildren). On a side note, when he left Disneyland, he stored his puppets with Bob Baker. Eventually Baker's theater bought the marionettes and they continue to perform in Bob Baker shows today.

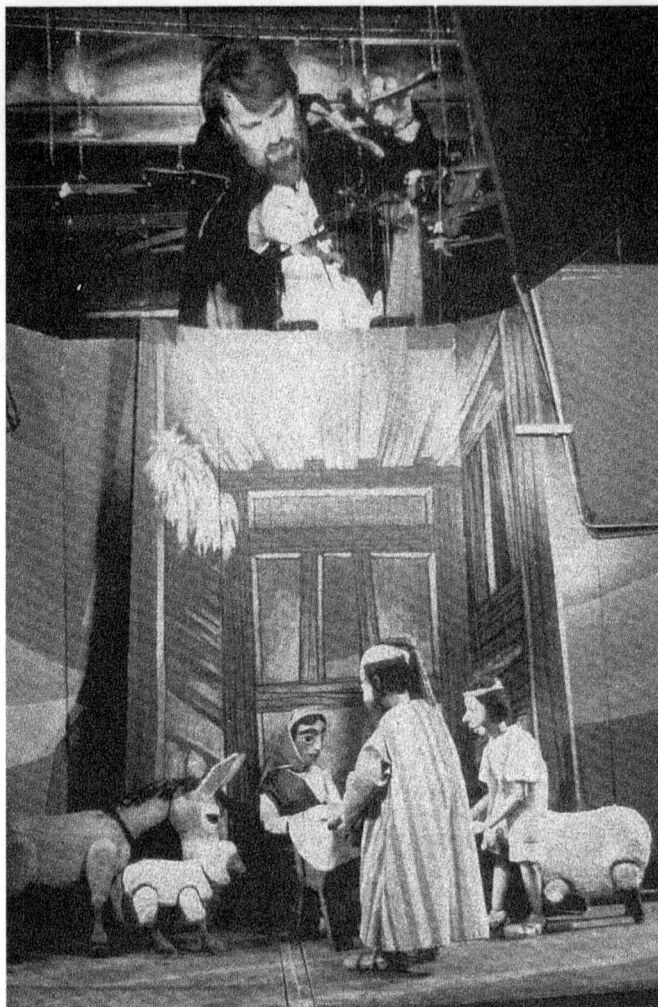

ROLAND SYLWESTER
1976

Roland Sylwester
1925–1998

Career: 1950–1998. Roland Sylwester and his wife Verna, school teachers at various Lutheran schools in California, found their calling by presenting religious teachings through puppetry. An artist and teacher, Roland was very impressed by a student marionette musical he saw at the California College of Arts and Crafts in Oakland in 1950. He realized the marionette could be used as a teaching aid. Devouring Marjorie Batchelder's *Puppet Theatre Handbook,* he set about carving his first puppets. Their early shows were more mainstream: *"Sylwester the Cat," "Alice in Wonderland"* and even a musical about freeways and pollution called *"And Then Came the Smog."* But that changed in 1966 when Roland was asked to present a religious-based show. He realized puppets were a tested way of teaching church morals and lessons. His shows were filled with what he called "reverent humor," never poking fun at spiritual things, only at our own human frailties.

Very soon the couple were presenting shows all over America for churches and spiritual events, as the Marionette Theatre of the Word. Roland wrote two popular books on theological puppetry, *Teaching Bible Stories More Effectively with Puppets* and *The Puppet and the Word,* plus many articles on the use of puppetry in the programs of the church. Roland and Verna produced close to fifteen religious puppet films including the popular titles *"He Really Lives!"* and *"I Will Take You to the Christ Child."* Roland's television specials have included *"The Stableboy's Christmas,"* based on his nativity play, and the KABC Los Angeles popular series *"Sunrise Ways,"* for which he received an Emmy nomination. He also created a series of humorous parables teaching basic Christian values titled *"The Bippity Boppity Bunch."* His shows were always filled with whimsy and were visually spellbinding.

In his spare time, Roland taught art and sculpture, and designed award winning Tournament of Roses parade floats from 1970—1974. He is remembered as saying "The idea of puppets in today's church may sound radical and new, but the association of puppetry and religion is as old as the recorded history of puppetry."

JIM GAMBLE
1995

Jim Gamble
1937–2016

Career: 1951–2016. James Gamble first decided he wanted to be a puppeteer when his mother brought him an article written by Bil Baird, from a *Woman's Day* magazine, in 1951. That year he built his first marionette. He was blown away when he saw his first professional puppet show, three years later, by Daniel Llords.

While attending the University of Oklahoma, Jim performed as the Jim Gamble Marionettes at Santa's Workshop, North Pole, in Colorado during the summers. After graduation, he served five years in the Air Force, stationed in Europe. He used this time to study the techniques of foreign puppeteers. In 1966, after being discharged, he settled in California and for 17 years he was a captain for Continental Airlines, while still pursuing his puppetry hobby on the side. Now he had the best of both worlds, a pilot by day and a puppeteer all over the world by night. In 1983 he established Jim Gamble Puppet Productions.

Jim received numerous awards for the library of puppet videos he produced. His titles include *"Peer Gynt,"* *"Nutcracker,"* and *"Hansel & Gretel."* Jim was a puppet consultant to Disney World and Disneyland, and created puppets for Disney parades and shows. He also did puppet work for film and television, and was a featured performer at many world puppetry festivals. Jim was honored with an UNIMA Citation of Excellence, and in 1991, the President's Award from the Puppeteers of America. He helped mentor the careers of Roger Mara, Hobey Ford, Greg Ballora, Christine Papalexis, Elizabeth Luce and Phillip Huber.

Jim will always be remembered for his remarkable smile and his willingness to share information, skills, new products and fellowship.

LEWIS MAHLMANN
1963

Lewis Mahlmann
1927–2014

Career: 1951–2014. Lewis Roy Mahlmann was born and raised in Chicago, where he was a friend of the famous Burr Tillstrom. As a child he presented puppet shows with marionettes bought at toy stores. He served in the Navy during World War II, and then sold real estate in San Francisco. In 1951, the book *Marionettes, a Hobby for Everyone* changed his life. From that point on Lewis managed his own puppet theater company, the Lilliputian Players. An accomplished singer, dancer, actor, painter and doll maker, he did very well at classical adult puppet theater. Lewis served two terms as President of the Puppeteers of America (1961 & 1963), one with Jim Henson as his Vice President. He was given the President's Award in 1988 and was a charter member of the San Francisco Puppetry Guild.

In 1967, Lewis became Master Puppeteer at the Children's Fairyland Storybook Puppet Theater. From 1967 to 2005, he brought to life through puppetry children's tales, classic novels, ballets, operas and original stories for the children of the San Francisco Bay Area. In 1990, Lewis and his apprentice/partner Randal Metz formed M Plus M Productions and co-directed the theater. His puppet patterns are available in the book *Making Puppets the Fairyland Way*. Lewis and his life partner, David Cadwalader Jones, also wrote five books of puppet plays from Fairyland and the Lilliputian Players. Four of these are out of print, and sought after by collectors.

Lewis also taught puppetry for several years at San Francisco State University, made and performed puppets for commercials and television, and mentored the careers of John Gilkerson, Michael Earl, Kevin Menegus, Jesse Vail, Evy Berman Wright and Alice Dinnean. In 2003, the Storybook Puppet Theater was dedicated to Lewis, and April 6, 2002 was Lewis Mahlmann Day in Oakland. In 2014, days before his death, the Oakland Heritage Alliance presented him with a Lifetime Achievement Award. He can also be found in the Arcadia Publications book: *Legendary Locals of Oakland*. Lewis' puppet shows, which numbered over 150, are still in repertoire at the Storybook Puppet Theater.

RAY & BETTY MOUNT
1956

Ray & Betty Mount
1918–2009 & 1918–2017

Career: 1951–2009. In 1950, Ray and his new wife Elizabeth settled in the San Francisco Bay Area, where the first thing they did was search out members of the newly forming San Francisco Bay Area Puppeteers Guild. Ray had an M.A. in English Literature from the University of North Carolina and a B.A. in English from Princeton. Betty was a theater major at Northwestern University School of Speech and held an M.A. from the Colorado State College of Education. Prior to marrying Ray, she had been a Navy WAVE during World War II, and also taught English, Drama and Theater Arts in Colorado, Nevada and Washington State. It's no wonder that almost all of the shows they created were focused on adapting Elizabethan plays into modern puppet shows. Betty was the director, voice coach and morale builder, while Ray was the main performer.

Through intellectual shows such as *"Sinbad the Sailor," "Reynard the Fox,"* and George Peele's *"The Old Wives Tale"* (renamed *"The White Bear")*, the couple sought to use puppetry in a creative, theatrical format (although they also tackled classic fairytales like *"Rapunzel.")*.

For the ten years they lived in California, the couple performed their art whenever possible. The Mount Puppets had been popular entertainers at Children's Fairyland since 1952, and were part of the first "Puppet Fair" at Fairyland in 1956. They were members of the San Francisco Bay Area Puppeteers Guild as well the Connecticut and National Guilds of Puppetry.

In 1960 Ray and Betty moved to Branford, Connecticut, where they continued to weave their magic. Ray wrote an article in the *Puppetry Journal* voicing his concern about what happens to puppets when the performer passes. His outcry inspired future puppet museums. The Mount Puppets are currently part of the collection in the Ballard Institute and Museum of Puppetry in Connecticut.

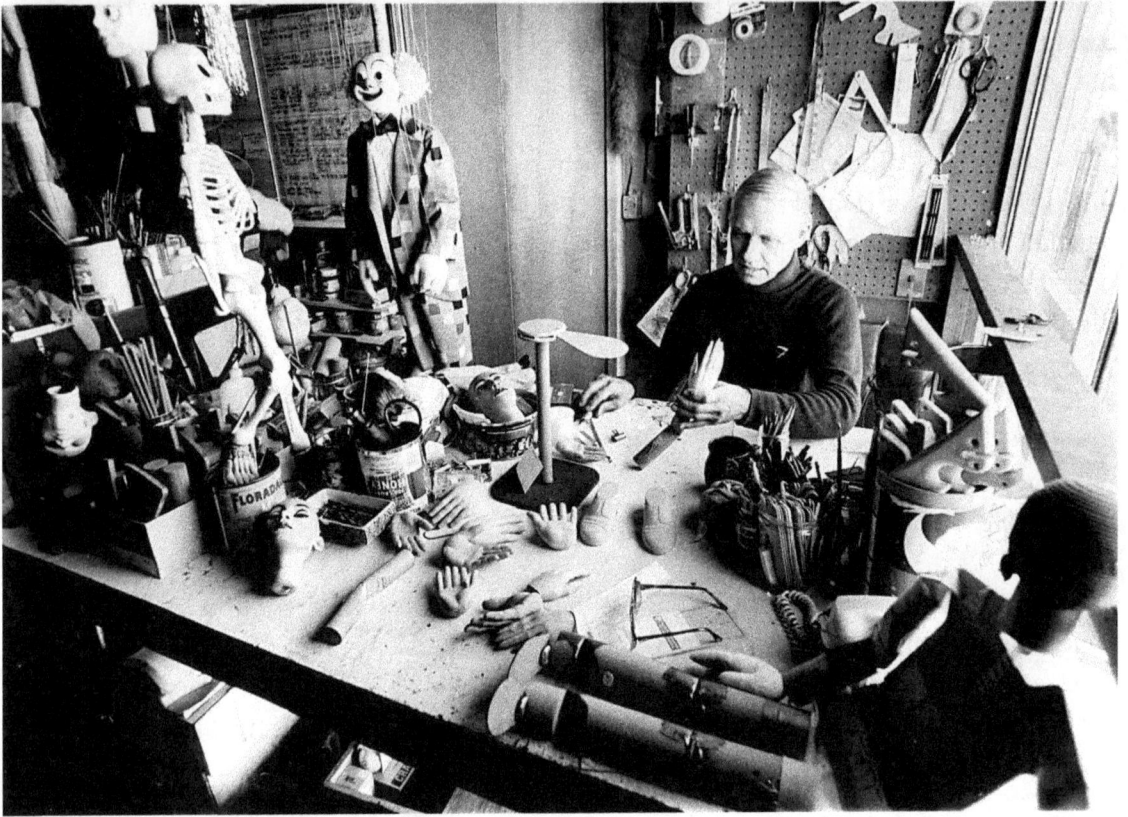

ROBERT LEROY SMITH
1980s

Robert LeRoy Smith
1927–2001

Career: 1951–2001. Robert Smith started his career in advertising and theater design before deciding to become a puppeteer. A Missouri native, he created elaborate paintings, etchings and silkscreens. Leaving his home state when he was 21, he traveled to Texas where he became a folk singer on radio and television. While working at a small theater in Houston, Robert decided to turn his artistic arts towards the puppet theater. He immersed himself in drawing, painting, lithograph and wood carving classes. In 1954, Robert moved to San Miguel de Allende in Mexico where he sold arts and crafts in a gallery while building marionettes and performing with them. He then returned to Texas and began working as an advertising artist Bullock's Department Store.

Robert continued to follow his dream of studying art and puppetry, touring Europe in 1957 to paint and perform folk music concerts, another passion. In 1962, he moved to Florence, Italy, where he was enthralled by Sicilian puppets. He returned to the U.S. in 1963, spending two years in Los Angeles before settling in San Francisco from 1965 to 1991.

In 1976 Robert formed Parnasus Puppets with his performing partner Edith Hartnett. They performed regularly at birthday parties, schools, hospitals and churches. He self-published books and pamphlets on puppetry such as *The Gun Control for Marionettes* (1983), *Fast and Easy to Make Marionette* (1984) and *Marionette Construction* (2000). In 1991 Robert moved back to Missouri.

Robert taught puppetry at the Music Arts Institute, worked with the Hazelle Project and performed for Young Audiences in the Kansas City area. He was often hired by the American Cultural Services to lecture and perform throughout the world. His marionettes are currently curated at the St. Louis Guild-run museum, the Puppetry Arts Institute, which also includes the Hazelle Puppet Museum.

BILL JONES
Aladdin
1968

Bill Jones
1935–present

Career: 1953–present. As a young boy, William Stuart Jones was given a book on rod puppets that changed his life. With rod puppets as his specialty, Bill and his twin brother began performing shows to finance themselves through college. With a Fine Arts degree from the University of Arizona, Bill specialized in makeup, wigs, costuming, doll making, appliqué, and puppetry. Armed with these assets, he moved to San Francisco in 1960 and quickly became a legend in the Bay Area. His credits include window display artist at Gump's department store and costumer for the Lamplighters' Music Theater.

Bill was Art Director for KQED, channel 9, for 20 years. He taught theatrical makeup design and costumes at San Francisco State University from 1975–1998, designed outlandish costumes and hats for Steve Silver's *"Beach Blanket Babylon"* for 20 years, and was the principal makeup artist for the San Francisco Opera from 1972–2017, working his talents on most of the opera greats.

Bill will always be remembered for the puppets he built for Dreusike-Stackpole Productions. In 1962–1963, Bill, Frank Dreusike and John Stackpole presented lavish puppet presentations of *"Aladdin and the Wonderful Lamp"* and *"Beauty and the Beast"* at the San Francisco War Memorial Veterans Building. Bill made the puppets, John directed and wrote and Frank designed and made the scenery, while members of the San Francisco Puppet Guild supplied vocals and manipulation. A film on the making of *"Beauty and the Beast"* was made for KPIX television. Bill's beautifully designed puppets are known for the theatrical makeup style painting applied to their faces. Bill also designed costumes and puppets for many of the puppet shows performed at the Storybook Puppet Theater in Oakland.

In 2017, Bill retired and moved to Arizona, but not before receiving a standing ovation for his makeup service from the patrons at his final performance for the San Francisco Opera. During his career Bill also designed the logo for the San Francisco Puppet Guild and the original hand logo for UNIMA-USA.

ART CLOKEY
with Gumby
1995

Art Clokey
1921–2010

Career: 1955–2010. Arthur Charles Clokey was born with the surname Farrington, but was adopted at age 11 by Joseph W. Clokey, a music professor and composer at Pomona College.

While studying film at the University of Southern California under the direction of Slavko Vorkapich, Art created an abstract 3½-minute animated film called *"Gumbasia"* (1955). The film, an homage to Disney's *"Fantasia,"* used clay stop-motion puppets. This film led to Art, and his first wife Ruth, forming Clokey Productions in the city of Glendora where he quickly established a crew of creative animators.

 Art's famous clay character, Gumby, debuted on *"The Howdy Doody Show."* It was so popular that Gumby (a clay boy) and Pokey (his horse) soon had their own show called *"The Gumby Show, or The Adventures of Gumby"* that ran from 1957–1969 and 1987–1989. After that came *"Davey & Goliath,"* a religious show sponsored by the Lutheran Church, aired 1961–1964 and 1971–1975. In the '80s, the popularity of Eddie Murphy's Gumby parody on *"Saturday Night Live"* sparked a revival of interest in the character. Clokey's second company, Premavision Inc., soon opened in Sausalito. 1995 saw Art creating *"Gumby: the Movie"* and all of the Gumby film archives were being aired again on Nickelodeon, Fox and the Cartoon Network.

Art's film process "Claymation," or as he called it "Trimensional Animation", utilized stop motion puppetry with clay figures and kinesthetic film forces, establishing a new form of film puppetry that has since inspired animators such as Nick Park, the creator of *"Wallace & Gromit."* Art used a special armature for each puppet and two 16mm cameras were used to film the 13½-minute segments. A new episode was produced every two weeks. Each puppet had sets of eyes made of self-sticking shelf paper and eyebrows and mouth of plasticine clay. Art trained many young animators, a few of whom took their talents to Pixar Studios. He is also the original voice of Pokey on the show.

MOLLIE FALKENSTEIN
1976

Mollie Falkenstein
1906–1992

Career: 1955–1992. Mollie Peck Falkenstein, who was born in England and schooled in Canada, was one of puppetry's world heroes. For most of her life, she was a professional ballet dancer. She had her own school of ballet, and toured the U.S. and Canada with several ballet companies. Mollie became the premiere danseuse, or head ballerina, of the Albertina Rasch Ballet, performing at the opening of the Ziegfeld Theater in "*Rio Rita*" in 1927. This led her to a job as a ballerina in the famous Ziegfeld Follies. She also danced in MGM movies, and stood in for stars such as Norma Shearer and Jeannette MacDonald.

When Mollie's daughter Jan was in elementary school, the two discovered a love of puppetry. To learn more, Mollie joined the Puppeteers of America, and this led to her training Jan and her friends. The girls performed as the Chiquita Puppeteers at many puppet events and a few even went on to careers in puppetry.

When Jan graduated from high school and left the puppets, Mollie became more immersed in the field. She founded the American Chapter of Union Internationale de la Marionnette (UNIMA-USA) as well as the Orange County Guild of Puppetry. While serving as General Secretary of UNIMA-USA, she initiated the chapter's magazine *A Propos* in 1970, which in 1995 became *Puppetry International*.

Besides her clever production of "*Goldilocks & the Three Bears,*" Mollie is best known for her finger and string ballerina puppet. This exquisite ballet puppet dancer with molded legs, attached to Mollie's fingers, had a head and arms controlled by strings. Mollie was a recipient of the Puppeteers of America's Trustees Award for Outstanding Service. In 1992, to honor her love of world puppetry, the Los Angeles Guild hosted an exhibition of puppetry at the John Wayne Airport. The exhibit, curated by Alan Cook, was called "*Puppets for Mollie.*"

NANCY COLE
1958

Nancy Cole
1935–present

Career: 1956–present. Nancy H. Cole has a M.A. from Stanford University with a B.F.A. from Carnegie-Mellon University in Drama & Dramatics/Theater Arts. Her thesis was on Guignol, a prominent puppet character in France with a personality much akin to Punch (not to be confused with Grand Guignol, the theater of naturalistic horror). Nancy, who is fluent in French, performed her Guignol show at the prestigious B. Altman and Co. on 5th Avenue in New York under her company name "Theater of the Little Hand." After leaving New York, she settled in Palo Alto, California.

Nancy has appeared many times on the *"Captain Kangaroo"* show and the *"Today Show."* When CBS television needed extra coverage for the Gemini 9 space landing, they asked Nancy to puppeteer a marionette of the classic NASA spaceship, trying to fill time along-side newscaster Walter Cronkite, while the landing was continually delayed. In 1976 she created Puppet Studio Theater (PST!) in Palo Alto to offer adults and children in the local area a live puppet "experience." At PST! Nancy met and mentored Elizabeth Luce with her early puppetry work.

Nancy likes to perform original, classic and traditional shows for children and satirical revues for adults. She has taught puppetry art at several universities and colleges, including New York University, the Spence School in New York, San Jose State and the American Conservatory Theater (ACT) in San Francisco. She has also performed in many TV commercials and produced promotional puppet shows. *Puppet Theatre in Performance*, Nancy's bestselling 1978 textbook on puppetry, gives the fledgling puppeteer everything they need to know about how to produce a puppet play. The book is still available online.

Although she still loves puppetry, Nancy established a second career as a forensic document examiner and handwriting analyst.

SUSAN FRENCH
1964

Susan French
1912–2003

Career: 1956–1967. Susan French Moultrie, daughter of show business lawyer Lloyd Moultrie, grew up among and was influenced by the many vaudevillians and movie stars her father represented. She was a stage, film and television actress, an art teacher, weaver, potter and photographer as well as being a puppeteer with the French Marionettes.

A graduate of the American Academy of Dramatic Arts in New York, French endeavored to bring a theatrical flair to everything she did. During her early career she was in two Broadway plays, worked in radio and was a photographer stylist for three national magazines.

Her television credits include popular shows such as the *"Alfred Hitchcock Hour," "Dallas," "L.A. Law," "Moonlighting," "Quantum Leap"* and *"Star Trek: The Next Generation."* Films include *"Jaws 2," "House," "Flatliners," "The Sting," "Airport 1975,"* and her most famous, *"Somewhere in Time,"* with Christopher Reeve. Susan played the older Elise McKenna, an older Edwardian Era stage actress and lover of Reeve's character.

In the late 1950s and early 1960s, Susan had a puppet theater at her home in Santa Monica. Producing a series of dramatized Greek myths with marionettes, she toured California sharing her magic. In 1964 she published *Presenting Marionettes*, by Art Horizons, Inc. This book, readily available in most public libraries during the '70s, launched the careers of many young puppet enthusiasts. Those inspired by the Muppets could now find a book that showed them, step by step with photos and illustrations, how to build their own puppet. French not only wrote the book and made the puppets, she illustrated and photographed each step herself. The textbook also includes a journey into the history of world puppetry.

JERRY JUHL
with Kermit the Frog
1970s

Jerry Juhl
1938–2005

Career: 1956–2005. Jerome Ravn Juhl moved from St. Paul, Minnesota to Menlo Park, California, when he was 14. He received a degree in theater from San Jose State College. As a teen, he organized his friends into the Menlo Marionettes. This led to the group joining the San Francisco Guild and performing at the very first "Puppet Fair" at Children's Fairyland in 1956. During 1958, Jerry had a popular puppet show on local station KNTV called *"Sylvie & Pup."* He was soon working alongside Lettie Connell Schubert for the Oakland Recreation Department's Vagabond Puppets. When she left the program, he took over and hired Oakland teen Frank Oznowicz to perform with him.

In 1961 Lettie was artistic director for a national puppet festival in Asilomar. She hired Jerry and the Vagabond players to present their current summer show. Jim Henson, the vice president of Puppeteers of America, attended the festival looking for talented puppeteers, and the rest is history!

Jerry packed his bag and left for New York to help Jim on his *"Sam and Friends"* show. His soon to be wife Susan Doerr, daughter of the Mayor of San Jose, joined him at Henson Associates in 1963. The fledgling company at that time consisted of Jim, Frank Oz (who joined after graduating high school), Don Sahlin, Jerry and Susan. Although trained to be a puppeteer, Jerry soon found writing was his true passion. He wrote all of Jim's television specials such as *"The Great Santa Claus Switch," "The Frog Prince"* and *"The Muppet Musicians of Bremen."* In addition to penning all the other Muppet venues, Jerry also wrote the films *"The Muppet Movie," "The Great Muppet Caper,"* and the *"The Muppets Christmas Carol"* and *"The Muppets Treasure Island."* From 1976-1981 he was head writer of *"The Muppet Show,"* and along with his wife Susan was writer and producer of *"Fraggle Rock"* from 1983-1987. Jerry also wrote all the segments for the Muppet characters on *"Sesame Street"* from 1969-1975.

Jerry won several Emmys for his writings, and also taught scripting seminars at colleges.

Frank Oz
with Miss Piggy
1977

Frank Oz
1944–present

Career: 1956–present. Frank Richard Oznowicz was born in Hereford, England, but was raised in Belgium and Oakland. He attended Oakland Technical High School and Oakland Junior College in hopes of being a journalist, but fate had other plans. Frank spent many years performing with his family, the Oznowicz Marionettes, at the Yosemite campground and other social events. When Children's Fairyland opened, he found a home there working alongside Dorothy Hayward and Tony Urbano. He and Tony built the puppets for a performance of Ravel's *"Mother Goose Suite"* by the Oakland Symphony Orchestra.

In 1960, Frank, and partner Jerry Juhl, directed the Vagabond Puppets of Oakland. The two performed at the Puppeteers of America National Festival, where Jim Henson saw them and hired them for the Muppets. Still in school, Frank stayed another year with Vagabond and finished his education. At 17, he created and performed *"Pinocchio"* for the Oakland Recreation Department Junior Theater and was a charter member of the San Francisco Puppet Guild. He credits his parents, the guild and Lettie Connell Schubert with mentoring him in puppetry.

Frank's history with the Muppets is well documented. Some of his most famous puppet characters are Grover, Cookie Monster and Burt from *"Sesame Street,"* as well as Miss Piggy, Fozzie Bear, Animal and Sam the Eagle from *"The Muppet Show."* In 1980, he gave life to one of the most famous fictional characters in history, the Jedi Master Yoda. Although retired from his other creations, Frank is still actively voicing and manipulating this *Star Wars* legend. For Children's Fairyland's 20th birthday, in 1970, he performed at the puppet theater with Burt and Cookie Monster. What the park thought would be a few kids attending turned into thousands!

Late in his career, with Jim Henson's help, Frank decided to become a film director. Working with Jim, he directed *"The Muppets Take Manhattan,"* and *"The Dark Crystal,"* and later *"Little Shop of Horrors,"* *"Dirty Rotten Scoundrels,"* *"The Indian in the Cupboard,"* *"In & Out"* and *"Muppet Guys Talking: Secrets Behind the Show,"* to name a few. Frank has received numerous Emmys and other awards for his work.

BRUCE SEDLEY
with King Fuddle
1959

Bruce Sedley
1925–2012

Career: 1956–2012. Bruce, known to thousands of baby boomers as "Skipper Sedley" (KRON-TV 1957- 59) or "Sir Sedley" (KTVU-TV 1962–1964) along with his well-known ventriloquist dummy "King Fuddle," was famous for his distinctive voice and crazy inventions. Sedley was a popular radio disc jockey and cartoon ventriloquist host on television in the San Francisco Bay Area. Bruce's vent dummy family was built by Al Dinsdale. As Bruce usually hosted *"The Three Stooges"* shorts on TV, the famous trio actually had him and all the other national television hosts perform in one of their films, *"The Outlaws is Coming!"* in 1965. The film also starred Adam West and Nancy Kovack. When Bruce was not on television with Fuddle, he was at Children's Fairyland in Oakland greeting the young fans and telling stories.

Perhaps Bruce's greatest invention was the Fairyland "Magic Key." As a TV host, he invited children to Fairyland to tell them popular nursery tales. What he thought would be a few kids became hundreds and led to one terrific case of laryngitis. So he created a plastic key, which when put in a metal box and turned, triggered a recording that told stories. In 1958, this idea spread like wildfire. Soon zoos, museums and parks all over America were using a "key-like" system to provide educational content. Bruce's "Talking Storybooks" were even used to promote educational booths at the 1962 World's Fair. But Fairyland had it first — and still has it. Not stopping at a plastic key, Bruce also invented the first magnetic keycard that was used for security at the 1968 Democratic convention, and later in hotels and offices. But that's another story.

In 2008 Bruce visited Fairyland to celebrate the 50th anniversary of the "Magic Key" as well as King Fuddle's 600th birthday. Fans flocked to see him and their puppet friend. Bruce is survived by his puppet Fuddle, who still lives today in the San Francisco Bay Area.

CHARLES TAYLOR
with Sugar the Dog & Hansel
1965

Charles Taylor
1940–present

Career: 1956–present. When Charles William Taylor was 16, he began working with Los Angeles puppeteer Margaret Fickling. She was so impressed that she insisted he also join the Los Angeles Puppet Guild. That led to him taking a puppet class from Harry Burnett and ultimately becoming a performer, stagehand, set designer, puppet builder and close friend for Harry and his Youth Turnabout Puppet Theatre, "The Turnabouters." Through his college days and beyond, Charles helped Harry build puppets and perform new shows.

Charles received the first ever Master of Arts degree in Interdisciplinary Studies, specializing in puppetry, from Cal State Long Beach. His final project, a production of *"Everyman,"* helped him become a member of the Phi Kappa Phi honor society. Charles, who has taught all grades since 1963 before retiring, taught puppet classes at Cal State from 1972–1982.

Charles has built puppets for Betsy Brown, Gayle Schluter and Howard Mitchell. He built a Bullwinkle Moose puppet for Jay Ward that later went on to be the design of the cartoon, as well as puppets for Jay Ward's *"Watt's Gnu"* television series. Charles has toured extensively in the Los Angeles school district as well as being an "extra" manipulator for the Kroffts' *"Les Poupées de Paris."* Forman Brown wrote a number of shows for Charles to perform, including the science fiction musical *"Morning in the Zoo or Let the Apes Plan It!"* His list of inspirational puppeteers includes the Beatons, Harry Burnett, Walton and O'Rourke, Tony Urbano, Bob Bromley, René Zendejas, Bob Baker, Ralph Chessé and Blanding Sloan — a veritable "Who's Who" of puppetry.

These days, Charles teaches classes on "Longevity Stick" exercises with senior citizens. His two daughters, Emily and Carol, are following in his footsteps, performing *"Punch and Judy"* with a stage and puppets they made together.

BILL CASSADY & HELGA WILLIAMSON
Berkeley Puppeteers
1961

Bill Cassady & Helga Williamson
1933–2015 & 1931–2012

Career: 1957–2015. Bill Cassady grew up in the San Francisco/Berkeley Bay Area, and graduated from San Francisco State College with a degree in art and philosophy. He and his wife, Helga Williamson, lived in Berkeley and were participants in the vibrant bohemian/hippie movement of the 1960s and '70s. With a deep interest in world culture, Bill fashioned his shows to be viewed as plays of dramatic merit rather than variety acts. As a photographer and writer, his puppets vividly reflected the cultures he was portraying. Many of his figures have been exhibited at the Detroit Institute of Art and the Lytton Center of Visual Arts.

Helga graduated from Barnard College in New York City with a concentration in Oriental civilization and languages. She introduced Bill to the art of the puppet through her family's love of puppetry. She made her first puppet in 1947 with the Marionette Project in Detroit. Their dynamic puppet repertoire, as the Berkeley Puppeteers, included *"Coyote," "Kasper & the Pirates," "Punch & Judy," "The Witch Who Lost Her Temper"* and Moliere's *"The Imaginary Invalid."* In 1965, on KQED Channel 9, they debuted *"The Net,"* an allegorical puppet tale about a hero trapped in a rope net of illusion, wandering the Earth looking for an explanation.

Bill and Helga separated after a 12-year career to seek other avenues of expression. Helga remarried and went on to a successful career in ecology and geology, traveling and teaching through her beloved Asia.

In 1969 Bill married Mea McNeil, moved to San Anselmo, and started the Morning Glory Puppeteers. Staying with his proven tales of culture, he and his wife Mea produced such classics as *"The Magic Twins," "The Popol Vuh," "Jasper"* and *"Ananse the Spider."*

GENII
1970s

Genii
1928–present

Career: 1957–present. Jean Cease, who later changed her name to Genii because it was "more magical," was an accomplished artist, singer, dancer, puppeteer and ventriloquist. In 1956, she suddenly became responsible for supporting her two children as a single mom. To make ends meet while doing something she loved, Genii decided to build a marionette show, in a theater she designed, where children could have catered parties and imaginative events. Geniiland officially opened in a small storefront in 1958 and eventually expanded to a huge storefront/warehouse setting. For 18 years Genii, with the help of her family, managed this unique entertainment venue in Los Angeles.

Genii was always recognized by her pink hair, which she had colored long before the style became popular. She not only created a living for her family through puppetry and ventriloquism, she used it to cure a stuttering problem that had plagued her through childhood to adulthood. For all of her shows at her theater, Genii would dress in her genie garb and lead the birthday children through adventures using puppets and song.

Genii has also self published 6 books on creating easy to make marionettes under the title *From One Puppet To Another*, as well as presenting a successful marionette dinner show for several years at the El Gato Mexican Restaurant in Van Nuys. Genii has also built puppets for television and commercials as well as performing at Disneyland and in Las Vegas. She credits Harry Burnett, Charles Taylor, Bob Baker and her family as her mentors.

Genii married a religious science school church reverend, Dr. Bill Townsend, and together they founded the Light Center and Ultimate Destiny University in Sedona, Arizona. She teaches woman's workshops & classes on empowerment, writes spiritual books, and of course, uses puppetry. Her daughter, Starr-Light, is currently carrying on the family puppet tradition as Fantasymakers in Nevada, since 1978.

BLAKE MAXAM
A Day in the Forest
2000

Blake Maxam
1944–present

Career: 1959–present. Blake Maxam grew up in Southern California, and moved to the Bay Area after graduating with a degree in Theater from California State University, Northridge. In the San Francisco Bay Area, Blake became an award-winning member of Actors' Equity, a voice-over performer and a professional magician and puppeteer who, among thousands of shows, has performed many times at the famous Magic Castle in Hollywood. Blake was inspired by early television and has a great love for fantasy and classic literature and a passion for collecting the original artwork for children's book illustrations.

Blake discovered the love of puppetry after witnessing the puppet talents of Bil Baird and Bob Baker. This was followed by a family puppet production of Baird's 1961 puppet script, *"The Magic Onion."* In the Bay Area, Blake's puppet career started while working on the cruise ship *Fairsea* with San Francisco puppeteer George Buchanan's Las Vegas marionette revue. After that came a Theater Specialist position with Oakland's Parks and Recreation, beginning as a member of the famous Vagabond Puppets team, touring recreation centers and libraries for five years with puppet director Earl Rhue. Blake took over the program in 1981, and except for 1985-87 (when loaned to the City Manager's Office to help coordinate Oakland's ADA Site Survey) produced Vagabond Puppets as well as other Oakland Parks & Recreation theater projects. Blake wrote and performed Vagabond Puppets longer than anyone else, producing such popular shows as *"The Brave Little Tailor,"* *"A Day in the Forest"* (with the Three Pig Brothers: Grouchy, Harpy & Cheeky), *"Hansel & Gretel"* and *"Ms. Riding Hood."* When Blake retired, Vagabond went into hiatus due to budget cuts.

As an actor, Blake performed with many notable Bay Area companies and lent vocal talents to KQED and to recordings used in the Children's Fairyland Storybook Puppet Theater. Blake has entertained from Canada to Mexico, New York to California, and in England and France.

Marian Derby

Career: Early '50s–Late '60s. As Party Puppets, Marian specialized in hand puppet birthday and Christmas shows. She helped design the basic hand puppet pattern, with Lewis Mahlmann and Lettie Schubert, that is used to this day at Children's Fairyland and internationally. Marian's television credits include performing Miss Busy Bee on the children's show *"Brother Buzz,"* as well as working with Benjamin Blake on the KPIX Special *"The Little Sweep"* in 1962. Under the name Marian Mountain, she authored *The Zen Environment–The Impact of Zen Meditation*, which is a classic for the field of Zen meditation.

Chuck McCann

Career: 1952–2018. Charles started his career as a child actor on radio, and then became a comedian on radio, nightclubs and popular television shows. In 1952 he found a love of puppetry teaming up with Paul Ashley in New York for shows: *"Rootie Kazootie,"* *"The Laurel and Hardy Show,"* *"The Gumby Show"* and *"Captain Kangaroo,"* acting as puppeteer/sounding board to many zany puppets. When Paul and Chuck dissolved their partnership in 1967, Chuck moved to California to work for the Kroffts in *"Far Out Space Nuts"* and doing vocals for Hanna-Barbera, Disney and other animation studios.

Gayle Schluter

Career: Early 1950s–present. Gayle Schluter's interest in puppetry began in the 1930s with a W.P.A. project she joined as a little girl. In the '50s she was mentored by Harry Burnett of the Turnabout Theatre and Betsy Brown in Pasadena. Gayle "officially" joined the puppetry world right after her first West Coast National convention in 1957. She has been Executive Secretary, Regional Director and National Festival Director for the Puppeteers of America, as well as their Membership Chair for 24 years. Gayle has also served on national and local boards and festival committees, providing invaluable leadership and organizational skills.

Jack & Elva Aiken

Career: Mid '50s–present. Jack is a cinematography professor and charter member of the Los Angeles Puppetry Guild. He and Elva met in college and formed the Aiken puppets, which later became Small Wonders Company with Elva and their daughter Laura specializing in birthday party shows. In 1957, Jack and Elva assisted Tony Urbano with *"Mary Louise"* for the puppet festival at UCLA, and in the early '80s, the Aikens worked with Virginia Curtis at the Puppet Theatre Workshop in Sierra Madre. Jack produced the documentary *"A Place to Pretend,"* a film on the artistry of Virginia Austin Curtis.

Beth Fernandez

Career: 1956–present. Beth Fernandez began her career performing puppets at Maca-bob's Toy Store in Pasadena for five years, before working for fifteen years at the Ge-niiland Puppet Theater in Van Nuys. Beth was mentored by John Zweers at a YMCA puppetry class, and then by Genii, eventually becoming an independent puppeteer performing one woman shows. Beth worked with the International Puppetry Museum, on the Board of Directors, cataloguing and photographing the many puppets. She is a charter member of the Los Angeles Guild, and served as Pacific Southwest Regional Director as well as being a columnist for the *Puppetry Journal*.

Pat McCormick

Career: 1958–1995. Pat McCormick was a television personality on KGO-TV and KT-VU-TV in the San Francisco Bay Area. During his tenure he was a weatherman, a host for the *"Dialing for Dollars"* movie, and best known for being the puppeteer for *"The Charley and Humphrey Good Stuff Hour"* (1972–1976). The show first started in a small Fresno station in 1959 with puppets made by Jack Shafton. Pat performed all the voic-es for his puppet characters. KTVU-TV also filmed him performing short PSAs (Public Service Announcements) with the puppets, centering on social awareness and morality, still seen today.

$\backsim 6 \backsim$

1960-69

THE 1960s WAS A time of turbulence and change. The Vietnam War, started in 1955, was a rallying point for theatrical parody, protest and student activism. It was the time to think "outside of the box." The National Organization of Women was finding a rallying cry as women were bolstered by the Equal Pay Act of 1963 and inspired by Betty Friedan's book *The Feminine Mystique.* And when you add the Civil Rights Movement and the assassinations of John F. Kennedy, Robert Kennedy, Malcolm X and Martin Luther King Jr., you have a generation shouting *"Enough is Enough!"* It truly was time for the Summer of Love and Woodstock.

On the big screen, film blockbusters like *"Cleopatra"* and *"Dr. Zhivago"* were giving way to psychological horror cinema such as *"Psycho"* and the Hammer Horror movies, while James Bond paved the way for *"Dr. Strangelove."* And eventually even the spaghetti westerns like *"The Good, the Bad and the Ugly"* moved aside as fantasy and science fiction broke through with *"The Planet of the Apes"* and *"2001: A Space Odyssey."* Meanwhile in literature, Dr. Seuss was producing fantasy children's tales that were aspiring to teach love and moral values through whimsy. Television was also taking up the moral agenda, and trying to show the follies of humanity, with Rod Serling's award winning *"The Twilight Zone"* and Gene Roddenberry's *"Star Trek."* And who better to help illustrate all of these images than the puppet? After all, puppet master Bil Baird was a smash hit with his singing marionette goats in the 1965 film musical sensation *"The Sound of Music,"* and his famous puppet volume *The Art of the Puppet.*

In this era, puppetry was changing through a global sharing of cultural entertainment. The Union Internationale de la Marionnette, which was founded in 1929, established its American chapter, UNIMA-USA, in 1966 to help promote international understanding and friendship through the art of puppetry. One of 101 UNIMA national centers, it was founded by American puppeteers meeting in San Diego. Art and puppets merged, giving birth to political puppet groups such as Peter Schumann's Bread and Puppet Theater of Vermont. The puppet was now politically active, being used as a tool to dramatically illustrate world views and protest the Vietnam War. Marionette and hand puppet shows were turning from amusements for children to adult spectacles. Punch and Judy were reverting back to their roots and giving voice to social outrage on the streets.

And while these larger elements of puppetry were effecting change, the Puppeteers of America was growing. College puppet classes were becoming popular and Frank Ballard, in 1964, began teaching the Puppet Arts Program at the University of Connecticut. This dynamic university eventually became home to the Ballard Institute and Museum of Puppetry as well as a home for future puppeteers to achieve a MA/MFA in the puppet arts. The 1964 New York World's Fair also helped to promote puppetry in America as Bil Baird, Frank Paris, Rod Young and Sid & Marty Krofft's *"Les Poupées de Paris"* presented the spectacle of the puppet. Walt Disney also presented his own form of the puppet, audio animatronics, as *"It's A Small World," "Great Moments with Mr. Lincoln"* and *"The Carousel of Progress"* came to life at the fair. And Marjorie Batchelder McPharlin published her addendum to her husband Paul's book on historical American puppetry, *Puppets in America Since 1948.*

Meanwhile, in California, the puppet was gaining a stronger foothold. Besides Fairyland's Storybook Puppet Theater, many other permanent playhouses were being opened. San Jose's Happy Hollow Park & Zoo opened its Puppet Castle in 1961. Bob Baker and Alton Wood debuted the Bob Baker Marionette Theater in 1963. Members of the San Diego Guild of Puppetry established a permanent puppet program at the Marie Hitchcock Theater in 1964. And Pat Platt's Puppet Playhouse, in San Diego, opened its curtains in 1965. Mel Helstein, professor of puppetry at University of California in Los Angeles, had also begun teaching puppetry as an elective for college students.

California puppeteers were now expanding the many styles of the puppet to include hand, rod, marionette, shadow, puppet body costumes and giant parade amusements, as well as experimental and avant-garde presentations.

And while all of this turmoil might be unsettling, hope was on the horizon. Jim Henson, creator of *"Sam and Friends,"* helped develop a television show that would soon become a classic. *"Sesame Street"* began airing on November 10, 1969. The puppet now became a new tool to teach children education, morality and social diversity. And the puppet evolved from friend to teacher, for millions of children all over the world. This launched a new age of puppeteers, as the young were influenced by Jim's puppets and envisioned puppetry careers of their own — in film, television, psychology, theology and even zoology. Puppetry would be used to teach and help. As the decade comes to a close, we'll take a moment to sing that popular 1967 hit from The Fifth Dimension (cue music please): "...*Harmony and understanding, sympathy and trust abounding ... This is the dawning of the age of ... The Puppet!*"

JAY JOHNSON
with Bob
2000s

Jay Johnson
1949–present

Career: 1960–present. When Jay Kent Johnson was 11, he discovered something magical: a natural ability to make a cousin's doll come to life. What began as an entertainment for his family eventually led the shy, lonely Texas boy with a mild form of dyslexia to working fairs and festivals as a ventriloquist. Soon Jay was performing at Six Flags Over Texas, Six Flags Over Georgia, and Astroworld. At age 18 he was mentored by master ventriloquist Arthur Sieving, who also made Jay's first vent figure. He went on to obtain a college degree, a B.B.A. in Marketing from the University of North Texas which has served him well in his business.

Jay is best known for playing Chuck Campbell with Bob his ventriloquist puppet on the controversial classic television series *"Soap,"* which ran for four years on ABC. Jay also played a violent police officer and ventriloquist on the CBS series *"Broken Badges."* He has starred in television series like *"Mrs. Columbo," "The Love Boat," "Simon & Simon," "The Facts of Life," "Empty Nest," "That '70s Show,"* and *"Hollywood Squares."* Jay has done over 30 commercials, hosted three comedy specials, two HBO Specials and two game shows. His countless live performances include comedy clubs and corporate shows all over the world. In 2006 Jay opened a show he wrote and performed on Broadway: *"Jay Johnson: The Two & Only!"*. This show won the Ovation Award in Los Angeles and the coveted Tony Award in New York.

Jay has also been honored by having the original Bob, his partner from *"Soap,"* inducted into the Smithsonian to sit next to Charlie McCarthy, Howdy Doody and Kermit the Frog.

Jay says, "I was not weird as a child. I did not use ventriloquism to trick my playmates. I had plenty of friends. Ventriloquist puppets are NOT creepy. And ventriloquism is not schizophrenia. And YES I did see all those *"Twilight Zone"* episodes which would dispute everything I have said about ventriloquism."

Luman Coad
& Bunyip
2007

Luman Coad
1942–present

Career: 1961–present. At age 20, Luman Coad was the youngest director appointed to the Fairyland Storybook Puppet Theater, after being assistant puppeteer of the Happy Hollow Park & Zoo's Castle Puppet Theater (1961-62). A native of Idaho, Luman came to California to study children's theater at San Jose State and San Francisco State Colleges. Luman directed the Fairyland theater from 1963–1966. During this time, he presented one of his shows, *"The Dog's Tail,"* at a Romanian puppet festival where it received first prize.

Mentored by Lettie Connell Schubert and Nancy H. Cole, Luman also worked with Benjamin Blake on his KPIX television special *"The Little Sweep."* Not long after, Arlyn Patricia Kuthan, his future wife and partner, invited Luman to move to Canada.

Coad Canada Puppets, established in 1966 by Luman and Arlyn, is considered one of North America's leading puppet theaters. Arlyn and Luman have performed across Europe, the Middle East, South America and the Pacific Rim. Luman has received both the Trustees and the President's Awards from the Puppeteers of America. He has also been awarded eight Citations of Excellence from UNIMA-USA. Coad Canada Puppets have been inducted as Pioneer Members in the British Columbia Entertainment Hall of Fame, and Luman's puppet work can be seen in the films *"Being John Malkovitch"* and *"The Never Ending Story."*

Luman has influenced the careers of many puppeteers through his showmanship and teachings. He has authored several books, *Theatre of Hand Puppets, Marionette Sourcebook: Theory & Technique, Chicago's Miniature Grand Operas,* and booklets *Puppets for Schools, Rod Puppets, Black Theatre* and *Puppet Theatre Management.* He is the owner of Charlemagne Press, which publishes new puppet books as well as reprints of puppetry classics. In 2012, Luman retired from performing but keeps puppetry alive through his publications. He is also the administrator for the Arlyn Award for Outstanding Design in Puppet Theatre.

PAM McINTIRE
Rumplestiltskin
1972

Pam McIntire
1910–2005

Career: 1962–2005. Pamelia Elizabeth McIntire was an artist/illustrator, a former painter of children's portraits and a greeting card designer. A graduate of the University of California Los Angeles, with a degree in English, she wanted to be a writer. In her early 50's, at an age when many start to think of retirement, Pam discovered puppetry. The art form brought all her talents together: writing, music, illustration, construction and doll making — and she embarked on an amazing career that stretched over the last 40 years of her life. As the McIntire Puppets, she created and performed close to 50 puppet plays for San Diego's children, including original works and adaptations of folk and fairytales.

Pam had fond childhood memories of *"Punch and Judy,"* and reading about how to make a cloth marionette from *My Book House for Children* by Olive Beaupre Miller, which later informed her puppetry career. Her speciality was making beautiful hand puppets with papier maché heads fashioned over balloons. Examples of her artistry grace puppet collections and exhibits across the country, and she designed and built for many other professionals. Pam was instrumental in starting the summer performance series at the puppet theater in Balboa Park in 1964 and was a favorite performer there for many years. Her murals grace Children's Hospital and an exhibit of her puppetry at the Children's Museum was the most popular event ever shown there.

Pam influenced the careers of many puppeteers in the San Diego area and was the longest active, and most beloved, member of the San Diego Guild. She also taught workshops at the Puppeteers of America conventions, and was a member of UNIMA-USA. For more than a quarter century, she designed characters and made the heads for many of the shows presented at the Oakland Children's Fairyland puppet theater. Pam's collection of puppets, props and extant shows were given to the Guild so her plays can be performed for new generations of San Diego's children.

JOHN GILKERSON
1978

John Gilkerson
1955–1989

Career: 1964–1989. At age nine, John Gilkerson became a child actor at Children's Fairyland in Oakland, portraying Prince Charming. There he met his mentor Lewis Mahlmann and began an amazing, but short-lived career in puppetry. A graduate of Dramatics from Chabot College, John loved everything about the theater. He was a dancer/singer for the San Francisco Gilbert & Sullivan Lamplighters, a costumer, set designer and choreographer for the Oakland and Joffrey Ballets, the Vienna Staatsoper, and the Dance Theater of Harlem. He also taught puppetry and drama in the Piedmont Unified School District.

As a puppeteer, John performed as the Gilkerson Puppets and the San Francisco Miniature Theatre. Besides running his own touring puppet theater, in 1984 he worked closely with Frank Zappa to build and design *"A Zappa Affair!"* The show married Zappa's music to the performances of ballet dancers wearing large puppet costumes which John created. John was also on the Emmy award winning children's show *"Buster and Me."* Under the directorship of Bay Area puppeteer and songwriter Robin Goodrow, John designed and built the puppets as well as playing "Russell" the Orangutan. The show, which aired on KRON TV channel 4 on Saturday mornings, centered around Robin, who was assigned with taking care of a house full of puppet monkeys who had problems most children could relate to. The show ran from 1979 to 1987. In his spare time, John built mascots for the San Francisco Giants, designed and made puppets for Children's Fairyland puppet shows, and produced mechanical figures for animated puppet Christmas windows at Gump's and I. Magnin Union Square department stores.

John's best friend at Skyline High was Tom Hanks. When Hanks accepted his 1994 Oscar for his role in *"Philadelphia,"* he credited John and their high school drama teacher for influencing his winning performance of representing a gay man in a positive way. John's puppetry continues on through television syndication and the repertoire of shows at Children's Fairyland.

BRUCE SCHWARTZ
1983

Bruce D. Schwartz
1955–present

Career: 1964–1995. Like most professional puppeteers, Bruce began performing shows for birthdays and kids in the neighborhood at a young age. This led to him performing yearly at the Renaissance Pleasure Faire in his late teens. When Bruce discovered the University of California Los Angeles offered classes in puppetry he enrolled in the program, but quickly withdrew from college after finding the classes were exclusively offered to theater majors. So he struck out on his own.

By 1972 Bruce began performing *"The Rat of Huge Proportions"* in his walk around puppet stage with hand puppets, but by 1973 he had switched to more intricate rod puppets. He has received three citations of excellence from UNIMA-USA, and has toured extensively in Japan, Europe and North America. Bruce thoroughly researches the style of costume, movement and music in his puppet vignettes and often composes his own music from his historical research. Japanese theater has greatly influenced his works.

Bruce was one of six international puppeteers to be profiled for the series *"Jim Henson Presents the World of Puppetry"* in 1985, and was twice on *"The Muppet Show."* Tired of the constant touring pace, Bruce looked forward to a quieter existence. In 1986, he laid aside his puppets to pursue his next love: yoga. In Pasadena, Bruce helped co-found the grassroots Pasadena Yoga Co-op, and sharpened his teaching skills at Yoga House.

In 1988, Bruce was the first puppeteer to receive a Genius Grant from the MacArthur Foundation. Since retirement he has built puppets for the film *"The Double Life of Veronique"* (1991) and Japanese dolls for *"The Ballad of Yachiyo"* (1995) at Berkeley Repertory Theatre. Bruce is known for characters with realism, humor and heart, which is not surprising since he admits to being influenced by Burr Tilstrom and Wayland Flowers. He will always be remembered for his exquisitely lyrical rod puppets, his bawdy Renaissance one man show, and an all-too-brief career in puppetry.

NICK LEFEUVRE
1990s

Nick Lefeuvre
1933–1998

Career: 1965–1998. Although Robert Cecil Lefeuvre was active in stage and screen since 1943, he did not pursue a puppet career until 1965. Nick was a man of many talents. He designed puppet festival posters, program books and personal logos for puppet companies and wrote many "how to" articles on puppetry, beautifully illustrated for beginners. Nick was also an accomplished painter and carpenter, known for his stage construction and miniature doll furniture. His miniature historical scenes can still be viewed in a popular Seattle underground attraction.

Nick started his puppetry career in Washington State. While living in Seattle, he ran a puppet theater for several years in a City of Everett shopping mall. He worked at a school for physically and mentally challenged students, creating puppets for stage shows which the students performed. Nick also worked on KOMO TV in Seattle for a show called *"Boomerang"* with singer Marnie Nixon, for which he received two Emmy awards for "Individual Achievement in Acting, Props and Puppetry." Nick preferred to work with hand and rod puppets, with his creative characterizations ranging from cute and stylized to extremely realistic and/or surreal. His puppets could have heads of round styrofoam balls with felt covering and sculpted felt hair or finely designed heads in plastic wood with chiseled features.

Nick and the Happy Unicorn Puppets finally settled in Monterey, California, where he also continued acting and design work along with teaching beginner puppetry classes at Monterey Peninsula College. Nick was known for his generosity, giving other performers sets of puppets, scripts or even memberships in the Puppeteers of America. Often unsatisfied with his beautiful creative work, he would threaten to quit puppetry, selling his puppets at ridiculously low prices, sulk for a few months, and then start over again. He built puppets for Lewis Mahlmann, Gayle Schluter, Peter Allen of Parasol Puppets, and the Seattle Puppetory Theater among others. Nick also designed and created many shows for the Children's Fairyland puppet theater.

ELIZABETH LUCE
Wizard of Oz
2012

Elizabeth Luce
1960–present

Career: 1965–present. When Elizabeth Ann Luce was five years old she was enrolled in an after school puppet program taught by Benjamin Blake. He helped her make her first sculpted rod puppet, and she was hooked. She taught herself puppetry by voraciously reading any puppet books she could find. In her teens she joined the San Francisco Bay Area Puppeteers Guild and apprenticed with Nancy H. Cole and her PST! (Puppet Studio Theater) youth puppetry program. This led to other work with recreation departments in her Palo Alto and Sunnyvale communities. Elizabeth went on to major in theater, and minor in studio art, at University of California Davis. She then earned her M.F.A. in set and costume design from UCLA.

After four years at Pepperdine University, designing shows while running the costume shop, teaching, and also working for Jim Gamble Productions, Elizabeth met Roger Mara and the two joined forces as Snapdragon Puppets. They returned to the San Francisco Bay Area, and for the next fifteen years she co-wrote, designed and sculpted all of the Snapdragon puppets. Elizabeth and Roger also produced two video productions: *"What's What Kid Dog,"* a children's TV pilot, and *"The Mousecracker,"* for which they earned an Emmy in 2000. When Roger passed in 2007, Elizabeth became Luce Puppet Company, a solo-performer entertainment for children and families, touring throughout California. She has built puppets for Fox television, the Disney Channel and various video projects.

Elizabeth and the Luce Puppet Company have received numerous awards, including the Los Angeles Drama Critics Circle Award for Puppet Design and the National Art Association Award for Excellence in the Theatrical Arts. She was given an Artist's Residency for masks and puppetry with Tutbat Theater in South Korea, and has worked with Chiodo Brothers and Swazzle as a freelance puppet builder and costumer. Elizabeth has also designed and costumed puppets for Kevin Menegus and the Fratello Marionettes, as well as for Lewis Mahlmann at the Children's Fairyland Puppet Theater.

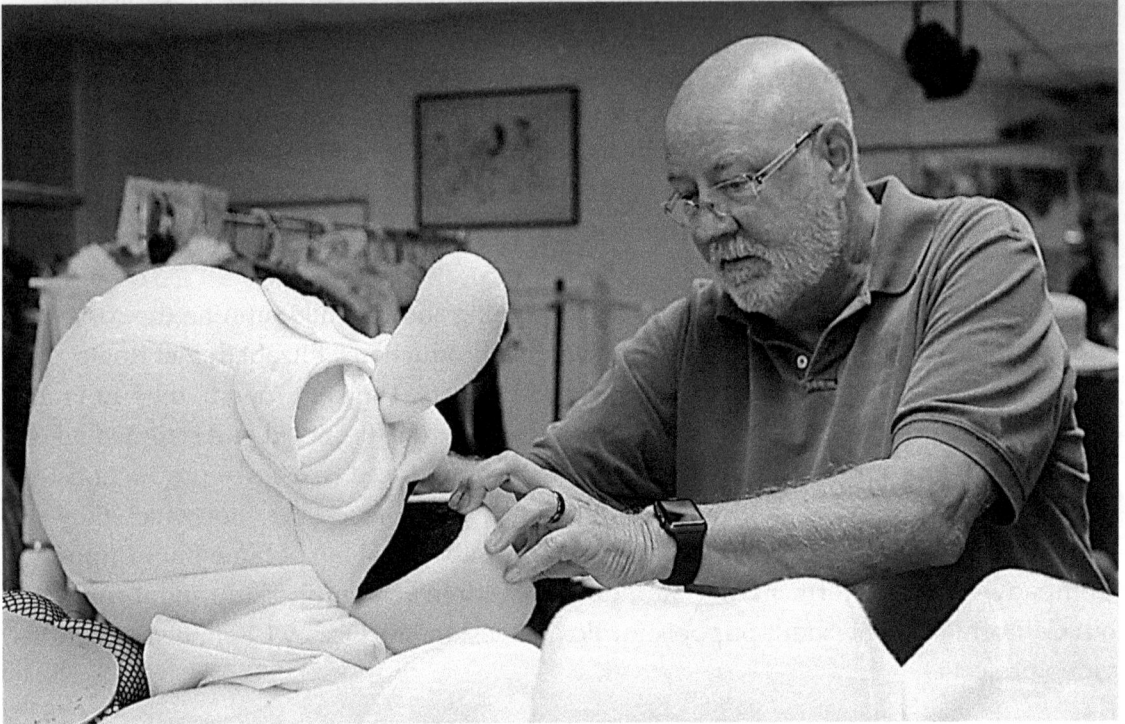

RICHARD BAY
2017

Richard Bay
1947–present

Career: 1966–present. At age four, Richard Bay was deeply inspired watching his grand-mother perform a production of *"The Frog Prince."* Both his mother and grandmother were puppeteers hired by the Works Project Administration to perform in the schools. As Richard grew, so did his love of puppetry. He has a B.A. and a M.A. from California State College Sacramento, , both in theater arts. He worked his way through college by performing puppet shows at Fairytale Town, the Sacramento sister park to Children's Fairyland. For his Master's thesis, Richard created a production of *"Doctor Faustus,"* blending puppetry with live acting — the style of production for which he later became known.

The Richard Bay Puppets have performed in the Sacramento area for many years, at birthday parties, fairs, television, shopping centers and stage theater productions. From 1976–2006 Richard was a professor of puppetry and theater arts at California State University Sacramento, creating with his students such memorable shows as *"Winnie the Pooh," "The World of Shalom Aleichem," "Tales of Poe"* and *"A Thousand Cranes."* He works primarily in the style of Japanese Bunraku, founded in Osaka in 1684, where the puppet-eers and puppet perform on stage together. Richard also helped develop a program that produced puppet opera for elementary school children in the Sacramento area. Its first show was *"The Girl of the Golden West"* in 1976.

Over the course of his career Richard has also produced ten puppet films for the state of California, teaching forestry and crime prevention. He has worked with many theater companies designing sets and puppets for such shows as *"Seussical"* and *"Little Shop of Horrors."* He also has designed California State Fair exhibits for over forty years. Richard is responsible for mentoring Art Gruenberger along with the puppetry careers of many students.

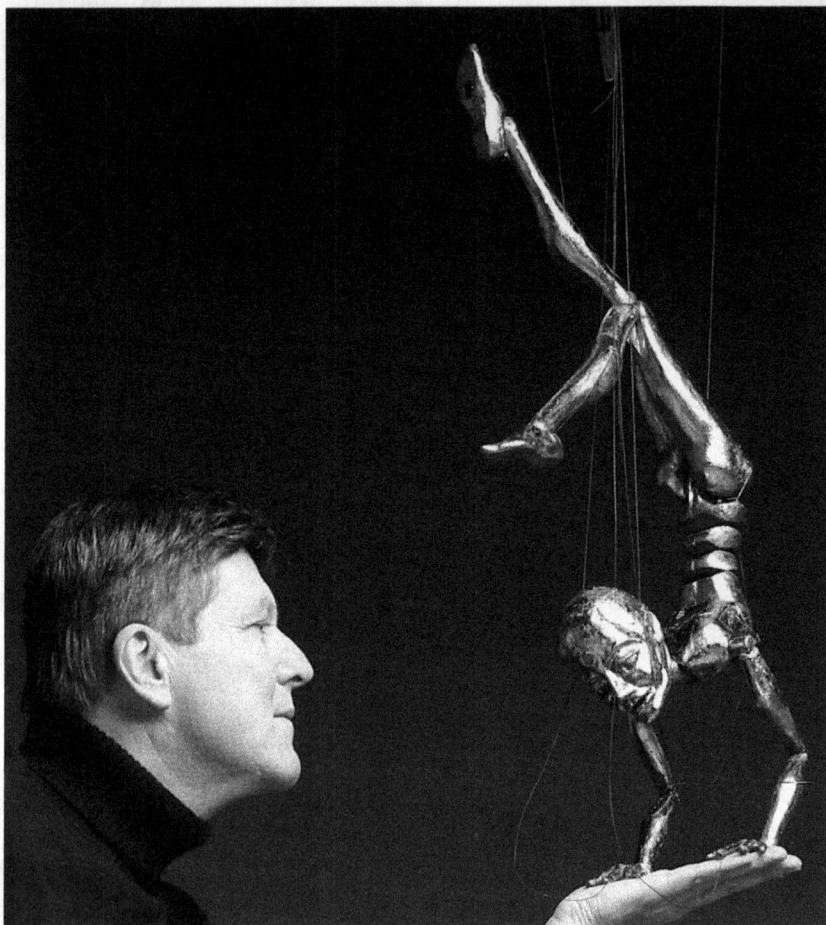

PHILLIP HUBER
with Oskar
2004

Phillip Huber
1951–present

Career: 1966–present. Although Phillip Huber spent most of his childhood working with puppets, it wasn't until 15 that he declared himself "a professional." Phillip majored in Theater and Education at Principia College where he created beautiful puppets for *"Tempest"* and *"The Magic Flute"* as his final projects. With a prepaid ticket and a job offer, Phillip left Illinois and headed for Hollywood and Tony Urbano Puppet Productions. For the next eight years he honed his craft working as the lead puppeteer and production supervisor for Tony's company. Phillip also spent time working for Jim Gamble Productions. While at Tony's, he met David Alexander, his partner, and together in 1980 they established the Huber Marionettes. Phillip credits the company's success to David's management and choreography skills.

Phillip has performed on many television shows including *"Dusty's Treehouse," "John Denver and the Muppets"* and *"The Tonight Show"* as well as performing many times at the prestigious Magic Castle of Hollywood. He sailed the high seas, performing his show *"Suspended Animation"* on cruise ships around the world, performed at the Lido in Paris and at Casino de Monte Carlo in Monaco. Phillip's puppets have performed on stage with Tommy Tune in *"Busker Alley,"* in *"That's Christmas"* with Sandy Duncan, and with Jim Nabors in *"Christmas with Friends and Nabors."* His film credits include *"Being John Malkovich," "The Legend of Tillamook's Gold"* and *"Oz the Great and Powerful."*

Phillip has lectured for the National Puppetry Conference at the Eugene O'Neill Theater Center as well as PuppetFest Midwest. He has also presented Master Classes at Stanford University, California Institute of the Arts, and Disney Feature Animation Studios. He has written many articles on puppetry for the *Puppetry Journal* as well as answered questions from aspiring puppeteers. Phillip has won the President's Award and an UNIMA-USA Citation of Excellence, and he thanks all the great marionette artists of Los Angeles for inspiring him.

GARY JONES

2017

Gary Jones
1942–present

Career: 1967–present. Gary Jones is a self-taught artist, sculptor, costumer, dancer, scenic designer, carpenter and closet poet. Gary was working in the department of an ad agency when, on a lark, he knocked on the door of the Kungsholm Miniature Grand Opera of Chicago. At 16 he had been mesmerized by these 12" puppet stars who performed full length operas on a grand stage. At 25 he became the first black apprentice puppeteer, and eventually moved up to a principal performer and scenic designer/builder for all new presentations. In his three years there, he designed the productions of *"Porgy and Bess," "The King and I," "Gypsy"* and *"Carmen."*

In 1975 Jones created Blackstreet USA Puppet Theatre and "The Yuppets!" — young urban professional puppets. Blackstreet sought to illuminate black culture through emotional song and dance, but soon redirected itself towards reinterpreting the classics of the traditional ballet canon. Gary follows two basic artistic principles: 1) Creating a new performance idiom with puppets based in an original movement vocabulary inspired by ballet, and 2) Using highly stylized black puppets to dramatically reinforce a positive self image among black people. Gary has performed in Iceland, Germany, Holland, Portugal, Honduras, Mexico, India and Japan. He also had two five-week engagements at the Smithsonian Institution Division of Performing Arts in Washington D.C. that broke attendance records. The shows featured five black puppeteers — Gary, Marcia Belton, Judy Qualls, James Olive and Robert Vines, performing with an entirely black puppet cast.

Gary moved his Blackstreet Puppet Theatre to Los Angeles in 1984. The company has been the recipient of numerous grants and awards including "The Crystal Castle" from Walt Disney Corporation for outstanding work with children. Gary was profiled by *People Magazine* in 1998. In his own words, "Art speaks directly to our souls...it is from this place that we can begin again in joy." For more on Kungsholm, you can read Gary's book *Subplot–Memoirs of Chicago's Kungsholm Miniature Grand Opera,* published by Charlemagne Press.

LARRY SCHMIDT
2018

Larry Schmidt
1953–2019

Career: 1967–2019. Larry was a third generation Californian, born in Berkeley on what he fondly called "The coattails of the Golden Age of Marionettes." He grew up watching *"Brother Buzz"* and *"Howdy Doody"* on television, while attending as many marionette puppet shows as he could at Children's Fairyland in Oakland. Larry's grandmother was a puppeteer in the Oakland churches and underserved districts of Oakland. As a teenager, Larry performed with puppets she helped him make for children's birthday party shows. He was also inspired by such greats as Ralph Chessé, Rufus Rose, Tony Urbano and Bil Baird.

Larry received a B.F.A. in fine art from California College of the Arts in Oakland, made costumes for the Oakland Ballet, and joined the San Francisco Bay Area Puppeteers Guild where he was further mentored by Lettie Schubert and Lewis Mahlmann. As a young man he studied Indonesian mask dance from Suzanne Suwanda, performed with Leonard Pitt, and then began building marionettes for a production of Stravinsky's *"The Firebird Suite."* In 2007, he first presented *"Driveway Follies,"* a Halloween marionette show, in the driveway of his Oakland family triplex. For the evenings of the performances, the roofs of his garages featured a *"Halloween Haunt"* populated with animatronic Halloween "dark ride" creations that Larry designed, motorized and sculpted.

"Driveway Follies" featured vintage trick marionettes designed in the style of classic marionette artists, and retro music from the '30s, '40s, '50s and '60s. Talented puppeteers including Robin Stevens, Kevin Menegus, Fred Riley III and Jesse Vail worked alongside Larry to provide this free Halloween puppet show in a safe environment for neighborhood children of all ages. At the time of Larry's death, the show was in its 12th year and had received funding grants from many individuals and organizations such as the City of Oakland and the Sisters of Perpetual Indulgence in San Francisco. The puppet show had become so popular that neighborhood streets had to be closed off due to crowd sizes. Videos of *"Driveways Follies"* can be found on Youtube.

JUDY FOLKMANIS
with Sea Serpent
2005

Judy Folkmanis
1941–2016

Career: 1968–2016. Judy Siegel met her husband Atis Folkmanis when they were both attending Antioch College. While Judy graduated with a B.A. in Biology, she always had a love for sewing and crafts. After college, she and Atis spent two years in Malaysia with the Peace Corps. That led to a year or so traveling in Europe and Asia before finally retuning to Massachusetts to raise a family.

"Sesame Street" had just started its run on television, and Judy was impressed by the way children responded to the puppets. Patterns for making Cookie Monster, Ernie & Bert in a *Woman's Day* magazine showed her how to make simple puppets. She started making them for her son's preschool and continued this practice to augment the family income, selling her puppets on consignment in Harvard Square.

When the family relocated to Berkeley in 1972 for Atis's extended education, Judy applied for a vending license and began hawking her puppets on the streets of Berkeley under the name Furry Folk Puppets. Atis noticed her hobby was producing quite a revenue, and suggested she think about going into business professionally. A very realistic looking beaver led to skunks, raccoons, bears, otters and squirrels, and then in 1976, a way of life. Atis happily gave up his career in science for pattern cutting and overseeing the new business.

Folkmanis puppets are now sold in stores, museums, and amusement attractions all over the world. Even though Judy has passed, the family still continues to create and produce puppets beloved by children worldwide. Located in Emeryville, Folkmanis Puppets Inc. is directly across the street from Disney's Pixar Studios. Judy's puppets are often seen being used by entertainers in shows ranging from puppetry, to magic, to ventriloquism and teaching animal lectures in school settings. The company's motto is *"Folkmanis Puppets ... Handle with Fun!"*

STEVE HANSEN
1980s

Steve Hansen
1946–2011

Career: 1968–2011. Steve Hansen took the puppet world by storm with his street savvy, satirical and theatrical presentations of *"Punch and Judy."* With a B.A. in Theatre Arts from San Francisco State, Steve knew how to bring his theatricality to the streets of San Francisco. What began as a politically satirical university project soon became a profitable street show at San Francisco's Fisherman's Wharf. At that time he was known as The Great Medicine Show Co. What could be funnier in the late '60s than Punch having his way with a puppet of Richard Nixon? Steve was a regular performer of *"Punch"* at the Renaissance Pleasure Faire and the Great Dickens Christmas Faire in the Bay Area. In 1972, Steve established his "one man–walking bag stage" and wandered off the streets and out into the world as the Puppet Man.

Steve apprenticed with such famous puppet companies as the Bob Brown Marionettes, Bil Baird, and the Muppets. At one time his *"Punch"* was seen performing for coin on Wall Street in the New York financial district. He performed at both Yosemite and Yellowstone National Parks and traveled with Punch through North America, Europe, Asia, Australia and New Zealand, finally settling at Walt Disney's EPCOT Center as a "puppet specialist and show consultant." Steve performed *"Punch"* as well as becoming a show producer and director at Disney World. His last *"Punch"* performance was at the Puppeteers of America Millennium Festival in Seattle, Washington.

Steve lectured on "Puppetry and Punch" in many locations, including the Museum of Modern Art, Stanford University, Tulane University and the DeYoung Museum of San Francisco. He appeared on *"What's My Line?"* as the Puppet Man and was a featured performer in Marlo Thomas' *"Free to Be You and Me."* He was also invited to perform at the Punchman's Convention in London, England. In 1991, Steve and his wife Judy moved to Canada and opened Peak Events, a corporate meeting and special event production company.

MICHAEL MALKIN
2019

Michael R. Malkin
1943–present

Career: 1968–Present. Michael R. Malkin is a writer, director, producer, documentarian and puppeteer. From 1974 to 2007, he was a professor and head of the Theater & Dance department at Cal Poly, San Luis Obispo. Michael has a B.A. in English Literature and a M.A./PhD in Theater from Tufts University in Massachusetts.

While working in Europe and Asia during 1968 and 1969, friends and other colleagues took Michael to a variety of puppet theater productions, including those featuring fascinating forms of traditional and folk puppet theater in what were often rural and relatively remote areas of Asia. When he returned to Europe and the United States, he avidly sought opportunities to see and learn about innovative contemporary puppetry. This also led to him and his wife, Pam, forming the Malkin Puppet Players.

Michael has written numerous books and articles on acting, directing and puppet theater, including *Traditional and Folk Puppets of the World*. He was the catalog author for the museum exhibition publications *PUPPETS: The Power of Wonder* and *PUPPETS: Art and Entertainment*. Michael is also a multiple award-winning screenwriter and was executive producer and co-writer of the video documentary, *"Puppets: Worlds of Imagination"* in 2001.

Michael served as director for two Puppeteers of America festivals at Cal Poly, and received an UNIMA-USA Citation of Excellence for one of his productions. He also helped create and organize a two-week-long workshop with the Muppets called *"A Survey of Puppet Theater Techniques"* for the CA State University's Summer Arts program and served on the board for UNIMA's periodical publication, *Puppetry International*.

Mentored by George Latshaw, Vince Anthony, Nancy Staub and Mike Oznowicz, Michael was influenced by Bil Baird, Albrecht Roser, Jim Henson and many others. Most of his work has advocated for and publicized puppetry and its practitioners.

CONRAD BISHOP & ELIZABETH FULLER
King Lear
2017

Conrad Bishop & Elizabeth Fuller
1941–present & 1940–present

Career: 1969–present. Husband and wife team Conrad and Elizabeth have led lives filled with music, theater, masks and puppets. They met and married as undergraduates at Northwestern University, where Conrad got a B.S. and M.A. in Theater. He later completed a Ph.D. at Stanford. Elizabeth, who was a childhood piano prodigy, turned her efforts to composing music and collaborating on theatrical endeavors. The two then spent two years teaching at University of South Carolina, and three at University of Wisconsin-Milwaukee. While in Wisconsin they became increasingly impatient with university theater and started the small ensemble Theatre X in 1969.

Theatre X used hand, and rod, as well as giant puppets for a series of short anti-war pieces. Then came a full production of *"Alice in Wonder"*, an adult version, in 1972. Because Conrad and Elizabeth's predominant work was in a variety of live-actor styles, as well as radio drama, they were a very obscure part of the puppetry landscape. Their puppets are controlled by one hand operating the head, the other as the character's live hand. This gave the figure a strong gestural life that allowed a fuller vocal expression than normally found in most contemporary stagings. Entirely self taught, the pair used puppetry only when it was the best medium for the particular story. Their full length puppet/mask shows include *"Macbeth," "The Tempest," "King Lear," "Descent of the Goddess Inanna"* and recently *"Frankenstein,"* as well as four collections of short pieces such as *"Rash Acts."* They also use puppets as elements in other plays.

Conrad and Elizabeth's company, The Independent Eye, was established in 1974 in Chicago. They later moved to Pennsylvania before settling in California. Touring has been the central focus of their work: the pair have performed in 38 states. They have produced over 78 works for over 3,500 performances and have authored several books on theater and their careers including the memoir *Co-Creation, 50 Years in the Making*.

MICHAEL EARL
2015

Michael Earl
1959–2015

Career: 1969–2015. Michael Earl Davis began his puppetry career at age 10. Before that he was a child actor in commercials for Curad Bandage and the Lipton *"Is It Soup Yet?"* kid. Michael changed his name to Earl, his middle name, when he was told by AFTRA and SAG that another "Mike Davis" was already a union member. He apprenticed at Children's Fairyland in Oakland with puppeteer Lewis Mahlmann, and from ages 10 to 17 he performed his own puppet shows using hand and marionette puppets. At 18 he moved to New York and apprenticed at Bil Baird's Marionette Theatre while also acting in commercials. The next year he started working with the Muppets on *"Sesame Street."* For three years he performed, and finally did the voice for Snuffleupagus. Michael also created the characters of Forgetful Jones, Polly Darton and Leslie Mostly, and served as understudy for Big Bird.

Michael is a four-time Emmy award winning puppeteer and writer/lyricist. He co-created, scripted and wrote lyrics for *"Ticktock Minutes"* on PBS, where he also played Dr. Ticktock. For stage he created the role of Noel Petard for Sid & Marty Krofft's live musical revue *"A Broadway Baby."* Michael's film and television work includes *"Muppets Take Manhattan," "John Denver and the Muppets: A Christmas Together," "The Jim Henson Hour," "Dinosaurs," "Team America: World Police,"* and *"Men in Black II."*

Michael acted with Whoopi Goldberg, danced with Gregory Hines and clowned with Victor Borge. In 1998 he created a biographical musical one man show: *"Pure Imagination"* that he staged in Los Angeles and New York. He founded Puppet School in Los Angeles with Roberto Ferreira, teaching TV puppetry to future puppeteers such as Drew Massey, Kevin Carlson, Camille Bonora, Sean & Patrick Johnson and Erik Kuska. Michael wanted to give back that "personal touch" he had received from his mentors Bil Baird, Jim Henson, Bob Baker and Lewis Mahlmann. His mission was *"To instruct, strengthen and encourage children of all ages through the imaginative use of music and puppetry."*

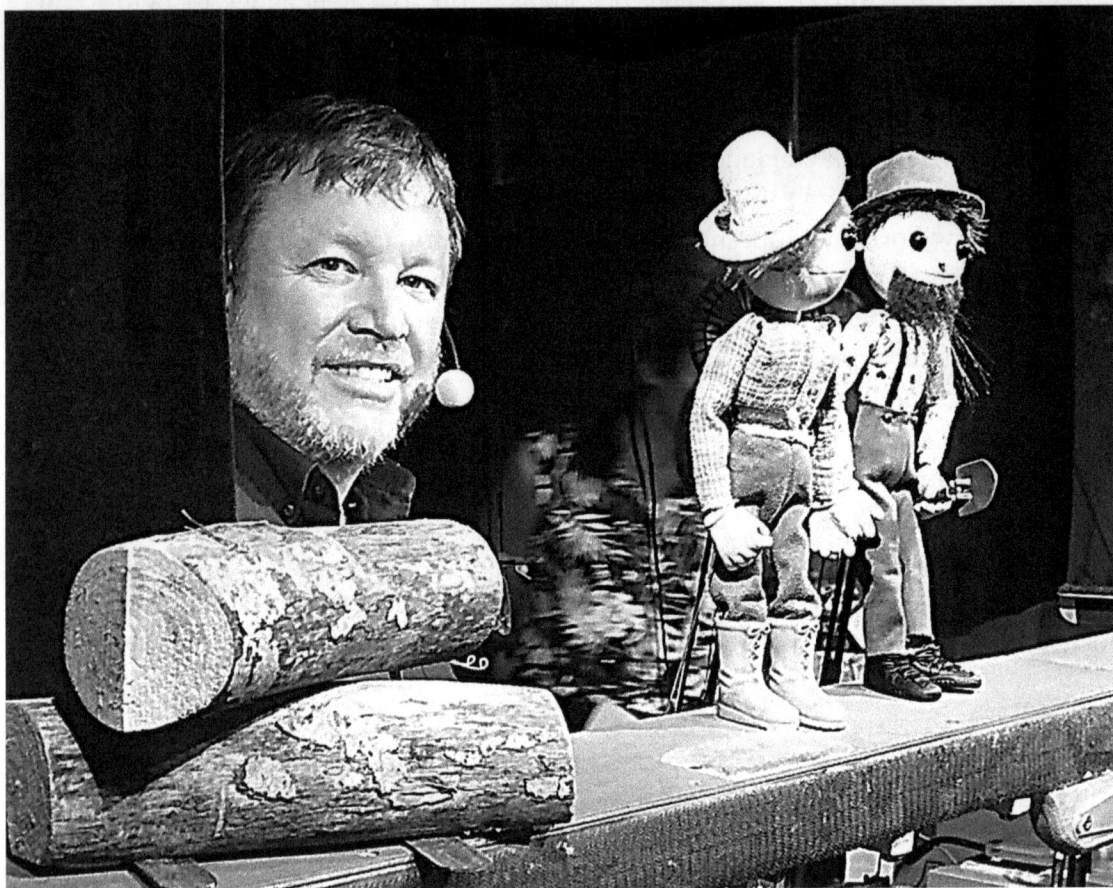

ROGER MARA
Tale of Paul Bunyan
2006

Roger Mara
1953–2007

Career: 1969–2007. In 1969, an actor still in high school, Roger was hired by Marla and Ellis Evans — The MarEl Marionettes — to perform the role of Emile the Fox in the PBS pilot *"Rockadaisy Den."* This led to him creating puppet shows for the Syracuse, New York Park and Recreation Department program, The Puppet Wagon, where he tested his skills designing and making puppets which toured the parks and playgrounds. A junior year abroad program in Paris allowed him to hobnob with foreign puppeteers and companies. Roger graduated with a degree in Social Anthropology from Columbia University, and through personal studies became an inventor and mechanical puppet genius. He credited French puppeteer André Tahon, German Albrecht Roser and American Dick Meyers as influencing his puppet talents.

In 1980 Roger moved to Los Angeles and began work for Jim Gamble Productions. He received an UNIMA-USA Citation of Excellence for his work on Jim's blacklight production of *"Peter and the Wolf."* Another show he created called *"Talk,"* an Ashanti story, debuted at the Hollywood Bowl Summer Children's Program. There, Roger met the show's puppet designer, Elizabeth Luce. In 1992 Elizabeth joined forces with Roger. They moved to the San Francisco area and started the Snapdragon Puppets. Their production *"The Mousecracker"* was filmed and made into a video, for which Roger and Elizabeth received an Emmy in 2000. Snapdragon Puppets had a 15 year career, first in San Francisco and then Seattle, Washington.

One of Roger's most well known innovations was his "popup stage." With a flip of the wrist, a 4' x 12' box transformed into a 7' stage with front, side and rear curtains, full proscenium and a built-in sound system. He opened his shows at puppet conventions with this presentation, and often got standing ovations. Although an entertainer for all ages, he believed performing for children was the only practical way to make a grant-free, dependable living as a full-time puppeteer.

Rand Bohn

Career: 1960–1995. Rand excelled at sculpting, mechanical knowledge of animation techniques, sound editing, mold making, costuming, design and performance. He began his career when he was eight. Rand worked for the Kungsholm Miniature Grand Opera of Chicago and also for Bob Baker and Tony Urbano in Los Angeles. Rand made the puppets for the hit television show *"The Magic Door"* on CBS, and his commercial clients included McDonald's, IHOP, Budweiser, Sun-Maid Raisins, and Walt Disney's World on Ice. He is most remembered for his variety show and his popular rod puppet version of *"Peter Rabbit."*

Van Charles Snowden

Career: 1962–2010. Van began his puppet career in 1962 performing as a puppeteer for Sid & Marty Krofft's *"Les Poupées de Paris."* This led to him being puppeteer and director for the Krofft's Six Flags Theme Park marionette shows. From 1969–1971, Van was *"H. R. Pufnstuf"* in the popular Krofft TV show. He was also in *"The Land of the Lost,"* *"Sigmund and the Sea Monsters,"* *"Lidsville,"* *"The Bugaloos"* and *"D.C. Follies."* Among his many credits, Van performed the puppetry for Chucky in *"Child's Play"* and the Cryptkeeper in HBO's *"Tales from the Crypt."*

David Cadwalader Jones

Career: 1963–2014. David began his career puppeteering and writing plays for Lewis Mahlmann's Lilliputian Players adult puppet theater. He then went on to adapt more than half the puppet plays that Lewis performed at the Children's Fairyland Storybook Puppet Theater. David taught many script writing workshops and his adaptations have been published in PLAYS, the Drama Magazine for Young People. He also co-authored four books of royalty-free puppet plays that can be presented by young puppeteers, and one book, *Scripts of the Lilliputian Players,* published by Charlemagne Press, of his adult plays.

Thom Fountain

Career: 1968–present. For seven seasons Thom Fountain was head puppeteer for Salem the Cat on *"Sabrina the Teenage Witch."* When he was ten or eleven in 1968, he saw Sid and Marty Krofft's marionette show at Six Flags over Georgia, and it changed his life. He became an usher and then a lighting man for the show, and finally, a puppeteer! Thom's movie and television credits include HBO's *"Tales from the Crypt,"* *"SpongeBob Squarepants,"* *"D.C. Follies,"* *"Muppets Tonight,"* *"Men in Black,"* *"Child's Play 3"* and *"Team America: World Police."* Thom has also taught puppetry for Disney Performing Arts.

Judy Roberto

Career: 1968–present. Judy Roberto began her puppet career being mentored by Betsy Brown. Afterwards, she spent many years teaching Arts & Puppetry in the Los Angeles Schools program. From 2006–2017, Judy was the director of the Happy Hollow Castle Puppet Theater in San Jose. As a Recreation Specialist for the city she taught puppetry and dramatic play along with shadow puppetry, developed and lead volunteer workshops, and did puppetry, scenic design and costume design for musical theater. Judy believes, and teaches, that puppetry combines the electricity of theater and the visual aesthetic of fine art.

Jackee Marks

Career: Late '60s–present. Jacqueline Marks is a sculptor, printmaker, author and puppeteer in Hermosa Beach. Mentored by Betsy Brown, she has presented shows through the Junior League's Programs, the Hollywood Bowl Family programs and the Los Angeles Symphonies for Youth RIFF program. Around 1990 her interest in puppetry extended to philanthropy. She is the Chief Financial Officer of the International Puppetry Museum, which supports the Cook/Marks collection of puppets and puppet paraphernalia. Jackee co-wrote the book: *Alan Cook, A Puppet Collector's Odyssey.* She's very interested in the art of shadow puppetry.

Joe Selph

Career: 1969–present. Known as Los Angeles's most unique children's entertainer, Joe Selph started his career as a clown, and was clown/magic consultant for the Puppeteers of America. A magician and performing member of Hollywood's Magic Castle, Joe has worked with the Jim Henson Company, Universal Studios, Sony Pictures and PBS. He eventually studied with René Zendejas as a puppeteer for birthday parties and private events. This led to becoming a team with René, taking their unique style of puppetry to events all over California. Today he continues the tradition of the René's Marionettes, performing annually.

Richard Stephen Weber

Career: 1969–circa 2005. Richard was a highly skilled classically trained puppeteer and puppet maker specializing in show design and staging of movement, as well as the design and manipulation of puppets in a broad range of styles and techniques. He began his career training with the Bil Baird Marionette Theatre for seven years. Moving to Los Angeles, he continued to work with Bob Baker, René Zendejas and Jack Shafton Productions. Richard was also an Emmy Award make-up artist and prop maker with credits including *"Deep Space Nine," "Voyager," "Madtv"* and *"Charmed."*

7

1970–1979

THE ERA OF THE 1970s is often called the "Me" decade. The populace thought not so much about the fixing of society, but the fixing of themselves. By 1973 America was out of the Vietnam War, even though that wouldn't officially end until 1975 with the fall of Saigon. A sense of community began with the launch of the Skylab in '73 and the resignation of Richard Nixon in '74. It was time to step back and view society, and ones' self, and figure out how to work together. In 1974 Bill Gates founded Microsoft and the following year the first personal computer, the Commodore PET, and the computer gaming console Atari 2600 went on sale. It was time to have fun and dream.

On the big screen, early 1970s war films like *"M.A.S.H.," "Patton,"* and *"Tora! Tora! Tora!"* gave way to the popularity of disaster films such as *"The Poseidon Adventure," "Earthquake"* and *"The Towering Inferno."* Films like *"Jaws"* and the *"Airport"* series scared us away from sea and air. And of course, don't forget all the gritty, naturalistic crime movies like *"The French Connection."* By the end of the '70s a breath of fresh air and welcome relief came with *"Star Wars."* And this opened the door for all the special effects fantasy films on the horizon. *"Close Encounters of the Third Kind," "Superman," "Alien,"* the Ray Harryhausen *"Sinbad"* films and *"Star Trek, The Motion Picture"* showed the youth of America they could be movie stars in a different way. Television also joined in, with the popular sci-fi series *"Battlestar Galactica"* and *"Buck Rogers in the 25th Century."* It is of special note that *"The Muppet Movie"* was the 10th highest grossing film of 1979. Meanwhile, in literature, H.P. Lovecraft, Roald Dahl, Maurice Sendak, Dean Koontz and Stephen King cast spells on us. Terry Brooks started his epic *Sword of Shannara* series, and artists Alan Lee and Brian Froud published *Faeries*, which led to many lavishly illustrated fantasy genealogies.

And what's happened with puppetry in America? One word — Muppets! With the success of *"Sesame Street,"* Jim Henson was able to launch television specials such as *"Hey Cinderella!,"* *"The Frog Prince"* and *"The Muppet Musicians of Bremen."* *"The Muppet Show"* began airing in 1976 and Jim Henson, Frank Oz and Jerry Juhl ushered in another Renaissance of puppetry. The youth of America felt a kinship with the Muppets, which led to the peak of membership in the Puppeteers of America in 1979. In an homage to *"Sesame Street"*, who were the "People in Your Neighborhood?" Why, they were puppeteers! The ME! of this decade could also stand for Muppet Explosion!

Polyfoam puppets suddenly became the choice of puppeteers producing shows, and affordable puppet making books were available in abundance. Kids ran to their local libraries to check out hidden puppet knowledge. Wayland Flowers and Madame, Ronn Lucas, as well as many ventriloquists sporting new dummies fashioned after the Muppets, established successful television and stage careers. In 1978 Vince Anthony opened the Center For Puppetry Arts in Georgia, the first of many puppet centers to be established across America. Guilds and puppet organizations flourished through the influx of puppeteers embracing the Muppets, television and the special effects film industry. And California produced a lion's share of that talent.

Since 1958 California has been the state with the largest percentage of Puppeteers of America members, with New York being the next. But "Muppet-like" puppets were not necessarily the choice of puppeteers in the Golden State. In 1972, the puppeteers held a National Convention in Oakland, featuring puppetry of all kinds. Its purpose was to highlight the various forms of the puppet through the "best of the best." At this convention, Dave Goelz talked to Frank Oz about joining the Henson group. And as Sid & Marty Krofft took over Saturday morning television with their puppet costume and stop motion specials, the San Francisco Bay Area saw other unique things happening. Larry Reed began performing his extraordinary shadow plays in San Francisco, while Bob Hartman captivated the crowds on the street at Ghirardelli Square with his satirical brand of puppet humor. And for those who wanted to begin performing shows without building their own puppets, Folkmanis Puppets opened their doors in Emeryville.

There is a saying in the puppet world that Jim Henson is the best and the worst thing to happen to puppetry. The best because he inspired and supported the art form and so many puppeteers and always brought out the best in a performance. Through his work, puppetry became a respected and honored profession in America. The worst because the Muppet style is what America thinks puppetry "is," even though Jim tried to open the eyes of the world to the different forms of the puppet. His 1985 television special *"Jim Henson Presents the World of Puppetry,"* so far only released on TV and videocassette, tried to show a mass audience the many venues of the puppet. International stars such as Holland's Henk Boerwinkel, Australia's Richard Bradshaw, France's Philippe Genty, Russia's Sergei Obraztsov, Germany's Albrecht Roser and California's Bruce Schwartz shared their many styles through Henson. But through the birth of the Muppet style, other techniques of puppetry became the forgotten children. But as we'll see in the decades to come, "what goes around, comes around."

Bob Hartman
2017

Bob Hartman
unknown–present

Career: 1970–present. Robert Hartman was raised in Oregon, but made his way to California where he graduated from the University of California with a degree in Field Biology. He was inspired to become a puppeteer after seeing the film, *"The Loon's Necklace,"* about Northwest Indian legends using Indian masks to tell the stories. Bob was a self-taught puppeteer, studying all the books he could find on art, theater and puppetry. His puppets are well known for the mechanical engineering of the figures that allows him to excel with their movements.

Bob began his career in the early '70s performing on the streets of San Francisco. His puppet theater could usually be found near Fisherman's Wharf, between Ghirardelli Square and the Cannery. His shows were so popular, that after many attempts to find a location to fit the huge crowds, the courtyard of the Cannery at Beach street welcomed him and it became his favorite location.

Bob was a San Francisco highlight for over a decade. In addition to working with hand and rod puppets, Bob loved to do short shadow presentations. His shows were for adults, although the kids loved the action. Bob was a favorite at comedy clubs, conventions and yearly performances in Marin at the Mill Valley Fall Arts Festival and the Mountain Play on Mount Tamalpais. A highly polished professional known for his great animation, humor, intelligence and charm, he was once described in a British puppet magazine as "...hysterically funny ... he pretends to be a haphazard amateur presenting his pieces in whatever order he stumbles upon his puppets!"

The Hartman Puppets, established in 1985, have toured extensively, and have been seen on Thames TV and the BBC in England as well as the Disney Channel and PBS. Bob has received an UNIMA-USA Citation of Excellence, and was a favored performer of Frank Oz and Robin Williams. A few of his well-known acts include *"Documentary of an Endangered Species,"* where he uses his biology degree to great laughter, *"The Race Between the Tortoise & the Hare,"* and his comedy routines with his Baby and Wolf puppets.

RANDAL J. METZ
1994

Randal John Metz
1959–present

Career: 1970–present. Randal knew he wanted to be a puppeteer at age 10 when he saw Lewis Mahlmann's production of *"Treasure Island"* at Children's Fairyland. But, how to do so? The answer: stay as close to the puppet theater as possible. And so for the last fifty years he has been working intimately with the Oakland park. Randal has served at Fairyland as a child entertainer, ride operator, recreation specialist, event planner, children's theater director, artistic director, puppeteer and historian.

In 1978 he and his puppet partner, Tom Royer, founded the Puppet Company to serve as puppeteers for the Oakland Knowland Park Zoo (1979-80). He feels honored to have had outstanding mentors: Lewis Mahlmann in classic puppetry, Lettie Schubert with hand puppets, Jerry Juhl for scriptwriting and Bob Baker in marionette performance. Randal has performed with the Big John Strong Variety Circus, directed one season of Oakland's Vagabond Puppets, and attended a two-week intensive puppetry course taught by Muppet performers, *"A Survey of Puppet Theater Techniques."* Since 1991, Randal has directed Fairyland's Storybook Puppet Theater, the oldest, continuously operating puppet theater in the U.S.

Graduating from San Francisco State University with a B.A. in Theater and Children's Theater, Randal has applied those teachings to puppetry, acting, stage direction and design in the San Francisco Bay Area. He has been fortunate enough to mentor several talented puppeteers including Kevin Menegus, Jesse Vail and Evy Berman Wright. Randal performs outside of the park, under the Puppet Company name, with puppetry partner Rhonda Godwin. Randal and Rhonda met in college where the two of them performed *"Punch and Judy"* and Commedia dell'Arte throughout California one summer.

Randal also creates puppets for rentals in shows and musicals such as *"Carnival," "Nunsense,""Sleuth,"* and *"Little Shop of Horrors."* He has written two previous books on puppetry: *Storybook Strings–50 Years of Puppetry at Children's Fairyland's Storybook Theater* and *Making Puppets the Fairyland Way*. In 2016, Oakland Mayor Libby Schaaf honored Randal with a proclamation for his services to Oakland.

LARRY REED
with Arjuna & Momosimok
1998

Larry Reed
1944–present

Career: 1970–present. Larry Reed received a Master's in film at the San Francisco Art Institute and is an actor in theater and film in the USA and Costa Rica. He's also studied at the Center for World Music, and attended Yale numerous times. In 1970, Larry saw his first Balinese Wayang shadow show performed by a dalang, a shadow performer. The images spoke to him and the music and puppetry transformed him. On his return to the States, he studied Gamelan and Javanese Wayang at Mills College in Oakland. He considers shadow play to be inherently cinematic: the original screenplay.

In 1972 Larry established Shadowlight Productions in San Francisco. He started as a solo performer, and after 20 years, decided to add four musicians and two assistants to his wayang performances. Shadowlight Productions does large scale modern shadow theater as well as regularly performing traditional Balinese shadows or wayang kulit. Larry invented the technique of using multiple lights to create live, edited "cuts" on shadow screens without seeing the actors or puppets enter the screen. Shadowlight is known for combining shadow technique with film, modern theater and dance styles. Larry has presented countless collaborations and ensemble shadow productions.

Larry was mentored by Pak I Nyoman Radjeg, a dalang from the village of Tabanan, as well as Viola Spolin in theater games and theory. He considers his influences to be Joseph Svoboda, Gordon Craig, Robert Edmond Jones, Dario Fo and Julie Taymor among others. He has received two UNIMA-USA citations of excellence, one for his production of *"In Xanadu."* As a filmmaker he has made dozens of documentaries about his work and shadow theater all over the world. Larry speaks Balinese and several other languages fluently, and was the first American acknowledged as a dalang, with the status of a priest.

He says, "Mythology, when reenacted, provides a place for public dreaming, ultimately linking everyday life with the sacred, the present with the past, and individual with the community."

PAUL ZALOOM
Punch & Judy
2009

Paul Zaloom
1951–present

Career: 1971–present. Paul began his puppet legacy in 1971 when he joined the renowned, Vermont-based avant-garde company, Bread and Puppet Theater. With Peter Schumann as his mentor, he began performing solo in 1977. His first piece was a found object puppet show, *"The World of Plastic."* Paul is recognized for his highly idiosyncratic work which utilizes techniques such as overhead projection, "picture performance", ventriloquism, and hand, rod, shadow, found object, and toy theater puppets. Although best known for his found object or "junk" puppet spectacles, he has also interpreted age-old puppet traditions such as *"Karagoz"* and *"Punch and Judy."*

Paul has written, designed and performed fifteen solo spectacles, including *"Fruit of Zaloom" "Zaloom, Sick but True," "The Mother of All Enemies"* and *"White Like Me: A Honky Dory Puppet Show."* With a B.A. in puppetry from Goddard College, he has also been involved with television and film. Paul appeared on the Emmy winning children's show *"Beakman's World"* (1992- 96) as Beakman the wacky scientist, and continues to perform the character in live stage shows in four countries. Paul also co-wrote, narrated and performed in the film *"Dante's Inferno"* (2003), a collaboration with painter Sandow Birk; a high definition, toy theater, feature-length puppet version of the epic poem, starring Dermot Mulroney and James Cromwell.

Paul has received four citations of excellence in the Art of Puppetry from UNIMA-USA, as well as being given a Guggenheim Fellowship in 1990. The National Endowment for the Arts, the Jim Henson Foundation, the Los Angeles Music Center and the New York State Council on the Arts have all supported his unique visions. Paul has been influenced by Bread and Puppet, Lord Richard Buckley, Marcel Duchamp, and Soupy Sales and Frank Natasi of *"The Soupy Sales Show."* Paul's self-professed mission as an artist has been to: 1) attempt to master almost every form of puppetry (excluding string marionettes) and 2) create funny and visually rich political and social satires that will generate unbridled mirth and awe about the things that are killing us all.

LEE ARMSTRONG
2008

Lee Armstrong
1952–present

Career: 1972–present. Lee Armstrong was born and grew up in Nova Scotia, Canada. After a year studying music at Mount Allison University, she decided to get a job in "The Arts." The next day, Mermaid Theatre, a local touring puppet company in schools, hired her and she started her puppetry career. This led to studying puppetry at the University of Ottawa with Felix Mirbt. Lee puppeteered with Nikki Tilroe's Frog Print Theatre from 1974–1980, as well as performing on Canadian TV shows. In 1977, she watched the taping of *"Emmet Otter's Jug-Band Christmas"* and knew she wanted to work with the Muppets. 1980 saw Lee receive a grant from the Canada Council to study acting at HB Studios and puppet construction on Julie Taymor's *"Haggadah"* in New York. When she returned home she was one of ten puppeteers — out of a few hundred who auditioned — to be chosen for Jim Henson's *"Fraggle Rock."* After three years on *"Fraggle"* (1982-1984), she left Canada for California.

Lee established Images in Motion in 1989 with collaborator Kamela Portuges. "At Images in Motion," Lee says, "I puppeteer and produce projects, coordinate video shoots, including scripts, bids, budgets, scheduling, organizing crews and equipment. I help build puppets, and I usually take out the trash." Clients have included the USDA Forest Service, Leapfrog Toys and Cartoon Network. Lee's credits include *"Being John Malkovich"* and *"Follow That Bird."* She has also produced films for the USDA Forest Service in Washington, D.C. Lee holds a degree in English and Theater from the University of Toronto and teaches *"The Art of Jim Henson"* and *"Pixar: Story Matters"* at U. C. Santa Cruz, and *"The Power of the Puppet in Performance"* at U. C. Berkeley. She has also taught many workshops on puppet video production.

Lee has won two Regional Emmys and numerous awards for her producing, writing, puppetry work, and coordinating of video projects on film and television. She credits Jim Henson with influencing her, and counts Lettie Connell Schubert, Mike Oznowicz, Nikki Tilroe and Felix Mirbt among her mentors.

STEVE AXTELL
with The Alien
2017

Steve Axtell
1958–present

Career: 1972–present. Steve Axtell, like many puppeteers of his generation, was inspired by the puppets he saw on television. Kukla, Fran & Ollie and the Muppets were his favorites, although Walt Disney, Dr. Seuss, Chuck Jones, Stan Winston and Mr. Rogers were also influential role models. Steve's first puppets were copies of his favorite *"Sesame Street"* heroes. And when the local paper did an article on this child puppeteer, his mother sent a copy and a photo to Jim Henson. Jim was touched by Steve's passion, and wrote back encouraging him to find his own designs rather than copying the Muppets like everyone else was doing. And that is how, in 1982, Axtell Expressions began.

Steve is now known for his own style of custom puppets that he builds for puppeteers, ventriloquists, magicians and amusement parks. His puppets get their signature look from the sculptural design and latex they are cast in. (It's amusing to him that "Axtell" can be arranged to form "Latex.") Axtell Expressions is very involved in animatronics and artificial intelligence for autonomous characters as well as projected interactive backgrounds called "Live Virtual Sets" for puppeteers and live stage performers. Besides making vent figures, Steve holds six patents for such inventions as the "Magic Drawing Board" that makes a drawing come alive, "The Bird Arm Illusion" and a "Bird Puppet Wing Flap Device." He also makes animated talking trees and dragons that breathe smoke for amusement venues.

Steve creates custom puppets for top ventriloquists such as *"America's Got Talent"* winner Terry Fator, Darci Lynne and Jay Johnson. He has built amusements for Disneyland and Legoland, Universal Studios and Six Flags as well as for the PBS television show *"Jack Houston's Imagineland."* As a pet project, in 2004, he created a TV show *"AxTelevision,"* which involved kids making puppets for their own shows and won over 12 awards. His mentors include Barbie sculptor Anthony Bulone, engineer Russ Robison, high school teachers Charles Casto and Nelson Roberts, as well as Gene Clark and figure maker Craig Lovik.

DAVE GOELZ
2016

Dave Goelz
1946–present

Career: 1972–present. After graduating from the Art Center College of Design in 1968, David Charles Goelz began his career as an industrial designer for John Deere, American Airlines and Hewlett-Packard. His first exposure to puppetry had been the television shows *"Time for Beany"* and *"Howdy Doody"* at age five. Twenty years later, after beginning his career in industrial design, Dave became fascinated with the design process that went into the Muppets on *"Sesame Street."* He attended the 1972 Puppeteers of America national festival in Oakland, where he met Frank Oz. A month later, he spent a week visiting the *"Sesame Street"* set in New York. Later that year, Dave met Jim Henson in Los Angeles, and showed him his design portfolio and puppets. Jim hired him for six months as a designer/builder and gave him after-hours training as a performer. His first puppet and character, Brewster, was in the *"Muppets Valentine Show"* on ABC.

Dave then returned to California and started his own business, building puppets for and performing in industrial films. His first client was the Raychem Corporation, for whom he built and performed "Ray, the Raychem Seal" in trade shows. Eight months later Dave rejoined the Muppets, where he continued his Raychem work and built such lovable *"Muppet Show"* characters as Animal, Floyd Pepper, Zoot, Uncle Deadly, and several puppets for *"Emmet Otter's Jug Band Christmas."*

Dave's character Gonzo the Great for *"The Muppet Show"* is his most memorable. The Gonzo puppet, originally known as "Cigar Box Frackle," had been built by Jim for Ed Sullivan's *"The Great Santa Claus Switch."* Dave gave him a voice, character and stardom. Dave has also performed Muppets Dr. Bunsen Honeydew, Zoot, Beauregarde, Chip the I.T. Guy, Boober Fraggle, Uncle Traveling Matt and Rugby Tiger. He also performed SkekUng in *"The Dark Crystal,"* Sir Didymus in *"Labyrinth"* and Digit on *"The Jim Henson Hour."* As a vocal actor, Dave voiced Figment in the *"Journey into Imagination with Figment"* ride at Walt Disney World, and with Frank Oz, voiced the "Subconscious Guards" in the Pixar film *"Inside Out."* Dave is the last original performer still working with the *"Muppet Show"* character group.

MARY NAGLER
2016

Mary Nagler
1953–present

Career: 1972–present. Mary Hildebrand Nagler first became interested in puppets while a freshman at the University of Santa Clara. The school was looking for someone to do a *"Punch and Judy"* show at their school Renaissance Faire and Mary thought, since she made puppets in Girl Scouts when she was 10, she was just the person to do it! That show started her career, which led to a B.A. in Fine Arts from Sonoma State, a degree in Buffoonery from Ringling Bros. and Barnum & Bailey Clown College, and eventually an M.F.A. in puppetry from the University of Connecticut. Mary was first influenced in puppetry when she saw a performance of *"Peter and the Wolf"* at the Happy Hollow Castle Puppet Theater in San Jose. She has been mentored by Ron Skolman of Happy Hollow and Santa Clara University, Jim Kroupa, Bart Roccoberton Jr., Glynn Tree Bartlett, and Michael and Valerie Nelson.

In 1972, Mary began performing with puppet partner Carlo Pellegrini as the Hildegrini Puppets. Since then she has worked for such prestigious companies as Images in Motion, the Fratello Marionettes, Furry Puppet Studio, Rick Lyon Studios, Puppet Heap and Michael Curry Design. In 2008, after receiving her Master's degree and returning to the Bay Area, she established Whorls of Wonder Puppet Theater. Her thesis presentation, *"Little Things,"* employed 47 puppets from all styles of puppet theater. Besides creating her own beautiful puppets, Mary builds for the theater stage as well as teaching college level puppetry and multicultural puppet classes.

Mary's recent show, *"Terran's Aquarium,"* about ecology and the fresh water crisis, received a 2011 Henson Foundation Family Grant. In 2015 her own versions of the puppets for *"Avenue Q"* were nominated for the Theater Bay Area awards in the Outstanding Creative Speciality Division. Mary has been influenced by Jim and Jane Henson, Ronnie Burkett, Lee Armstrong and Kamela Portuges as well as the San Francisco Bay AreaPuppeteers Guild.

MIKE QUINN
with Skek-Na
1982

Mike Quinn
1964–present

Career: 1972–present. Michael Quinn began performing magic and puppets for his family and friends at the age of eight. By 15 he was regularly visiting the set of *"The Muppet Show,"* since he lived nearby in England. In 1980, at 16, he officially joined the Jim Henson Company, helping to puppeteer on *"The Great Muppet Caper."* Since the Muppets were signed on for a two-film contract, Mike was next assigned the job of designing and building "Podlings" for *"The Dark Crystal."* He also performed the role of SkekNa, the Slave Master. These successes led to Mike helping Frank Oz puppeteer Yoda in *"Return of the Jedi."* Mike also created the role of Nien Nunb, Lando Calrissian's co-pilot.

In late 1989, Mike joined forces with fellow puppeteer David Barclay creating Ultimate Animates, a production company specializing in new building and performing techniques for internal and external puppet productions. Soon he was acting as "Chief Hand Puppeteer" for *"Who Framed Roger Rabbit?"* The job was called "Chief Hand" because that's often all they filmed. Mike spent his time helping to create the illusion showing where an animated Roger landed when jumping on the bed, or he worked fragmented puppets that animators later removed and drew over.

For Henson's *"Fraggle Rock,"* Mike performed Gobo Fraggle and Uncle Traveling Matt, when they ventured out into the human world or "Outer Space", for many French and U.K. segments. He also worked Sprocket the dog on several German and French episodes. This meant traveling to various countries to film with all the different hosts used on the international shows. In 1997, Mike moved to San Francisco to work with Pixar as a Character Animator for *"A Bug's Life"* and *"Toy Story II."* Mike also was employed with Industrial Light & Magic as an animator, first working on *"Jurassic Park III"* and *"Attack of the Clones,"* and later reprising his role as Nien Nunb for the final Disney *"Star Wars"* film trilogy. Mike still works with the Muppets, and can be seen puppeteering in Jim Carrey's *"Kidding"* on Showtime.

ALLAN TRAUTMAN
Jungle Book
with NEEL SETAI
2016

Allan Trautman
1955–present

Career: 1973–present. While studying physics at Washington University, Allan decided to add a drama major to his goals. The next day, he saw an opening posted on the drama school's community audition board for a children's educational TV show, *"The Letter People."* They were willing to train actors who showed some talent with puppets and could do voices. Allan auditioned, was hired, and began a successful career in puppetry. After graduating, he went on to earn an M.F.A. in Acting from the California Institute of the Arts.

After arriving in California, Allan was hired by Sid & Marty Krofft Productions after he took part in their puppet school taught by Tony Urbano. After his time with the Kroffts he found employment with the Jim Henson Company, where he worked on the Disney project *"Muppet*Vision 3-D."* Allan's work can be seen on the television shows *"D. C. Follies"* and *"Dinosaurs,"* where he worked the animatronics for Fran Sinclair, and he has directed episodes of *"Splash and Bubbles"* and *"Sid the Science Kid."* His puppetry film work includes *"Muppets from Space,"* *"The Flintstones in Viva Rock Vegas,"* *"Doctor Dolittle,"* *"The Country Bears,"* and most recently *"The Jungle Book"* and *"The Happytime Murders."* Allan has worked with the Jim Henson's Creature Shop since 1991 on many animatronic puppet related projects.

Allan is a founding member of Henson Alternative's puppet improv show, *"Puppet Up!"* (a.k.a. *Stuffed and Unstrung*), touring to such places as Melbourne and Sydney, Australia. Having spent two years performing at the Colorado Shakespeare Festival, he was well prepared to play one of the most "iconic" zombies to ever appear on the large screen. Allan portrayed "The Tarman" in both *"Return of the Living Dead"* films. He is happy to pass on skills he learned from his mentors, King Hall, Tony Urbano and Patrick Bristol Hall.

Allan occasionally teaches Puppet Technique to new employees of the Jim Henson Company. He has also taught improvisation at College of the Canyons in Santa Clarita, California, and an online course: Understanding Theatre. Currently he is working as lead animatronic puppeteer for Ned on *"Earth to Ned"* for the Disney+ channel.

STEVEN M. OVERTON
2011

Steven M. Overton
1958–present

Career: 1974–present. When Steve Overton was six years old, he crawled under a puppet stage to see what was going on behind the scenes. And he's stayed there ever since. This fascination for puppets led him to form the Castle of Tiny Children in 1968, where he performed plays with Pelham Puppets on the military base in Germany where his family was stationed. He returned to the puppet world in 1974 with the Olde World Puppet Theatre, after his high school art teacher convinced him to build his own shows. He was living in Oregon at the time, and five years later became the puppeteer for the Portland Zoo.

In 1981, Steve moved to Hawaii where he met his life and puppet partner, Martin Richmond. After a year the two moved to California and settled in Pacifica. Steve spent time traveling between Los Angeles and San Francisco sharpening his talents. He worked with René and his Artists at Knott's Berry Farm and collaborated with Frank Paris and Bob Baker on projects. In the Bay Area, Steve and Martin performed at Macy's department stores for ten years. They toured libraries, elementary schools, fairs and malls throughout California in the '80s with *The Tales of Belvuria*," seventeen interlocking puppet shows detailing this imaginary Renaissance land. In 1992 they returned to Oregon, where they built the puppets for Walt Disney World's *Hunchback of Notre Dame*" stage show, which had a six year run, and also built puppets for the *Wee Sing Under The Sea*" video. They have also produced a DVD movie titled *Witch Key, a Prince's Adventure*," and *The Enchanted Ring, A Princess's Adventure* puppet photo book, all based on their Belvuria shows. In 2012 they opened Ping Ping's Pint Sized Puppet Museum, featuring shows and exhibits.

Steve's mentors include Frank Paris, Phillip Huber, Bob Baker, Lewis Mahlmann and Michael Curry. He says his influencers have been opera, Shakespeare, Tony Sarg, classic fairytales and Pelham Puppets. Steve created "Maraku," a puppet performance style combining the western technique of marionettes with Japanese Bunraku.

HENRY SELICK
with Coraline
2009

Henry Selick
1952–present

Career: 1975–present. Henry Selick is a stop motion director, producer and writer, best known for directing Tim Burton's *"Nightmare Before Christmas"* (1993) and *"James and the Giant Peach"* (1996), as well as LAIKA's *"Coraline"* (2009). He also worked on the films *"Monkeybone"* (2001), *"Life Aquatic"* (2004) and *"Moongirl"* (2005). Henry studied science at Rutgers University, and art at Syracuse University and Central Saint Martins College of Art and Design in London. He also studied Experimental Animation at California Institute of the Arts under Jules Engel. His student films *"Phases"* and *"Tube Tales"* were nominated for Student Academy Awards.

Henry was influenced by shadow puppeteer Lotte Reiniger's's film *"The Adventures of Prince Achmed"* and Ray Harryhausen's stop-motion puppetry in *"The 7ᵗʰ Voyage of Sinbad."* His early career contains work as an "in-betweener" and animator trainee on the Disney Studio's *"Pete's Dragon"*, and *"The Small One"*, as well as main animator on *"The Fox and the Hound."* Dissatisfied with cell animation, Henry left Disney, and in 1986 established his own company, Selick Projects. As a freelancer, he worked on commercials for Pillsbury, Ritz Crackers and John Korty's *"Twice Upon a Time."* He also storyboarded the film *"Nutcracker: The Motion Picture"* with designs by Maurice Sendak, and the fantasy sequences for Walter Murch's *"Return to Oz."* But it was his work animating MTV Station IDs, for which he won a Clio, and an award-winning animated series called *"Slow Bob in the Lower Dimensions,"* that caught Tim Burton's eye.

In 2010, Selick joined Pixar and the Walt Disney Company with a long-term contract to exclusively produce stop-motion films. His new studio was called "Cinderbiter Productions" and produces great, scary films for young ones. He is currently working on the features *"The Shadow King,"* Adam Gidwitz's *"A Tale Dark and Grimm,"* and Jordan Peele and Keegan-Michael Key's *"Wendell and Wild."* In 2017, he was selected to direct the pilot and episodes of *"Little Nightmares"* produced by the Russo Brothers, which debuted in 2019 based on the popular video game.

PHIL TIPPETT
Return of the Jedi
1983

Phil Tippett
1951–present

Career: 1975–present. Phil Tippett is an American movie director and Oscar and Emmy Award-winning visual effects supervisor and producer, who specializes in creature design, stop-motion puppetry and computerized character animation. Phil was inspired by the work of Ray Harryhausen and Willis O'Brien's *"King Kong."* After receiving a B.A. in Art from the University of California, he began work at Cascade Pictures animation studio in Los Angeles. His first success was designing the stop-motion characters in the chess scene for *"Star Wars."* In *"Empire Strikes Back"* he brought to life the Tauntauns and the sinister AT-AT Imperial Walkers, and in 1983 he led the famed Lucasfilm Creature Shop, winning his first Oscar for his work on *"Return of the Jedi."* Phil created the fish for Roger Corman's *"Piranha,"* modeled the Dark Overlord creatures in *"Howard the Duck"* and animated the CBS documentary *"Dinosaur!,"* for which his studio won an Emmy for Outstanding Special Visual Effects. In 1981 he created the dragon for *"Dragonslayer,"* where he developed his own form of stop-motion called "Go Motion Technique," which incorporates motion blur into each frame of film that involves movement.

After working for Industrial Light & Magic, Phil formed Tippett Studio in 1984. After several successes, in 1995 Tippett Studio began work on the giant bugs in *"Starship Troopers."* This led to Phil directing the sequel, *"Hero of the Federation."* Phil's puppet animation can be seen in the *"Star Wars"* trilogy, *"Jurassic Park,"* *"Willow,"* *"Evolution"* and the *"RoboCop"* trilogy. When he first saw the CG dinosaurs from Steven Spielberg, Phil was blown away.

Phil is busy combining computer graphic techniques with stop-motion, as well as influencing Tippett Studio VFX supervisors and crew as they create monsters, aliens and appealing creatures for numerous films that wind their way through the Tippett pipeline. Since 2017 he has been working on his own stop-motion series, *"Mad God,"* which was imagined in 1990 and funded through Kickstarter.

LYNNE JENNINGS
2000s

Lynne Jennings
1943–present

Career: 1976–present. Lynne has been the Executive Director of the San Diego Guild of Puppetry for more than 20 years, helping guide its growth from its early "club" days, to its current firm focus on bringing free puppetry programming to underserved communities, while procuring grant funding to compensate its teaching, performing and guest artists for their expertise. Programming includes: shows and workshops for all ages, school residencies, giant puppet parades, summer camps, exhibits and festivals.

Lynne discovered puppetry as a Girl Scout, and later was part of her sorority's performing troupe at Middlebury College in Vermont (where she got her degree in Biology). Although most of her work is now administrative, Lynne spent many years as a builder, a teaching artist in the schools, and was for ten years, the designer/ builder/director of San Diego Opera's puppetry outreach program. She still works with local theaters, schools and colleges when their shows involve puppetry. Lynne has served 13 years on the UNI-MA-USA Board, with six as Vice President and five as Citations Chair. She was involved with most of the Puppeteers of America festivals from 1978-2004, and was ongoing staff of PuppetFest MidWest, an independent festival held annually from 2003–2012. She has directed two Pacific Southwest Regional Puppetry Festivals and in 2015 co-directed the Guild's first festival for the general public in downtown San Diego.

Lynne has studied with the Henson artists in a summer intensive, *"A Survey of Puppet Theater Techniques"* at Humboldt State in 1994: and at the National Puppetry Conference at the O'Neill Theater Center from 1995-97. She has a number of Guild shows to her credit, most notably her shadow puppet memory piece, *"Season of the Swan"* and the Henson Grant production on elder abuse: *"Goldilocks: The Nursing Home Version."* Lynne is a firm believer in the power of puppetry to change lives in profound and positive ways and credits her major puppet influences as Pam McIntire, Bruce Schwartz, Caroly Wilcox, Luman Coad, Eric Bass and Paco Parecio.

RANDEL McGEE
with Groark
2018

Randel McGee
1954–present

Career: 1976–present. While on a tour of Europe, Jack Randel McGee became enchanted with the Salzburg Marionettes. When he returned to Brigham Young University to receive a B.A. in Theater and Children's Theater, he joined a puppet troupe and class offered there, and began doing puppetry in elementary schools. After college he did variety shows combining shadows, hand/mouth puppets, rod and marionettes. He also did ventriloquism, developing a vent partner, Groark the Dragon, to help emcee the show. Soon, the other puppets were dropped in favor of just the vent act. As Randel McGee & Groark, Randel has performed at the Center for Puppetry Arts, and has also been a featured ventriloquist at both the International and Japanese (yes, he speaks Japanese) Ventriloquist Association Festivals.

Known as McGee Productions, Randel and Groark have appeared, and taught workshops, in Singapore, Malaysia, the Philippines, Brunei, Taiwan and India. Randel has been the artist in residence for the California Arts Council and the Treehouse Children's Museum in Ogden, Utah, designing, building and directing puppet productions. He has produced a video series *"Getting Along with Groark"* that deals with character education for elementary school children, and has been bestowed numerous honors and awards. Besides vent work, Randel still does shadow puppetry presentations and teaches workshops on many different styles of puppetry, while occasionally performing storytelling as Hans Christian Andersen.

Randel has performed at national and regional puppet conventions, and has received the Trustee Award for Outstanding Service to an Organization from Puppeteers of America, as well as a Citation of Excellence from UNIMA-USA. His influencers include Paul Winchell, Jimmy Nelson, Shari Lewis and the Muppets, and he was mentored by Dr. Harold R. Oaks, puppet class director at Brigham Young, and Seattle puppeteer Rob D'Arc. Randel currently resides in Hanford, a small town near Fresno, *"where the only culture is agri-culture! (wink)"* and hopes that he has contributed a little bit to California's rich artistic legacy. His son Matthew McGee currently continues the family puppet tradition in Washington D.C.

WENDY MORTON
The Little Dragon
2005

Wendy Morton
1956–present

Career: 1976–present. In 1976, Wendy Morton attended a workshop taught by puppeteer Margo Rose at the famous O'Neill Theater Center. She was interested in performance and specifically experimental theater combining art, masks, puppets and found-objects. Wendy began working in the Bay Area, with George Coats Performance Works, doing object manipulation. Having been influenced by shadow master Lotte Reiniger, Wendy formed her own company The Shadowmakers. Her shadow piece *"The Little Dragon"* was commissioned by Bose and performed in the Boston Area and at the International Shadow Theatre Festival in Germany.

In the style of Bread and Puppet, Wendy has used masks and puppets to perform in the Berkeley Hills Tilden Park with *"The Wildcat Creek Project."* She has worked with Larry Reed as designer and lead puppeteer for his award-winning shadow production *"In Xanadu,"* and did character voices for *"The Wild Party,"* as well as a commissioned shadow performance of *"Coyote Stories"* that toured England as part of a music festival.

For thirteen years, 1993–2006, Wendy worked at Industrial Light & Magic as a puppeteer, model and creature maker doing visual effects. Her work includes giant pigeons for a Superbowl commercial, the Energizer Bunny, and the Wampa in *"The Empire Strikes Back Special Edition."* She has performed and constructed for such films as *"Fire in the Sky,"* *"Congo,"* *"The Mummy,"* *"A.I. Artificial Intelligence,"* *"The Lost World: Jurassic Park,"* *"The Phantom Menace"* and the first 3 *"Pirates of the Caribbean"* films. Her puppet building and puppeteering for the Hefty commercial, *"The Gingerbread Man,"* received a Clio award.

Wendy has a Theater Arts degree from Grinnell College in Iowa, and was mentored by shadow artists Larry Reed and Richard Bradshaw and puppetmaker Judy Folkmanis. She has collaborated with Jay O'Callahan, Art Gruenberger, Nick Barone and Raven Kaliana. Wendy has been the Shadow Puppetry Consultant for the Puppeteers of America, and has taught shadow puppetry workshops. Her shadow production of *"The Jungle Book"* received a Arlyn Citation of Recognition in Puppet Theatre Design. She's currently a Project Manager at Folkmanis Puppets.

MICHAEL & VALERIE NELSON
1980s

Michael & Valerie Nelson
1953–present & 1955–present

Career: 1979–present. Valerie was teaching and Michael was a cabinet maker when they decided to put on a show for the children at Valerie's school. Michael had studied Jungian psychology at Hampshire College in Amherst, while Valerie had majored in voice at Napa Valley College. Having no puppetry experience besides playing with puppets as children, they decided to create a full marionette show, which also included hand puppets in a higher, second proscenium. The show was greatly enjoyed by the children, who literally rolled on the floor laughing. This prompted the Nelsons to further explore this art form, and they eventually founded Magical Moonshine Theatre as a professional, touring theater.

In the early 1980s, the Nelsons sought to simplify Japanese Bunraku (3 puppeteers to a single puppet) to one puppeteer, and finally to a puppeteer using table top puppets, live music and singing, with the performer's face visible. This puppetry presentation style was not universally accepted by the puppet community, but soon other puppet companies began performing in the same style and it became more mainstream. The Nelsons have also performed with shadows, hand, rod and giant parade puppets. Their shows include *"Animal Folktales of the Americas,"* as well as adult works such as *"Orpheus Ascending," "Cannibal Island"* and *"Canterbury Tales."* In the 1990s, the Nelsons began to explore toy theatre, and through several of life's twists and turns they formed their second company, Little Blue Moon Theatre, which featured intimate shows revolving around various erotic themes in the style of paper theater.

The Nelsons were influenced by the Carter Family Marionettes, and were mentored by Lettie Connell Schubert and George Latshaw. Michael studied puppetry with Jim Henson at the International Institute of Puppetry in France. They have toured Europe, India, Asia, and Latin America, as well as coast to coast in North America. Beginning in 2009, the couple started hosting the popular puppet slams, *"Forbidden Puppet Cabaret"*, in Vallejo.

CHRISTINE PAPALEXIS
2019

Christine Papalexis
1956–present

Career: 1979–Present. Christine Papalexis started working for the Bob Baker Marionette Theater after completing a degree in Sociology at University of California, Santa Barbara. She hadn't planned to be a puppeteer, but working at Bob's sparked this new passion and over the next three and a half years she became entangled in the puppet world. Christine continued to pursue her career and has worked in movies, television and commercials as a professional puppeteer, puppet builder and costumer. She has performed with a variety of puppets including hand/rod puppets, cable, animatronic and hydraulic puppets, though marionettes are her first love.

After performing at the Queen Mary in Long Beach, and for Jim Gamble Productions, Christine forged a path in the film world. Her skills can be seen in some of the most beloved creature films including: *"Batman Returns,""Alien Resurrection," "Hollow Man," "Annabelle 2, Creation," "Men in Black II," "Team America: World Police," "The Santa Clause II & III" "Bedazzled", "The X-Files" "Michael"* and more. Her television work includes *"Kidding", "Crank Yankers," "The Muppets," "D.C. Follies," and "Timmy the Tooth."* She also built puppets for Timmy, and played Annette-Full-of-Jello. She worked for various studios including Amalgamated Dynamics, Inc., Stan Winston Studio, The Character Shop, and many more. Christine's favorite form of puppetry is found object theater. She produced two marionette shows using found objects, *"The Witch's Egg"* and *"Amaterasu."* The latter, based on a Japanese folk tale, marked her film directorial debut. It was supported by Heather Henson's Handmade Puppet Dreams, which showcases independent puppeteers who use film to present live-action puppetry.

Christine's major influencers have been: Bob Baker, Jim Henson, Bil Baird, visual artists Judy Chicago and Joseph Cornell, and mentored by Phillip Huber and Michael Haimsohn. Christine served as President of the Los Angeles Guild of Puppetry for six years as well as being Regional Director for Puppeteers of America. She regularly contributes to local and national/international puppet publications. Since 2011, she has produced puppet slams for the Guild in the Los Angeles area.

Outstanding Ovations!... 1970s

Julie & Richard Greene

Career: 1971–Early '80s. The Greenes were known in the Bay Area as the Puppet House, performing at schools, parties and any social gathering. Besides their own productions, the two were the directors of the famous Oakland Vagabond Puppets from 1973–1975. Being vocal actors they flourished at bringing live puppetry to Bay Area children. The Greenes also taught puppetry workshops for children, teens, adults and the handicapped. In 1971, Julie and Richard began touring with Nick Coppola and the Nicolo Marionettes of New York, who trained them. Richard was also trained as a clown and as a nurse.

Jack & Christopher Fredericks

Career: 1972–present. The Walden Marionettes, a father and son team, began as part of the Walden School Program in San Mateo. They were at one time the puppeteers for the San Francisco Zoo, and have entertained children and adults from the Canadian to the Mexican border. Jack and Christopher were mentored by the famous marionettist Albrecht Roser of Germany. Jack toured Germany at the close of World War II with an elaborate puppet production of *"A Christmas Carol."* He was also featured in a short segment with Muppet character Uncle Traveling Matt, on Jim Henson's *"Fraggle Rock."*

Scott Land

Career: 1972–present. Since age 12, Scott Land (as the Scott Land Marionettes) has performed at convention centers, theme parks, corporate events and of course cruise lines. In addition to sculpting and carving, Scott designs all his creations. Scott is honored to be one of few puppeteers asked to perform at the legendary Magic Castle in Hollywood. He has even performed for the Dalai Lama. Recently, Scott moved to Las Vegas and opened Team Land Productions, where his wife Lisa paints all of his caricature puppets. Scott has been mentored by Bob Baker, Tony Urbano and Albrecht Roser.

Michael Baroto

Career: 1973–present. Michael Baroto is a sought after artist, puppeteer, costumer, sculptor, writer and animator. His career includes work in special costume effects and puppet design for theater and amusement parks, as well as costume effects and puppets for NBC, CBS, Paramount, Universal, Disneyland and Mattel. Michael's company, Spectacular Dimensions, specializes in the design and creation of puppets, dolls, costumes and illustration for entertainment media. He trained with Bil Baird as a puppeteer and puppet manufacturer, and with Sid & Marty Krofft as a puppet designer. Michael has also written several articles for the *Puppetry Journal* illustrating his craft.

Pat Brymer

Career: 1973–2020. Patrick worked with Hanna-Barbera in the costume department and as a principal performer and builder for Sid & Marty Krofft and their live stage shows at Six Flags Amusement Park attractions. His film work includes *"Team America: World Police"* and the infamously impish gopher in *"Caddyshack."* Pat has also performed with Thom Fountain, playing various puppet characters on the live children's stage show *"The Crayon Court."* He worked with Shari Lewis as her puppet partner, fabricator and personal puppeteer for twenty years, creating puppets for *"Lamb Chop's Play-along"* and *"The Charlie Horse Music Pizza."*

George Buchanan

Career: 1973–1992. Born George Lee Dalton, Buchanan began his career as a ventriloquist. After seeing Tony Urbano perform, he switched to adult marionette revue. George appeared on *"The Tonight Show"* and toured the world on cruise ships. He headlined casino revues in Vegas, Reno, Lake Tahoe, the Bahamas and Mexico. He often headlined at San Francisco's famous Finocchio's nightclub, which featured female impersonators and unique acts. George's most famous marionette was Richard Nixon dressed in a business suit with diamond earrings and a pink feather boa singing "I did it my way."

Joe & Ronna Leon

Career: 1976–present. Joe and Ronna Casey Leon formed the Caterpillar Puppets in the Bay Area. With Joe's degree in art and Ronna's in literature, the couple are perfectly paired for puppetry. The two were selected to represent young American puppeteers at an International Puppetry Conference in Moscow, and have been awarded grants from the National Endowment for the Arts and the California Arts Council. Ronna was co-director of the international/national Puppeteers of America convention at San Francisco State in 1993. They've been featured puppeteers at Marine World/Africa U.S.A. in Vallejo, and the California State Fair.

Robin Goodrow

Career: 1977–present. Robin is a puppeteer, storyteller, songwriter and actress at children's parties, libraries and other gatherings. She went from the puppet proscenium to the television proscenium with her show *"Buster and Me"* on KRON TV, which aired for 20 years with syndication. The show explores problems in a family–Robin and two monkey children, Buster and Vanilla, and their friend Russell. It has received Parents Choice Awards, numerous Emmys and the prestigious Iris Award for "Best Local Children's Show in America." Buster even made a cameo appearance in Robin William's *"Mrs. Doubtfire."*

Peter Brizzi

Career: 1979–2010. When Peter was a child, he was influenced to be a puppeteer by two things: *"Howdy Doody"* (which he saw taped in person) and a touring puppetry troupe that visited his school. Inspired, he and his wife Teena formed P & T Puppets, performing puppetry for their small Sunday School program. Eventually, they started appearing at events and libraries. Peter loved to perform rod puppets under blacklight, and mixed classical tales and music such as Gilbert & Sullivan. His show specialty was using visual gizmos and mechanics with his scenic effects to spellbound the youngstersAbove

Above: ART GRUENBERGER
Don Quixote

Left: MARY NAGLER
Gwenderfigg
1995

8

1980–1989

THE 1980s WAS an era defined by conservative politics, the rise of computer technology and the end of the Cold War. Due to advances in technology and a worldwide move away from planned economies, the country was letting things take their own course and heading towards laissez-faire capitalism. By 1982, technology was a major industry thanks to the production and popularity of computers, "walkman" cassette players and boomboxes. In 1981, MTV television was launched and reshaped pop culture through its film techniques and innovations. The world was slowly becoming digital. The internet was still in the hands of the military, but in 1989 the World Wide Web was invented (although it wasn't released to the public until 1991). Meanwhile the entertainment world was fragmenting and redefining itself.

"Star Wars" ignited the rise of puppetry and effects in film. Overnight, puppeteers, animators and film artists became "the stars." Hit films such as *"E.T. the Extra-Terrestrial,"* *"Raiders of the Lost Ark,"* the *"Back to the Future"* trilogy and the *"Batman"* movies were spellbinding us with their film effect images. Of course, teen flicks like *"The Breakfast Club,"* *"Fast Times at Ridgemont High,"* *"Ferris Bueller's Day Off"* and *"Sixteen Candles"* still captured significant attention. But the success of action film franchises such as *"Terminator,"* *"Alien,"* *"Predator"* and *"RoboCop"* were about to ensure that puppeteers were a necessity in Hollywood.

This is the decade where cable television became accessible, and with it, HBO and Showtime. Popular writers such as Tom Clancy, Robert Ludlum, Thomas Harris and Clive Cussler were supplying the genre with imaginative tales ripe with images. And in the literary world, Terry Pratchett took us to new fantasy kingdoms while monumental illustrative artists such as Maurice Sendak, Greg & Tim Hildebrandt and Michael Hague were busy with the brush recreating classic novels and fairytale images.

The film industry had a dramatic effect on puppetry. Jim Henson began building puppets with servos and gears that made them more animatronic. His research and experimentation on *"The Dark Crystal"* and *"Labyrinth"* soon gained recognition. Of special note was his creation of "Waldo", a mechanical device to control a puppet's movement at a distance via electronic connections. George Lucas of *"Star Wars"* fame partnered with Henson to build new fantastic cinematic creatures such as Yoda. The Walt Disney company even profited from his designs and built superior animatronic attractions. Eventually the medical industry also looked to these three giants for ideas in better mechanical appendages and advancements. Industrial Light & Magic, George Lucas's effects company, began to employ puppeteers as designers, miniatures craftsmen and performers as work demands increased. Computer graphics for a completely digital character were still advancing, and "practical puppetry" was the process used to create fantasy characters in real time with the actors.

Now that Henson was pushing puppetry into the popular culture, the Puppeteers of America felt it was time to do their share. *"Puppets–Art & Entertainment"* was a beautiful puppet exhibit that toured eleven American cities from 1980–1983. Nancy Staub was project director for the tour, which was co-curated and managed by Alan Cook of Los Angeles. It played in each city for several months and featured shows, workshops and lectures presented by local puppet performers. The Puppeteers of America also transferred all of its puppet film archives onto videocassettes, the popular medium at that time, giving members access to hundreds of hours of puppet history videos. And puppet shows were finding a new home in the libraries of America, as librarians used the puppet to entertain and teach youngsters. Since the '30s, children's librarian training involved puppets and storytelling. Many libraries built their own puppet theaters for children's librarians. In the '70s, puppetry became an elective rather than a required subject for library degrees. Since fewer librarians studied the art form, it opened the door for many professional puppeteers to start performing regularly in their local libraries. Puppetry was vibrant across the States! And the beauty of the marionette was given new life as Phillip Huber, Ronnie Burkett, David Simpich and Joe Cashore used these puppets to their full theatrical extent.

Meanwhile in California, with puppeteers now entering the movie industry, Tony Urbano and Bob Baker were working feverishly with the Screen Actors Guild to create a niche for puppeteers in the union by 1989. This would establish that a professional puppeteer, not a prop man or stage hand, must manipulate any form of puppet on screen, and that the puppeteer receives credit as being a principal performer. Stan Winston also led the way for more practical puppetry on film through his makeup/effects company the Stan Winston Studio. Puppets were taking over almost all the entertainment venues, even the Broadway stage, as "Audrey II" — the man-eating puppet plant by Martin Robinson — created a sensation when *"Little Shop of Horrors"* opened off-Broadway in 1982. Steve Axtell established Axtell Expressions in 1982, and promptly began supplying ventriloquists, magicians and puppeteers with high quality puppet figures. In 1986 Pixar Films was founded in Emeryville by George Lucas, advancing the art of virtual puppetry. Before long the Chiodo Brothers began making films with puppets, while Phil Tippitt turned stop-motion into "Go-Motion" animation. And in 1989 Lee Armstrong and Kamela Portuges opened Images in Motion in Marin with the theme of "one-stop shopping for all your puppet film needs."

In the next decade the life of the puppet came full circle, and once more became a popular attraction on the theatrical stage in all its various venues.

Tim Blaney
with George Clooney
2004

Tim Blaney
1959–present

Career: 1980–present. Tim Blaney is a voice-over artist, puppet builder, puppeteer and actor. Tim studied painting, drawing and sculpture at UCLA, but withdrew during his third year to seek a better fit for his future. When investigating employment options, he responded to a job posting from Tony Urbano Productions. Thinking he would be hired for set painting, Tim soon became a working puppeteer.

His first puppetry work was performing for Tony at the annual Laguna Beach Festival of Arts . Tim's knack for vocal characterizations soon had Tony casting him in a commercial for Home Savings and Loan of Arizona, where he both manipulated and voiced his puppet character. (At that time, a puppeteer had to either perform the voice or own the puppet itself to receive residuals. By late 1989, the Screen Actors Guild agreed to contractually recognize puppeteers as principal performers, with the same benefits as actors.)

Tim's film work includes principal puppeteer and voice of the robotic star Johnny Five in *"Short Circuit,"* as well as the voice of Frank the Pug in the *"Men in Black"* films and the voice and puppeteer of the Puckmarin in Disney's *"Flight of the Navigator."* Other film credits include *"Team America: World Police," "How the Grinch Stole Christmas,"* and the voice of Goofy Goober in *"The SpongeBob SquarePants Movie."* Tim's television credits include *"Dinosaurs," "Muppets Tonight!," "Community," "Angel," "Mystery Science Theater 3000"* and *"Crank Yanker*s." He also voiced numerous characters for video games.

Tim's puppet/voice influences include *Monty Python* and Tony Urbano's Emmy-winning children's show *"Dusty's Treehouse."* Tim was mentored by Tony Urbano, Rick Baker and vocal legend Daws Butler.

KEVIN CARLSON
with Warehouse Mouse
2009

Kevin Carlson
1962–present

Career: 1980–present. Kevin Carlson's first involvement with puppetry was demonstrating Christian puppets at the Broadway department store in Los Angeles while working for a company that produced puppets for religious ministries. This inspired him to audition for Sid & Marty Krofft. After being one of the 25 chosen out of 500 who auditioned, Kevin went on to participate in the Krofft Puppet School taught by Tony Urbano. Through the Kroffts, he became Grandpa Fudge on the *"Oral Roberts Celebration Specials."* This led to a national tour with Irlene Mandrell where he starred as Truck Shackley, a puppet Tony Urbano originated for television on *"The Barbara Mandrell Show."*

Most of Kevin's work has been with Muppet-style puppets, although he has manipulated marionettes for special shows with Tony Urbano. Tony also helped Kevin get membership in SAG-AFTRA (Screen Actors Guild–American Federation of Television and Radio Artists). His television work has included building puppets for the McDonald's television commercials. He was also involved with *"Muppets Tonight!,"* *"Dinosaurs,"* *"D.C. Follies"* and *"The Mr. Potato Head Show,"* where he played Mr. Potato Head. Kevin can be seen as Conky, Clockey and Floorey on *"Pee Wee's Playhouse"* and as Timmy on *"The Adventures of Timmy the Tooth."* He was heavily influenced by *"The Muppet Show,"* and was in both *"Muppet*Vision 3-D"* by Disney and *"The Muppets"* film.

Kevin has a B.A. in Speech Communications from Cal State Fullerton. He was a member of the Jim Henson Company's *"Puppet Up!"* and has performed live with the Muppets at the Hollywood Bowl and at the O2 Arena in London. His film work includes *"Doctor Dolittle 2,"* *"Men in Black II,"* *"Cats & Dogs,"* *"Batman Returns,"* *"Team America: World Police",* *"Beetlejuice,"* *"Child's Play 2"* and *"Forgetting Sarah Marshall."* He thanks his puppet mentors Tony Urbano and Van Snowden for all their shared knowledge.

EDWARD, STEVEN & CHARLES CHIODO
2004

The Chiodo Brothers
1952, 1954 & 1960–present

Career: 1980–present. Chiodo Bros. Productions was established in 1980 when three brothers, Charles, Stephen and Edward Chiodo, from New York moved to Los Angeles to pursue their dreams of filmmaking. Stephen is the company's director, Edward is the producer and Charles is the production designer and illustrator. Their company specializes in projects involving puppets, from scriptwriting to production to post-production. They work primarily as stop-motion animators, using puppetry, animatronics and makeup effects as well.

The Chiodo brothers became involved in puppetry because of the demand for fantasy characters performing live with actors. Hand puppets and cable-operated puppets, then computer-operated animatronic characters all became apparatus in their film toolbox. The three of them created many of the iconic characters we have come to love. The brothers brought to the screen Large Marge in *"Pee-Wee's Big Adventure,"* as well as the Rankin Bass stop-motion tribute in the movie *"Elf."* They produced and built the puppets for *"The Mr. Potato Head Show"* for Fox television and Hasbro Toys, and amused us with demonic voodoo dolls coming to life in Spike Lee's *"Tales from the Hood."* The company is also known for sculpting and painting the "Gremlin" animated puppets.

Another type of puppetry the brothers use is full-costumed animatronic creatures for Fox television's *"Teenage Mutant Ninja Turtles"* or the villains in their cult classic science fiction comedy *"Killer Klowns From Outer Space."* Other film credits include all of the *"Critters"* movies, *"Team America: World Police"* (they built the puppets) and the mice dioramas in *"Dinner for Schmucks."* The Chiodos have also done many clay animation stop-motion segments for *"The Simpsons."*

The brothers were influenced by Ray Harryhausen, *"King Kong," "Godzilla,"* and *"The Thing,"* and swear they were mentored by Forry Ackerman's Famous Monsters of Filmland magazine. As kids, the Chiodos made Super 8 movies in New York featuring toys. Today, they run a studio in the Los Angeles area where many aspiring puppeteers come to learn, design and create.

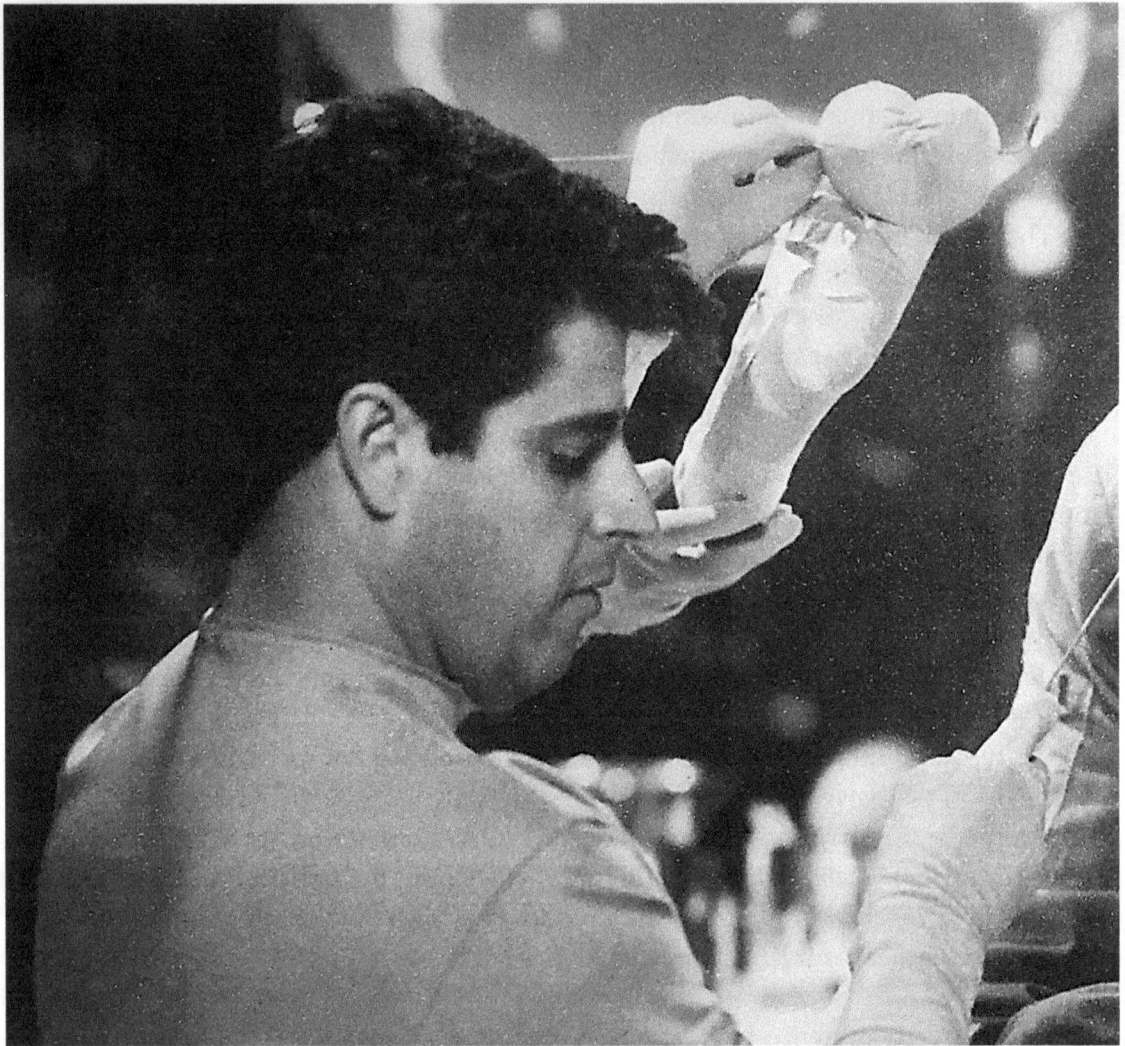

BRUCE LANOIL
1990s

Bruce Lanoil
1960–present

Career: 1980–Present. Bruce Lanoil is a puppeteer who also excels at improvisation, theater and voiceover work. While a theater major at Cal State Northridge, he applied for a job with Sid & Marty Krofft Productions. He was one of 16 out of approximately 900 applicants chosen by Tony Urbano to be part of their puppet school. Bruce then honed his craft working on many McDonald's Chicken McNugget commercials alongside Tony Urbano. He also traveled on a Krofft National tour with Irlene Mandrell, helping to bring to life Truck Shackley and the Texas Critters, an all-puppet country western band.

In 1990, Brian Henson chose Bruce as head puppeteer for Charlene Sinclair in *"Dinosaurs."* Animatronics and facial puppeteering ruled his next decade, as he traveled the world courtesy of the Jim Henson Creature Shop, with numerous film and television appearances. Bruce's movie work includes *"Dr. Doolittle," "Adventures of Pinocchio," "Jack Frost," "Cats & Dogs I & II,"* where he was the face perfomer for Mr. Tinkles, *"Happytime Murders," "Muppet*Vision 3-D," "Muppets Most Wanted"* and *"Theodore Rex"* with Whoopi Goldberg. His television highlights include *"The Wubbulous World of Dr. Seuss (Cat in the Hat)," "Muppets Tonight!"* and *"The Adventures of Timmy the Tooth."*

Bruce helped pioneer real-time puppeteered CG animation with Henson's HDPS-Digital Puppetry System in shows like *"Sid the Science Kid"* and movies like *"Where the Wild Things Are,"* where he partnered with Dave Barclay Studios in England. He's done voices in *"Looney Tunes Back in Action"* (Pepe Le Pew) and he is a voice double for Timon from *"Lion King"* on Disney shorts and video games.

Saturday morning cartoons, sugary cereals, magazines, Jerry Lewis flicks and classic *Star Trek* have influenced his career, while Tony Urbano, Paul Sills, Avery Schreiber and Harvey Kalmanson have mentored him. Bruce is extremely grateful for a career sharing so much whimsical joy and laughter, and remains committed to our unique, dynamic, artistic puppet community.

GREG BALLORA
Team America: World Police
2004

Greg Ballora
1964–present

Career: 1983–Present. Gregory B. Ballora is a Los Angeles based puppet builder and performer. He discovered a love for puppetry while working on various productions in college. After graduating from the Theater Arts department at UCLA, Greg immediately immersed himself in the film business. He is an actor, a special effects performer and a puppet builder. For fifteen years, Greg worked with puppeteer Jim Gamble building and performing puppet shows and directing the videos Jim produced to sell. Greg has also been a puppet performer for the Jim Henson Company's improvisational, live show, *"Puppet Up!–Uncensored."*

Greg's film work includes *"RoboCop 2"* as part of the robot monster crew, *"The Flint-stones," "Dolls," "Stuart Little"* and *"Spiderman 2"* where he manipulated the many arms of Doc Ock. He has also lent his vocal and puppet talents to *"The X-Files," "Happytime Murders," "Men in Black II"* and was a lead puppeteer in *"Team America: World Police."* His television work includes *"Timmy the Tooth," "The Crayon Box"* and *"Greg the Bunny."* He has also played the role of Baloney on *"The Mr. Potato Head Show"* and was puppet captain for Disney XD's production *"Crash and Bernstein."* Greg has been a puppet master for the Disneyland Resort, building puppets, training and teaching performers, creating parade choreography for puppets and large floats.

Greg has worked alongside fellow puppeteers Michael Paul Ziegfeld and Kevin Carlson. He has also taught puppet production at UCLA, Pepperdine University, Penn State and Cal Arts as well as numerous workshops at Puppeteers of America conventions. In 1993 Greg was one of twenty-five artist/dancer/puppeteers chosen to participate in a two-week intensive puppetry course taught by Muppet performers: *"A Survey of Puppet Theater Techniques,"* at Humboldt State University. He has also performed with the Muppets in *"The Muppets"* film and on the *"The Muppets"* television series. His work can be seen on the Henson Company television show *"Earth to Ned"* for the Disney+ channel.

Greg considers his biggest influences to be Jim Henson, Hobey Ford, Michael Earl, Tony Urbano and Ronnie Burkett.

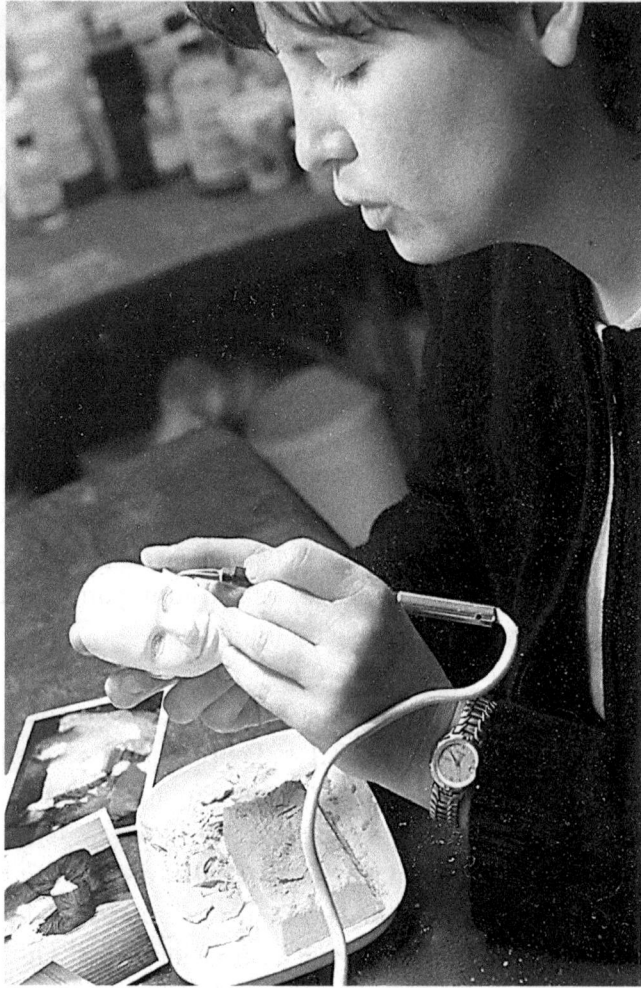

KAMELA PORTUGES-ROBBINS
2008

Kamela Portuges-Robbins
1963–present

Career: 1983–Present. Kamela Portuges was influenced by Pat McCormick and his *"Charlie and Humphrey Good Stuff Hour"* puppet show on local Bay Area television. This led to her seeking out the San Francisco Bay Area Puppeteers Guild at one of their puppet events. There, she met Lee Armstrong, who was holding a workshop on television puppetry. The two women combined their talents to create Images in Motion, a puppet production company in Marin. With an M.A. in Theater and Marketing, as well as a B.S. in Business and Marketing from Humboldt State University, Kamela is quite prepared to run one of the most successful puppet companies in the state.

As a designer and sculptor she has had numerous jobs in the film and the toy industry. Kamela has worked at Chris Walas Studios on *"The Fly II,"* supervised and was lead sculptor for the marionettes in *"Being John Malkovich"* and sculpted stop-motion maquettes for *"James & The Giant Peach"* and *"Monkeybone."* Kamela has sculpted dolls, action figures, toys and sculptures for Leapfrog, Playalong, Pottery Barn, Crayola, San Francisco Music Box Company and Galoob Toys. She has also illustrated children's books and coloring books. As her other skills include 3D modeling and 3D printing for puppets and other projects, Kamela supervises this work at Images in Motion. 3D printing clients have included the Academy of Science San Francisco, Event Network, Paleo Mill, the Black Hills Institute, Industrial Light & Magic and another well-known animation studio. Related work includes sculpting toy products and celebrity dolls, paint masters, radio and cable control mechanisms, 2 and 3D animation, masks, molding and casting, armatures, etc.

Kamela and Lee have performed their own live puppet shows *"Big Bad Bruce," "Water Works"* and *"What in the World"* in local California libraries. Puppeteering credits include *"Being John Malkovich," "The Life Aquatic with Steve Zissou"* and numerous commercials for Disney, Mattel, Electronic Arts, Round Table Pizza, Mercedes Benz, Cartoon Network and ILM. She has won several Regional Emmys for her work, as well as other awards and recognitions. Kamela considers being able to do what she loves her greatest accomplishment.

RICK LAZZARINI
with Cougar
2012

Rick Lazzarini
1960–present

Career: 1985–Present. Rick is a puppeteer, puppet builder, puppet director, movement choreographer, production manager and suit performer. Rick is the founder and chief creative officer of The Character Shop, and has created fantastic creatures, puppets and animatronic effects on film for many years. Whether it's traditional hand, rod, marionette; or more advanced animatronic, radio-control or electronic; whimsical, stylized or realistic; Rick has proved adept in just about every style of puppetry. He was mentored by Stan Winston and has worked and taught puppet skills at the Stan Winston School of Character Arts. Rick also heads the Animatronics Institute, and has taught courses at University of Southern California, UCLA and the American Film Institute.

Rick has built and puppeteered creations from the six-inch replica of Julia Roberts as Tinkerbell for *"Hook,"* to life-sized elephants for *"Operation Dumbo Drop."* He built and performed the chicken puppets for the Foster Farms *"Amazing Chickens"* commercials, the Budweiser Frogs commercials, and designed, created and puppeteered the head of the queen alien in *"Aliens"* as well as the puppeteering mechanisms for the running face-hugger and opening eggs. In Mel Brooks' *"Spaceballs,"* Rick is responsible for the animatronic ears on John Candy as Barf the Mawg, as well as performing Pizza the Hutt. Other films he's built puppets for include *"Snakes on a Plane,"* *"Mimic,"* *"Hocus Pocus,"* *"Ghostbusters 2,"* *"Ghostbusters 2016"* and the *"A Nightmare on Elm Street"* series. He created the "Facial Waldo", a groundbreaking device that allows animatronic puppets to lip-synch and mimic a puppeteer's facial expressions.

Rick lends his time as a residuals advocate, helping union puppeteers battle unfair film practices. He has been sought out, advised and consulted with many puppeteers on these issues, helping them with their grievances and claims to win back what was rightfully theirs. Rick's goals continue to be to entertain, amaze, stimulate, bring joy and excitement and connect, through performance and an elevated sense of fantastic reality, on a personal, human level.

MaRia Bodmann
with Self Portrait & Grim Reaper
2010

MaRia Bodmann
1952–2019

Career: 1986–2019. MaRia Elena Bodmann was an artist, musician, performer and business manager. She held a BFA and MFA in Multidisciplinary Art and Music from California Institute of the Arts, studied music at the Hochschule der Kunste in Germany, and shadow theater in the village of Sukawati, Bali. MaRia's specialty was shadow theater. She told stories, sang, played gamelan music, made shadow figures of all kinds and choreographed traditional, contemporary and experimental shadow performances.

While studying as an interdisciplinary art/music student in the early 1980s, MaRia took advantage of the other departments within the Institute. She performed work study duties in the theater set and costume shops and attended classes in mask-making and scenic painting. While building an ensemble of non-traditional percussion instruments made from industrial scraps, MaRia heard Indonesian gamelan music and was totally drawn to it. Not long afterwards she was introduced to traditional-style Balinese Wayang Kulit shadow play performed by Larry Reed.

After graduating in interdisciplinary art, MaRia received Fulbright and Indonesian Department of Culture and Education grants. From 1986 to 1988 she studied shadow play (performance and building), gamelan gender wayang (the musical accompaniment) and gamelan tuning in Bali. Upon her return she presented a full-length shadow play as part of her master's thesis. In 1988, Maria and her partner, Cliff DeArment, formed Bali & Beyond, a company of Los Angeles performing artists inspired by the cultures of Indonesia. Ten years after MaRia started performing traditional style Balinese wayang, she debuted *"Alice in the Shadows,"* a psychedelic rock 'n' roll shadow play. Western elements such as additional lighting, projections and liquid light projectors were added to present a totally unique and new performance art.

MaRia was influenced in her work by Eric Martin, Connie Hatch and Larry Reed. Her mentors include I Wayan Nartha, I Wayan Loceng and I Wayan Sarga.

NICK BARONE
Puss in Boots
2007

Nick Barone
1967–2014

Career: 1986–2014. Nicholas Joseph Barone built his first puppet when he was five years old, but for many years didn't realize he was building puppets. He wrote short stories and made home movies featuring his hand-made puppets, immersing himself in as many art forms as he could find, and later became known for his strong sense of scenic design and his painting skills.

Nick ultimately moved to Hollywood, California, and began painting sets for the television industry. But puppetry was still his biggest love. He eventually settled in San Diego and became a prominent member of the San Diego Guild of Puppetry. Nick was a featured performer at the Marie Hitchcock Puppet Theater in Balboa Park. He worked alongside various puppeteers for nearly ten years, developing his craft and sharing his own self-taught skills, particularly in creating foam moving-mouth puppets.

In 1996, Nick met his future wife, Rose Sage, at a regional convention and soon moved to the San Francisco Bay Area where she resided. With Nick Barone's Puppets, he began to make a name for himself as one of the premier puppeteers in the Bay Area. Nick built puppets for film, television and live theater, including the Marin Theater Company's production of Gilles Segal's *"The Puppetmaster of Lodz."* He received a Regional Emmy for his work on Roger Mara's Snapdragon DVD Production of *"The Mousecracker."* Nick's productions included *"T-Rex Thunderlizard's Wild West Review," "Puss in Boots," "Tales from the Enchanted Forest"* and *"Tricks & Treats,"* which still performs in repertory at Children's Fairyland.

Besides designing his own mechanisms for puppets, Nick composed all of the original music and songs for his productions. He also manipulated his computer to record all of the voices, which he performed himself, changing the pitch and rhythms to create his characters. Nick served terms as President of the San Diego and San Francisco Bay Area Puppeteers Guilds and was well known for his engaging workshops.

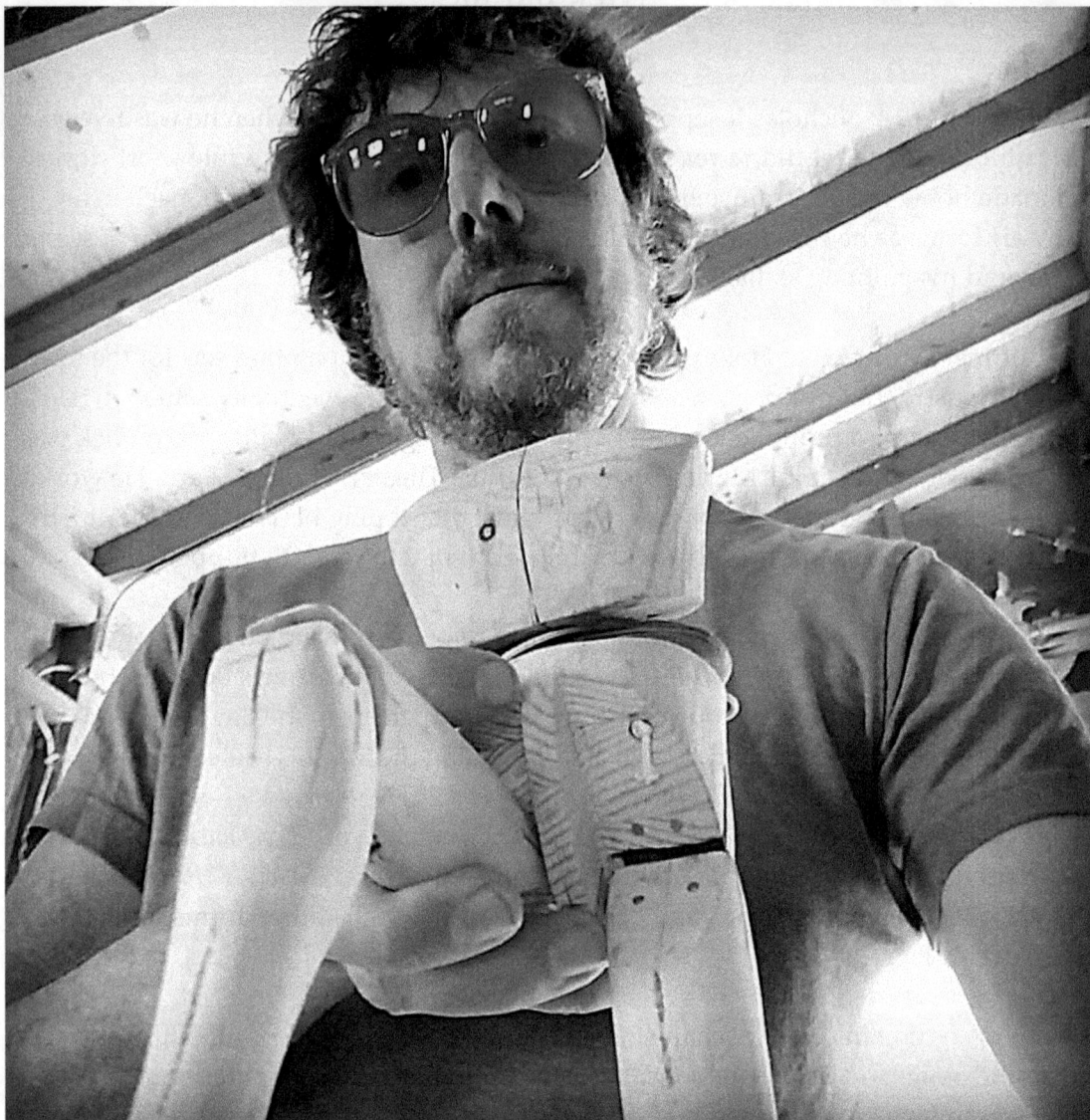

Fred C. Riley III
2018

Fred C. Riley III
1970–present

Career: 1986–Present. Fred C. Riley began his puppet career in his sophomore year of high school when he joined with fellow students Ron and Brent Binion to help with their puppet productions. After several successful shows, including a sold-out Christmas show at a local theater, he never looked back. Fred's motto is *"I'll try anything once."* After 33 years he has mastered skills as a puppeteer, director, writer, builder, musician, sound engineer and photo and video editor.

Fred has worked and trained with many prestigious companies, and with many forms of puppetry. From Czech black theater puppetry to marionettes, intimate to spectacle, he approaches every role with passion. Fred worked with Janet and Reg Bradley and their Tears of Joy Theatre, where he toured and taught residencies for children all over Oregon, Washington and Idaho. After that, he worked for four years with Jon Ludwig and Vince Anthony at the Center for Puppetry Arts in Atlanta, where he was a resident puppeteer and taught classes for adults and teens in puppet theory and movement. Fred also produced his own works, *"Nox"* and *"Bar,"* as part of the Center's Xperimental Puppet Theater. Following that success, he became a puppeteer, choreographer and trainer for the famous Obie Award-winning theater Ping Chong and Company.

In 2007, Fred returned to the Bay Area and performed with the Fratello Marionettes and Children's Fairyland's puppet company. He's currently constructing and performing for Larry Reed and Shadowlight Productions. He was also a builder, performer and assistant director for *"Feathers of Fire,"* a tale of Persia told through Balinese shadow puppetry, which has toured several countries. Fred was also a marionette builder, performer and director for Larry Schmidt's *"Driveway Follies"* in Oakland.

Fred was mentored by puppeteers Ron & Brent Binion, Larry Reed and Ping Chong, and has been influenced by Teatra Drak, Jon Ludwig, Jainie Geiser and Laurie Anderson. He has spoken on the art of puppetry at Western University and Stanford. "I want to give people not just inspiration, but the tools to use that inspiration," he says. "This art has so much untapped potential."

LAURIE BRANHAM
2017

Laurie Branham
1956–present

Career: 1987–Present. Laurie Branham grew up surrounded by an artistic family. Working with her father, a professional artist and art director, she learned at a very young age how to draw, paint and design. When Laurie was 10, her father presented her with a beautiful little marionette theater he had built from wood, along with a complete cast of Pelham Puppets.

In 1987, Laurie found herself working for the Bob Baker Marionettes in Hollywood, who mentored her further in marionette construction. And in 1990 she established the Puppets & Players Little Theatre.

Laurie and her father built a traveling Italian Baroque Marionette Theater — "a marionette theater on wheels" — so she could live the life of a gypsy, performing puppet shows around the country. She has performed with this puppet theater since 1991, entertaining at special events. Her shows include *"Thumbelina," "Scooter's Circus Adventure," "Puff the Magic Dragon"* and *"Magical Moments from Oz."* The Puppets & Players Little Theatre calls Orange County its home but is also perfectly at home performing all over the western United States at fairs, festivals, theme parks, corporate events, parties, libraries and schools.

As main puppeteer, director, original script writer, set designer, choreographer and many of the voices, Laurie also designs and builds the marionettes, sets and back drops for the productions.

Laurie graduated with honors from the Drama Studio of London and also attended the Artes Instituto Allende, a visual arts school in Mexico. Her influences include her father and his love of theater, the many workshops attended through Puppeteers of America, and her mentor Bob Baker. She is proud to be on the roster of the Segerstrom Center for the Arts, performing marionette shows and puppetry making workshops for the schools in Southern California. Her goal has been to revive traditional puppet theater, an art form that has entertained and educated young and old for centuries.

MICHAEL PAUL ZIEGFELD
2018

Michael Paul Ziegfeld
1971–present

Career: 1987–Present. Since he was three years old, Michael was puppeteering for his own entertainment and exploration, and watching *"Sesame Street"* to study the manipulation and to dissect the technology. At age 16 Michael began his career in local television, as well as performing at parties and schools. He has since honed his craft touring with such names as James Brown, Lisa Lampanelli, Joan Rivers and Don Rickles to become a comic-ventriloquist headliner in over 40 countries along with television credits on *"The Tonight Show"* and *"Saturday Night Live."* Most recently, he was seen on *"America's Got Talent,"* performing with Willie, his puppet "International Bird of Prey."

Michael's film career includes motion pictures such as *"27 Dresses"* opposite Katherine Heigl, *"The Ten"* co-starring with Winona Ryder and Paul Rudd, and Kevin Spacey's *"The Ventriloquist."* He's also lent his voice or hands to Pixar and Jim Henson Productions (*"Sesame Street," "Muppets Take Manhattan," "Muppets Tonight."*) and is well known for creating branded puppet characters including Willie, Nadia Coma: "The World's Oldest Gymnast" and MTV's *"CJ and Peanut."* Much of his puppeteering career has been through his Las Vegas ventriloquist act.

Based in Los Angeles, Michael has been fortunate enough to continue to learn and experiment in real time. He works in movies, television and as a comedy writer and script and show consultant, providing script coverage and/or directing for the Disney Channel, CBS Comedy Division, Robert DeNiro, Jennifer Hudson, Joshua Rush, Bradley Cooper, David Letterman, Bill Maher, and the Comedy Central Roasts. He has taught classes at University of California Los Angeles, Pace University, SAG-AFTRA's Master Class and the Eugene O'Neill Puppet Conference.

Michael's published works include comedic editorials for *USA Today, Huffington Post, LaughSpin* and his new book *Breaking Out of Show Business: What I Discovered by Not Being Discovered.* He feels fortunate to include Richard Hunt, Greg Ballora, Caroll Spinney, Mike Quinn, Frank Meshkuleit and Ronnie Burkett among his puppet career influencers and mentors.

KEVIN MENEGUS
with Redd Fox
2018

Kevin Menegus
1976–present

Career: 1989–Present. Kevin Menegus became intrigued by puppetry after receiving a puppet as a gift at age six. A craftsman, carpenter and musician, Kevin found puppetry to be an art form that could express many of his talents.

Kevin holds a Bachelor of Music degree in percussion performance from the University of the Pacific Conservatory of Music, which comes in handy for selecting and orchestrating the right accompaniment for each marionette performance. He has traveled throughout the United States performing classical, jazz and new music, has appeared in symphony orchestras in the Bay Area and toured with the Sonos Handbell Ensemble.

In 1989, Kevin established his own professional puppet touring company, the Fratello Marionettes, and made his Puppeteers of America debut in 1993 at age 16, performing in the Young Performers Showcase at the San Francisco National Festival. He was mentored by Tony Urbano, Randal Metz, Lewis Mahlmann, Lettie Schubert and Bob Baker, learning from them while developing his own unique styles of puppet-making and performance. Kevin worked for the Bob Baker Marionettes and performed around the world on cruise ships with Tony Urbano and his marionettes before devoting himself full-time to the Fratello Marionettes. In 1999 he appeared on the revived *"Gong Show,"* winning first place for "Helen High Water," his hula dancing stripper grandmother marionette.

The Fratello Marionettes tours the Bay Area and beyond, entertaining at symphonies, fairs, festivals, libraries and schools. Performances include *"Aladdin," "The Frog Prince," "Carnival of the Animals," "Vaudeville Follies," "Peter & the Wolf," "Mother Goose Land"* and *"Spooktacular!"*

Kevin has written many articles for the *Puppetry Journal*. In addition to building puppets for his own use, he runs a small business restoring marionettes and toy puppets. He also has a large collection of professional and toy puppets and marionettes.

Camilla Henneman

Career: 1980–present. Camilla Henneman is an accomplished film artist, creating creatures, puppets and costumes. From 1980–1988 and from 1991–1994 she supervised makeup artist Rick Baker's Costume & Fabrication Shop, taking a break in between to pursue other projects. Camilla has also worked for the Jim Henson Creature Shop. Her film credits include *"Batman Forever," "The Blob," "George of the Jungle," "Ghostbusters II," "Harry and the Hendersons"* and *"Captain EO"* as well as television projects *"Michael Jackson's Thriller"* and *"Buffy the Vampire Slayer."* She currently writes articles for the *Puppetry Journal*, and is active running her own puppet company.

Jamie Keithline & Bonny Hall

Career: 1980–present. In 1982, Jamie and Bonny established Puppetwork in San Francisco. When the couple moved to the East Coast in 1989, they became Crabgrass Puppet Theatre. They each graduated with a Bachelor of Fine Arts from the University of Connecticut, and have been awarded two UNIMA-USA Citations of Excellence. In 2008, Bonny received a Citation of Merit from the Arlyn Award for Outstanding Design in the Puppet Theater. Their secret? The use of puppetry, masks, storytelling and mime to create fanciful tales. Bonny teaches creative dramatics and puppetry while Jamie specializes in acting, clowning, mime and storytelling.

Karen Prell

Career: 1980–present. As a Muppet performer, Karen Prell is most widely known for playing Red Fraggle on *"Fraggle Rock"* from 1983–1987. She has also applied her skills to quite a few Muppet classics including the *"Muppet Christmas Carol," "Dreamchild"* and *"Labyrinth."* In 1997, Karen transitioned into computer animation, working on Pixar films including *"A Bug's Life"* and *"Toy Story 2."* Karen has also worked on Disney's *"Enchanted"* and with Phil Tippett Studio on *"The League of Extraordinary Gentlemen"* and *"Son of the Mask."* Her television credits include *"Sesame Street"* and *"The Muppet Show."*

Kirk R. Thatcher

Career: 1981–present. Kirk R. Thatcher is an Emmy award winning writer and producer, an award winning television commercial and viral video director, and a creature maker and designer for films and television. Film credits include *"Muppet Treasure Island," "Return of the Jedi," "Star Trek II, III & IV," "Poltergeist"* and *"Gremlins."* Kirk also designed the characters for Jim Henson's *"Dinosaurs."* He has the distinction of having worked in various production capacities on three of the most successful franchises in entertainment history: *Star Wars, Star Trek* and the *Muppets.* Kirk admits being influenced by creatures, spaceships and broad comedy.

Joyce Hutter

Career: 1985–present. Joyce Hutter is a writer, designer, prop and puppet maker, and mask crafter for human and puppet theater. She brings socially responsible puppet theater and innovative puppet performances to children and adults through her company Strings and Things Puppet Theatre. Working as a member of Rogue Artists Ensemble, Joyce received a distinguished Achievement Award from the Los Angeles Drama Critics Circle for mask and puppet design. *"The Comical Tragedy or Tragical Comedy of Mr. Punch," "The Story of Frog Belly Rat Bone"* and *"The Gogol Project"* are just a few of her successes.

Ron Binion

Career: Mid '80s–present. Ronald Binion is a puppeteer, performer, designer and fabricator for film, television, theater and humanitarian puppetry. Ron trained as a resident puppeteer and head puppet builder for the Center for Puppetry Arts in Atlanta from 1991–1995. He has also lent his talents to the Jim Henson Company on many projects. From 2007–2011, Ron worked as an Overseas Puppet Workshop trainer and puppeteer for No Strings International in Indonesia, Cambodia, the Philippines, Kenya and Haiti. His credits include *"Crank Yankers," "Bear in the Big Blue House," "Muppets Tonight!," "Muppet Treasure Island"* and *"Book of Pooh."*

Steven Ritz-Barr

Career: Mid '80s–present. Steven is a visiting animation instructor at UCLA, specializing in marionette films from classic stories. *"Faust," "Don Quixote"* and *"Joan of Arc"* are just a few of the exceptional film adaptions produced by Classics in Miniature, the company he formed in 2007. His epic puppet films have been given three UNIMA Citations of Excellence, and Steven received a grant from the Henson Foundation for his live show *"An Evening with Edgar Poe."* Mentored by puppet masters Jean-Loup Temporal and Jim Henson, Steven also studied movement, mime and theater in France.

Talib and Olivia Huff

Career: 1986–present. Talib and Olivia have performed their puppet magic all across the Western United States as Tinker's Coin Productions. The Huffs have taught children and adults in schools, museums, workshops and conferences about the puppet arts and a wide variety of other subjects. They have traveled to several countries sharing their puppetry and teaching international puppet skills. Their live "Renaissance Fair" style show, *"The Three Billy Goats Gruff,"* done with simple rod puppets and the eager help of their audience, has become a real crowd pleaser. Talib also portrays Father Christmas at events during the holidays.

9

1990–1999

THE 1990s ARE OFTEN characterized by the rise of multiculturalism and alternative media. This was the decade of digital technology, cell phones, personal computers and the World Wide Web. Through this sharing of technology the world became more connected–leading to the wider discovery of different cultures and communities. The popularity of the "Slacker" and "Valley Girl" movements introduced "California Culture" to the rest of America, and heavily influenced it throughout the decade. But the '90s weren't all "totally tubular." The Gulf War began in 1990, the World Trade Center and the Oklahoma Federal Building bombings took place in 1993 and 1995, and the President Clinton and Monica Lewinsky scandal rocked the nation in 1998.

With the rise of digital technology, including the release of compact discs in 1982, the film industry began to see the death throes of stop-motion and practical puppetry. Digital effects replaced puppeteers, and matte painters gave way to "green screen" filming. With the success of the movies *"Terminator 2: Judgement Day" "Jurassic Park"* and *"Toy Story,"* filmmakers were free to create lush and fantastic creatures and settings without an actor actually in the environment on set. But puppetry was still important, as Stan Winston and Phil Tippett helped integrate both digital and practical puppetry into *"Jurassic Park."* In literature we were seeing the meteoric rise of the Japanese animation style anime, as well as the increased popularity of graphic comics with Neil Gaiman's *"Sandman"* series. Timothy Zahn relaunched the *"Star Wars"* phenomenon in books with the *"Thrawn Trilogy"* while Michael Crichton, Anne Rice and J. K. Rowling held us spellbound with tales of technology, vampires and wizardry. R. L. Stine's *"Goosebumps"* tales did same for the little ones. And illustrative artwork such as James Christensen's *A Journey of the Imagination* inspired puppeteers with their own fantasy characters and worlds.

In the 1990s, puppetry continued to thrive but also started looking back at its roots. At Humboldt State University in California, members of the Muppets team taught a two-week intensive class on puppetry and theater examining all aspects of puppetry from construction to performance, stage to film, classical to avant-garde, and all forms of the puppet. Experimental and found object puppetry became popular entertainments as art, film, theater and spectacle drew bigger and bigger audiences. In 1991 prominent members of the puppet community introduced the first National Puppetry Conference, held at the Eugene O'Neill Theater Center in Connecticut, as a yearly seminar to explore the growth of puppetry as an art form. To keep up with the digital era, and to better promote itself and puppetry, the Puppeteers of America officially opened its website in 1997. In film and television, puppets with better expression and lifelike movements filled the screens, foreshadowing the next decade where animatronics and facial puppeteering would dominate the industry. This was also the decade in which the Jim Henson Industry morphed and changed after Henson's death in 1990. He had been in the process of merging his company with the Disney Company in late 1989, but the deal was cancelled when the two entities couldn't come to terms after Henson's passing.

While Julie Taymor was dazzling audiences with her *"Lion King"* Broadway show featuring puppet designs, California puppeteers Bruce Schwartz and Basil Twist had put their own artistic brands on the theatrical stage. Schwartz, then Taymor and Twist each received MacArthur Foundation Fellowship "Genius Grant Awards." These visionaries were leading the way for the prominence of puppets in Broadway shows. And on a smaller stage, in 1997 Steve Meltzer of Los Angeles opened the Santa Monica Puppetry Center.

At a time puppet effects were becoming scarce in feature films, movie directors Tim Burton, Phil Tippett and Henry Selick, inspired by Ray Harryhausen and George Pal, attempted to bring back the magic of stop-motion to the silver screen. In 1993 the Puppeteers of America held a national convention in the San Francisco Bay Area, hosting some of the best puppeteers from America and across the world. The gala laced international event was co-directed by puppeteer legends Mike Oznowicz and Lettie Schubert with the help of Ronna Casey Leon. In 1999, the Conservatory of Puppetry Arts (COPA) opened in Pasadena, featuring the Alan Cook/Jacqueline Marks puppet collections with over 5,000 puppets and 1,200 puppet related books and pamphlets. By 2011, COPA would become the International Puppetry Museum and move to the Northwest Puppet Center in Seattle, Washington.

As the 1990s wound down we began to see that since the 1920s, the art of puppetry established a circular cycle. From classical puppetry, to marionettes, to stop motion, to political expression, to Muppet style, to film and television, to the theatrical stage and back to the classical forms once again. And as it circled, it was exciting to see the future puppeteers adding their own touches to this vibrant art form. But as the century came to a close, the new millennium was soon to usher in a new trend of puppet performance and style.

ALICE DINNEAN
Turkey Hollow
2015

Alice Dinnean
1969–present

Career: 1990–Present. Alice Catherine Dinnean grew up in Piedmont. In the late '80s she worked at Children's Fairyland painting attractions while playing with puppets, and sang in Gilbert & Sullivan productions and also the prestigious Oakland Youth Chorus. Her love of puppets began in the second grade, when she won a pig puppet for a story submitted to Cricket Magazine. And she developed a fascination for puppet theater while performing with her sister Carol and voicing puppets. Alice also created puppet projects for drama at Oberlin College, where she studied studio art and art history. After college, she and Carol became resident puppeteers at the Atlanta Center for Puppetry Arts. This eventually led to Alice finding a job with the Jim Henson Company.

Soon Alice found herself on *"Sesame Street,"* where she played Goldilocks and Groogel as well as Sherry Netherland, the owner of the Furry Arms Hotel, for many years. She also played Snizzy on *"Aliens in the Family,"* Gabriela Cordova in *"Sid the Science Kid"* and Grandma Flutter on *"Bear in the Big Blue House."* Her other Muppet credits include *"Muppets Tonight,"* *"Muppets from Space,"* *"It's A Very Muppet Christmas Movie,"* *"The Muppets Wizard of Oz"* and *"The Muppets Movie."* For PBS she played Julie Woo & Sizzle the Cat on *"Puzzle Place"* as well as performing and writing for *"Jack's Big Music Show,"* where she also plays Mary. Her other film and television credits include *"Country Bears,"* *"Team America: World Police,"* *"Happytime Murders,"* *"Buffy the Vampire Slayer"* and *"Angel."*

Alice is not only a puppet performer, she is also an actress and creative writer for film and television. She spent several years, studying and working at the National Puppetry Conference held at the Eugene O'Neill Theater Center. Currently she is the principal puppeteer for Brea, one of the lead characters in Netflix's *"Dark Crystal: Age of Resistance."* Alice prefers performing to building puppets.

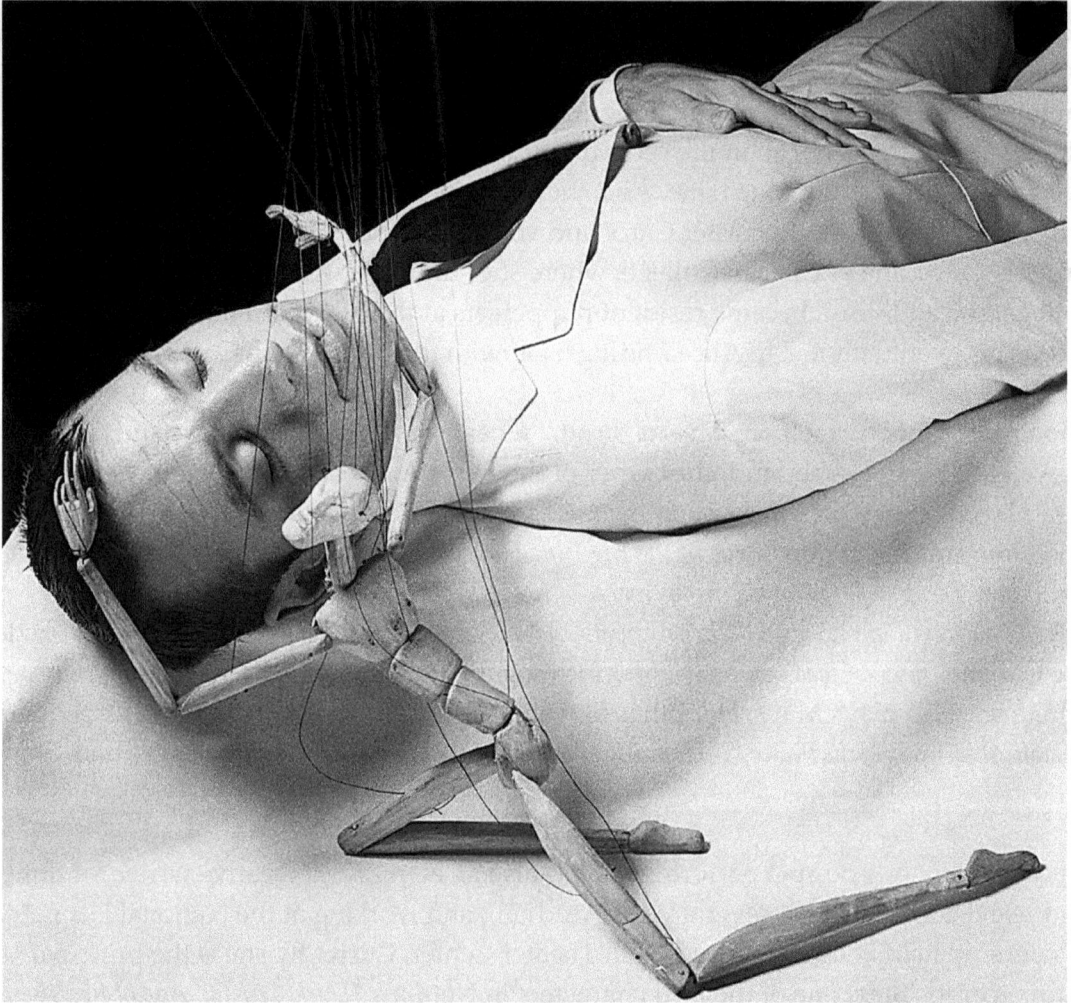

BASIL TWIST
with Stickman
1990s

Basil Twist
1969–present

Career: 1990–Present. Basil Twist is a third-generation performer, born into a family of puppeteers, who is known for revitalizing puppetry as a serious and sophisticated art form through his imaginative experiments with materials, techniques and uses in both narrative and abstract works. Basil's shows range from productions of classic stories to abstract visualizations of orchestral music and are informed by puppetry traditions from around the world, including hand puppets, bunraku and string-and-rod marionettes. Basil received a degree from the École Nationale Supérieure des Arts de la Marionnette (ESNAM) in Charleville-Mézières, France, where he was trained in set design, costume design, dramaturgy, music and acting. He was awarded a MacArthur Fellowship Genius Grant in 2015, and has also won Obie, Drama Desk and Bessie Awards.

Basil's work includes *"Symphonie Fantastique"* (1998) which uses pieces of fabric, feathers, plastic, vinyl and fishing lures in a small tank of water to simulate imagery to music. He contributed to the magic of Alfonso Cuarón's *"Harry Potter and the Prisoner of Azkaban,"* creating the Dementors, which were first filmed underwater, and later were finalized on computer using his stylistic model. Basil has produced the shows *"Petrushka,"* the Japanese *"Doguagaeshi"*(screen flipping), *"Rite of Spring," "Hansel & Gretel," "Arias With A Twist"* and *"La Bella Dormente nel Bosco."* He was awarded Henson Grants for his productions of *"Master Peter's Puppet Show"* and *"The Araneidae Show."*

Basil works in both New York and San Francisco. He has taught puppet classes at Stanford, Duke, New York and Brown Universities. Since 1999 he has served as artistic director of the Dream Music Puppetry Program at the HERE Arts Center in New York City. Basil has worked with puppeteer/directors Theodora Skipitares, Roman Paska and Julie Taymor. He credits Jim Henson, Philippe Genty, European puppetry and a festival of puppetry and music in France as his influencers. Basil was recently awarded the Rome Prize from the American Academy in Rome.

BILL BARRETTA
2000s

Bill Barretta
1964–present

Career: 1991–Present. William Paul Barretta was raised in Yardley, Pennsylvania and never imagined he'd become a puppeteer. His brother Gene, an award-winning children's book author and illustrator, was the creative driving force that enlisted Bill on many artistic productions as kids. In 1974, Gene Barretta wrote to Jim Henson, asking how to make a Muppet. Jim sent back instructions along with an encouraging letter, and soon the brothers were putting on shows for their large Italian American family. Bill never thought this would become a part of his journey in life.

In the summer of 1981, Bill became close friends with Brian Henson. They worked together at Sesame Place, a children's theme park in Pennsylvania. This led, years later, to Bill auditioning for his friend in 1991 and landing the suit performer role of Earl Sinclair on the hit show *"Dinosaurs."*

Since then, Bill has become one of the core Muppet performers for the Jim Henson and Disney Companies. He created such characters as Pepe the King Prawn, Johnny Fiama, Bobo the Bear and more, as well as inheriting the roles of Rowlf the Dog, Dr. Teeth and the Swedish Chef after Jim's passing. Bill performed in the hit Henson shows *"The Wubbulous World of Dr. Seuss," "The Animal Show"* and *"Muppets Tonight,"* as well as being executive producer for the ABC series *"The Muppets."* Bill also co-produced and performed in the films *"Muppet Treasure Island," "It's a Very Merry Muppet Christmas Movie," "Muppet's Wizard of Oz," "The Muppets,"* and *"Muppets Most Wanted."*

Most recently, Bill appeared as Detective Phil Phillips in *"The Happytime Murders"* and as himself in the Frank Oz documentary *"Muppet Guys Talking."* He's also done voice-over work for such shows as the Disney Channel's *"Kim Possible"* and as a featured performer in the Henson adult improvisational show *"Puppet Up!–Uncensored."* Bill was trained at the Neighborhood Playhouse in New York City under the late, great Sanford Meisner. He's a nice Italian boy whose favorite Muppet has always been Guy Smiley.

ART GRUENBERGER
with Rusty the Dog
2018

Art Gruenberger
1969–present

Career: 1991–Present. Art Gruenberger has been an actor since 1979. He holds a B.A. in Liberal Studies with a minor in Theater from California State College Sacramento, and an MFA in Acting from University of California, Davis. In his final year of college he decided to take a puppetry class thinking it would be an easy 'A'. The course was taught by master puppeteer Richard Bay, a puppet builder, performer and director who became Art's mentor. Richard recognized Art's passion for performing and cast him in a show called *"A Thousand Cranes."* Performing a serious and beautiful piece of theater with puppets opened up Art to puppetry beyond the silliness of the Muppets. He also attended *"A Survey of Puppet Theater Techniques,"* a two-week intensive puppetry course taught by Muppet performers.

Since 1994, Art has mainly developed one-man performances for children with his company Puppet Art Theater. His repertoire of sixteen children's tales are being seen throughout California and beyond, and he has also produced blacklight productions. Art has worked for Larry Reed's Shadowlight Productions and with Wendy Morton, taking a large-scale shadow production to the UK and Germany. Art also produces and presents shows seasonally at Sacramento's Fairytale Town children's park. He was a guest artist for the National Puppetry Conference at the Eugene O'Neill Theater Center in 2016, where he workshopped *"Sweeney Todd"* with life-size puppets. He has also been a guest director at UC Davis and CSU Sacramento where he produced *"Avenue Q"* and *"Man of La Mancha"* featuring life-size puppets.

Art has served the Puppeteers of America as Vice President in 2010, as well as President of the San Francisco Bay Area Puppeteers Guild in 2011. He's been influenced by the puppetry of Richard Bay, Nick Barone, Jim Henson, George Latshaw, Marty Robinson and Wendy Morton. Art cowrote *The Actor's Lab Book, A Practical Supplement for the Beginning Actor* with Sheldon Deckelbaum in 2006. He is also a freelance writer for educational videos and live puppet theater.

Evy (Berman) Wright
with Skeeter
2014

Evy (Berman) Wright
1969–present

Career: 1992–Present. Evelyn Claire Wright wanted to be a puppeteer, but didn't know how to go about training for the profession. In order to learn more about puppetry and building techniques, she applied to be a puppeteer at Children's Fairyland through an Oakland jobs program. For two years she studied with mentors Randal Metz and Lewis Mahlmann, helping plan events, build puppets and paint scenery and play sets for the park. She also spent time working in Bay Area theater as a scenic designer and prop specialist.

Evy eventually left California and moved to Georgia to become a resident puppeteer at the Atlanta Center for Puppetry Arts. In 2000 she co-founded Curious Moon Puppets with fellow puppeteer Reay Kaplan. Her signature character, Skeeter the dog, has entertained thousands of children of all ages throughout the southeast where she has provided original puppet productions and workshops for children, families and adults. She's also worked on a freelance basis on projects for film, television and video games. Evy's puppetry work can be seen in the CD-ROM video game *"Dinotopia"* (1995) and the movie *"Muppets from Space"* (1999). She also built all of the puppets for *"The Lady from Sockholm"* (2005), a feature-length all-sock-puppet film noir comedy about a sock puppet detective who finds himself knee-high in debt and praying for a big case. Evy has also worked on ads for Coca Cola and has appeared on the Cartoon Network.

Evy has been a featured performer at the Puppeteers of America Southeast Regional Festival, and the 1993 National Convention in San Francisco. She credits Carol Burnett and Lily Tomlin as influencers. For 12 years Evy appeared with the Big Apple Circus Clown Care Unit in Atlanta, Georgia as a hospital clown. She recently moved to West Virginia where she is pursuing a master's degree and is the Activities Coordinator at West Virginia University (WVU) Medicine.

SEAN & PATRICK JOHNSON
Jack Rabbit & Prairie Dog Pete
2018

Sean and Patrick Johnson
1977–present

Career: 1993–Present. Twin brothers Sean Johnson and Patrick Johnson began their careers in 1993. Greatly inspired by the work of Jim Henson, the brothers attended their first National Puppetry Festival in San Francisco, spending the majority of their time in workshops learning the basics of foam puppet construction and television puppetry. This led to the creation of the Johnson Brothers Puppets in 1993, internships with puppeteers in the Bay Area such as Henry Selick, and countless performances in libraries and schools, and in events. The brothers even earned the rank of Eagle Scout by using puppets in their relevant community projects. After studying film, television and animation at DeAnza Junior College, the duo left San Francisco to pursue work in Southern California.

In 2004, the brothers co-founded Swazzle Inc., a Glendale-based puppet company offering a wide range of services, including live puppet shows, theatrical puppet rentals and custom designed and built puppets. They also produce original puppet content for stage and screen. The duo have created two large-scale theater productions: *"The Little Prince"* and the bilingual family musical *"Dream Carver,"* which have been performed in theaters and performing arts centers across the United States. Some notable puppet projects they have worked on include the Showtime series *"Kidding,"* starring Jim Carrey, *"The Pee-wee Herman Live Show"* on Broadway, and the Aquarium of the Pacific's *"Pacific Pals."* They've created characters for various television commercials and recently built the puppets for *"Crank Yankers"* on Comedy Central. Large-scale productions include *"Dinosaur Train Live"* and the 2019 Netflix series *"The Dark Crystal: Age of Resistance"* with the Jim Henson Creature Shop. Film work includes *"The Happytime Murders."*

In 2005, Sean and Patrick became involved in the Jim Henson Company's puppet improv group, *"Puppet Up!"* Along with building and refurbishing several principal puppets for the improvisational adult theater show, the Johnsons also served as puppeteers, puppet wranglers and puppeteer instructors. Their work has led to many other puppet projects at Jim Henson's Creature Shop in Burbank. But their greatest joy comes from creating their own original work.

LEX RUDD
with Lion
2009

Lex Rudd
1978–present

Career: 1994–Present. Alexis Rudd is an actor, costume designer, illustrator, model maker, prop master, puppeteer and voice artist who has made and performed in creature costumes since 1994. She emigrated to the United States from England in 2004, settling in Guerneville. In 2009, when Lex was making a short film that needed a puppet character, she discovered the Puppeteers of America and its local guilds.

Lex has a B.S. in Special Effects from Southbank University London, and a Higher National Diploma in Interactive Arts from the University of Wales, Newport. In 2004 she formed Primal Visions Design Studio, designing and producing puppets, costumes, plush toys and other creature effects. She mainly concentrates on building puppets but has also performed them in commercials and infomercials. Lex also collaborates with New York puppeteer Arthur H. Poore on various stage shows. She has built puppets for companies including the Jim Henson Creature Shop and Disney Imagineering as well as designing plush toys for Hasbro Toys and Folkmanis Puppets. Lex designed one puppet for a private client that sold $800,000 worth of product in the first 10 days. Her work includes fabrication on one of the returning lead characters in the Netflix series *"The Dark Crystal: Age of Resistance"* and an animated deer figure she puppeteered for a series of Colorado wildlife commercials. Her creations can be seen in the films *"The Brothers Grimm,"* *"Oscar's Hotel for Fantastical Creatures"* and Jim Henson's *"Turkey Hollow."*

Lex has received numerous toy industry awards for her Folkmanis puppet designs and creations. She lists her biggest influences as early British puppet television shows: *"Rainbow"* with Zippy, George and Bungle, *"The Sooty Show,"* *"Round the Bend"* with Doc Croc, Zig and Zag, *"Roland Rat: The Series,"* and of course *"The Dark Crystal."* She was also a contestant on the *"Jim Henson Creature Shop Challenge"* on the SyFy Channel in 2015.

LESLIE CARRARA-RUDOLPH
with Lolly Lardpop
2018

Leslie Carrara-Rudolph
1962–present

Career: 1996–present. Growing up in Pleasant Hill, California, Leslie Jolene Carrara-Rudolph experienced her first puppet show at Children's Fairyland, where puppet master Lewis Mahlmann introduced her to a wolf marionette made out of a gourd. She was hooked and started making puppets out of whatever she could find.

A love for all things arts and puppetry took a backseat as a teenage Leslie developed her character and musical theater chops in Fantasy Forum Actors Ensemble before designing her major at San Francisco State University: "Child Development Through the Arts."

Upon graduation, Leslie joined the cast of *"Beach Blanket Babylon,"* worked as an improviser at Disney World, and wrote and performed her show *"Life in Other People's Shoes"* at an HBO Workspace. It was this show that led her to her first professional puppetry job when Bill Barretta convinced Brian Henson to hire Leslie on *"Muppets Tonight."*

Leslie found herself mentored by Muppet legend Jerry Nelson and working alongside her future husband, and future musical director, Paul Rudolph. She joined the L.A. Puppetry Guild, and soon after created her signature character, candy-loving Lolly Lardpop, who performed regularly at the Cavern Club Theater and hung out with Chuck McCann.

Leslie developed and starred in Disney's *"Wahoo Wagon"* at the El Capitan Theater and is a founding member of *"Puppet Up."* Puppetry roles in *"The Wubbulous World of Dr. Seuss," "Forgetting Sarah Marshall," "Johnny and the Sprites,"* and *"Splash and Bubbles"* soon followed, but it's Leslie's five-time Emmy nominated role as *Sesame Street's* Abby Cadabby that has allowed her to reach children globally. Leslie and writing partner Jamie Donmoyer spread joy with their podcast *"Lolly's Radio Playdate," "Bizarre Brunch Cabarets"* and outreach projects.

Leslie received an UNIMA Citation of Excellence in puppetry for her one-woman show *"Entertaining a Thought."*

LIEBE WETZEL
Cirque du Celery
2002

Liebe Wetzel
1960–present

Career: 1996–Present. Liebe Wetzel began her puppet career as the clown Too Too Tomato. She decided to become a puppeteer after attending Avner the Eccentric's Clowning Workshop in 1996, as the group only responded when she included a puppet in her act. The instructor declared, "You're not funny as a clown, but your puppets are." In 1999, Liebe founded Lunatique Fantastique, a group of found object puppeteers. She cites breath, movement and focus as the three rules of object puppetry.

Liebe is a graduate of the Dell'Arte International School of Physical Theater in Humboldt County, and has studied at the Cornish College of Arts in Seattle, WA. Besides holding a BA in Biology and Biochemistry from Rice University, she is a master at mime, melodrama, masks, stilts, juggling and assorted theatrical skills. Using items found in everyday use and bringing them to life on stage, Liebe has created a niche for herself. Who would've thought an audience could feel deeply for a bra, or be moved to tears by a plunger and a few rolls of toilet paper? Her shows, including *"Snake in the Basement," "Brace Yourself Frances, It's Polio," "Beauty and the Breast," "Object Odyssey," "Naked Foam," "Objects in Predicaments"* and *"The Wrapping Paper Caper"* portray social problems. *"Stump"* is about returning from the Iraq war. *"Chicken Stock"* is about Bird Flu. Liebe has found the use of object puppets to tell a story makes difficult material more readily accessible.

Liebe calls Dada master Marcel Duchamp the great-grandfather of her work. He took found objects and turned them into art, helping us to see the world in a different way. She has earned a "Goldie," an outstanding local discovery award from the *San Francisco Bay Guardian*, and won "Best of Fringe" in the 2001 San Francisco Fringe Festival. Liebe believes an artist's job in the community is to talk about things no one else will talk about and make it entertaining.

SAM KOJI HALE
2016

Sam Koji Hale

1970–present

Career: 1999–Present. Sam Hale is a master storyboard artist, illustrator, digital post-production artist, production designer, writer and puppet fabricator. His forte is creating puppet movies using live puppetry and stop motion in digital worlds. Hale lived for a decade in the San Francisco Bay Area, earning a Master of Fine Arts degree from the Academy of Art University in 2000. While studying illustration at the college, a professor suggested Sam do a puppet film. Sam sought out the San Francisco Bay Area Puppeers Guild, meeting Muppet legend Dave Goelz and eventually Muppet writer Jerry Juhl, who mentored him in scriptwriting.

In 2009 Sam founded Mighty Pug Studio in Los Angeles. Influenced by Japanese folklore, mythology and motifs, he has created many Asian fantasy films. His puppet skills include classic puppetry, shadows, stop motion and Bunraku table top puppetry as in his show *"The Fox Lantern."* His films include *"Yamasong,"* mythic steampunk film *"Monster of the Sky,"* and *"Yamasong: March of the Hollows,"* a feature film executive produced by Heather Henson and Toby Froud and released in 2019. Sam says, "Most people working in film will tell you filmmaking is challenging work. We just complicate it a tad with puppets! Where do we hide puppeteers, or light a shot with puppets if the puppeteer is visible? How do we use digital effects to take out rods and puppeteers? How do we nuance a performance that requires a puppet changing props? How do we overcome the very limitations of the puppet style–strings for marionettes, rods for tabletop, etc.? These are all challenges for certain, but I think those of us working in puppetry appreciate a good challenge!"

Over the course of his career Sam has been a producer for Heather Henson's Handmade Puppet Dreams, digital effects lead for the Disney Channel's *"Bite-sized Adventures of Sam Sandwich,"* production manager at Chiodo Brothers Productions and artistic director on the Cartoon Network's show *"Annoying Orange."* He also used to teach Theater Arts at Cal State San Bernardino.

Brian Patterson

Career: 1990–present. Brian is the son of Phyllis and Ron Patterson, founders of the Renaissance Pleasure Faire and Great Dickens Christmas Fair. It's no wonder that Brian has been heavily influenced by the stylings of the Italian Commedia dell'arte. Brian has a walk-around stage and a stationary Punch stage. In 1990, he and partner Heidi Wohlwend formed the Piccolo Puppet Players. Piccolo presents the *"Tragical Comedy or Comical Tragedy of Punch and Judy"* in the traditional British style. Brian is the puppet professor, while Heidi acted as the bottler, providing music and authentic sound effects.

Drew Massey

Career: 1993–present. Andrew Massey was a performer on *"Sesame Street"* in 1993 and then joined the Jim Henson Company. He was Sid in *"Sid the Science Kid"* as well as Stuff in *"Mutt & Stuff."* He's worked on the *"Men in Black"* films and performs Count Blah in *"Greg the Bunny"* as well as being one of the two Foster Farms Chickens. Drew built his first puppet in second grade with help from Muppeteer Michael Earl. Today, Drew is a standup comedian, actor, director, producer, singer, musician and voice actor and has studied industrial design, illustration and film.

Jesse Vail

Career: 1994–present. Jesse Vail is a puppet builder, performer and consultant as well as a vocal actor and teaching artist. He is also a professional prop maker for local theater including high schools and the American Music Theatre of San Jose. Jesse started his puppetry career working as a clown and balloon artist known as "Bino" before discovering Children's Fairyland's Storybook Puppet Theater. There he was mentored by Lewis Mahlmann and Randal Metz. From 1997–2004, Jesse was the director of the Happy Hollow Castle Puppet Theater in San Jose. In 2004 he founded Fool Moon Puppetry Arts.

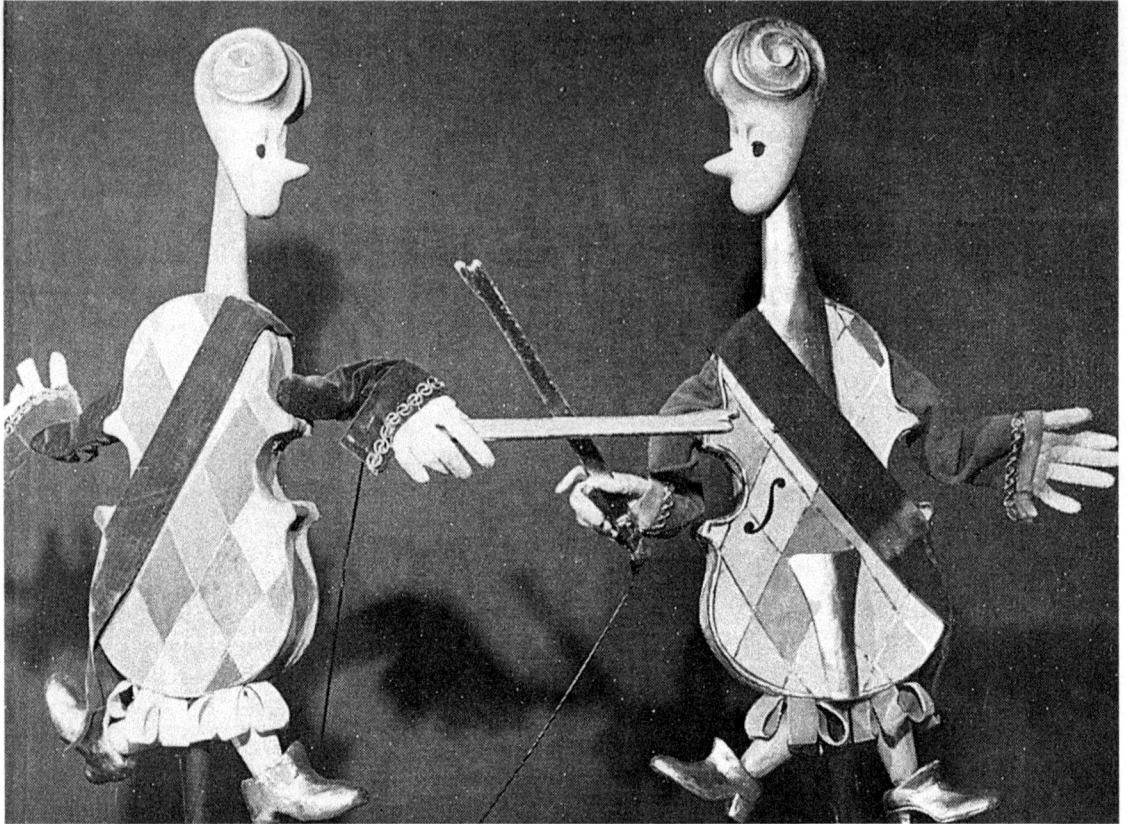

BENJAMIN BLAKE
Dueling Violins
1966

$\backsim$ 10 $\backsim$

The 2000s

WECOME TO THE 21st century! The world is now changing quickly, and everyone seems to be moving faster to keep up with it. At the turn of the century, Y2K, or the Millennium Bug, was a serious concern. When computing technology was invented, nobody had considered a change in century — and now everyone was afraid the new technology would not register the change from 1999 to 2000. Apocalyptic conditions were predicted: Computers would crash, banks would fail, and planes would fall from the sky! Of course, that didn't happen (at least not connected with Y2K), although we did have our share of newsworthy items in the "aughties." The World Trade Center was destroyed in 2001. The Great Recession hit in 2007 for 18 months. And on a positive note, we elected our first black President in 2009. Meanwhile, news and opinions continued to be exchanged on an increasingly sophisticated internet. With technology prices becoming easily more affordable, and the introduction of Facebook (2004), Youtube (2005) and the iPhone (2007), social media was redefining how puppetry was evolving.

And what about movies and literature? Digital characters were here at last, relegating practical puppetry to "has-been" status. Lucasfilm, and the Weta Workshop in New Zealand, created aliens, dynamic landscapes and illusions through the introduction of motion capture. In motion capture, digital markers are attached to an actor to plot their filmed movements. Later, the animation data was mapped to a 3D model so the model performs the same actions as the actor, creating a computer graphic performance that is integrated into the finished film — an upgrade to the older process of rotoscoping. Actor Andy Serkis became the master of these performances with his portrayal of Gollum in *"The Lord of the Rings"* and the *"Hobbit"* trilogies. Computer graphic animation took over from classic line drawn animation. The *"Pirates of the Caribbean"* and new *"Star Wars"* series along with the many Marvel Superhero movies set the bar high for the special effects industry. Puppetry became relegated to specialized films such as *"Team America:*

World Police" and *"The Happytime Murders."* But the biggest change of all came when Disney bought the Muppets in 2004. After the previous German media company, EM.TV, backed away from their deal, Disney soon owned Kermit and *"Bear in the Big Blue House,"* although not the *"Sesame Street"* characters or the Jim Henson Company. "The Mouse" soon also gobbled up Marvel comics in 2009 and Lucasfilm in 2012. The Disney Company effectively now owned everyone's childhood.

And the world of books was changing also. E-books were becoming popular with the computer driven populace. Amazon Kindle appeared in 2007, with Barnes & Noble Nook and iBooks becoming available in 2009 and 2010. And authors continued to turn out captivating tales that captured the imagination. George R. R. Martin's *A Game of Thrones* series and the easy reading adventures of James Patterson became popular. And for the younger set, Daniel Handler penned Lemony Snicket's *A Series of Unfortunate Events.*

In the puppetry world, chat sites such as "Puptcrit" and "Puppet HUB" provided a virtual space where puppeteers could blog and socialize. Puppetry began to see a renaissance through the internet powered instant communication and information exchange. After purchasing the Muppets, Disney decided its amusement parks should feature more practical puppetry. Disney became a big employer and trainer of puppeteers, leading the way for other major amusement parks to follow their lead. Everyone was suddenly a puppeteer. To help keep perspective on the growth of the profession, the Puppeteers of America published *A Timeline of Puppetry in America* in 2003. This informational magazine was published as a special edition of the Puppetry Journal. 2001 is the year the brothers Mark and Tony Mazzarella released on PBS their one hour film documentary *"Stories of the American Puppet,"* the evolution of puppetry from colonial times to the 21st century. 300 years in the making! The other major growth spurt for puppetry in America was the creation of popular adult puppet talent shows such as puppet slams and Henson's Puppet Up! A slam is an evening of short form, live puppet theater for an adult audience – a way for fledgling or professional puppeteers to share their talents. Each act is five minutes or less, and can be works in progress, polished gems, or anything in between. And on Broadway, puppets were featured as a "necessity" in stage shows such as *"Little Shop of Horrors," "Avenue Q," "War Horse"* and practically all of Julie Taymor's productions.

Puppetry continued to prosper in California, although primarily in the Los Angeles area where the Jim Henson Company is based. Through the use of the Henson Digital Performance System (HDPS), digital puppet shows were being created in "real time." Unlike film's motion capture system, the Henson process required two puppeteers working in sync to bring a digital puppet to the screen. One puppeteer wears a giant digital marker puppet suit which captures their physical movements, while the lead puppeteer manipulates a computer system to capture the facial expressions, voice performance and mouth movements via a hand control. This was used to perfection in the show *Sid the Science Kid"* to bring digital puppets to the screen. Heather Henson was also uniting puppeteers with her Handmade Puppet Dreams film series which supported puppet films designed and directed by puppet artists. California puppets and puppeteers also found a home on the internet through amateur or professional "Webisodes" — online series, sort of like a television series with a lower budget. And L.A. puppeteer Grant Bacioccio created the ongoing podcast *Under the Puppet,"* speaking with different professional puppeteers each month about their careers and experiences, preserving puppetry through their personal stories.

To sum all of this up, the future of puppetry is continuing to expand while at the same time hearkening back to its roots. Classical, live puppet theater is coming back, supported by parents who appreciate having the opportunity for their children to take a break from the constant rush of CG and video games. And film and television puppeteers are finding themselves attracted to the simpler forms of puppetry as a new means of expressing themselves, as there are only so many jobs available in the film industry. From the streets, to minstrel shows, to vaudeville and burlesque, to the theatrical stage, and from radio, to television, to movies, puppetry has experienced an exciting and stimulating evolution. But we do have to watch out for this digital world. With so many finding themselves glued to the computer screen, the idea of a mentor, or of a coming together of puppeteers in a social gathering such as guilds or conventions, is being threatened by a device that can keep you at home with instant tutorials and video content. Nothing can replace the feeling of being present for a live, theatrical puppet presentation. But in the meantime, sit back and laugh, enjoy the antics of a perhaps very soon to be virtual reality *"Punch and Judy."*

Grant Baciocco
with Toiley T Paper
2017

Grant Baciocco
1974–present

Career: 2000–Present. Grant Patrick Baciocco is an accomplished comedian, actor, writer and singer/songwriter who grew up in the San Francisco Bay Area watching his favorite puppet shows: Robin Goodrow's *"Buster and Me,"* Pat McCormick's *"Charlie and Humphrey Good Stuff Hour"* and the Muppets. In 2000, Grant decided to build his first professional puppet for his girlfriend, so he ordered a foam puppet book off the internet and began building. That led to the creation of a puppet for a dog training DVD.

In 2003 the Jim Henson Company asked Grant to participate in a sizzle reel announcing a new show, *"America's Next Top Muppet,"* a spoof of *"America's Next Top Model"* directed by Bill Barretta. This led to Grant meeting Brian Henson and Leslie Carrara-Rudolph, who became his mentors. Leslie recommended Grant for Henson training and he was soon a performer and host on Henson's *"Puppet Up–Uncensored,"* aka *"Stuffed & Unstrung."*

In 2006 he was hired to produce and host the official Henson Company podcast, which sparked his idea to have a podcast interviewing working puppeteers. Grant's monthly *"Under the Puppet"* podcast features puppeteers talking about the art and business of puppetry. Grant also regularly puppeteers the character Crow T. Robot on the new Netflix version of *"Mystery Science Theater 3000,"* both in the show and in touring company productions. Other puppet credits include *"Wet Hot American Summer: Ten Years Later,"* *"Last Week Tonight with John Oliver"* and *"The Happytime Murders."* Grant also produces his own content and performs live shows with his puppet character Toiley T. Paper, who has an online following of more than 1.3 million fans.

Grant has a BA from California State University Long Beach in Theater, specializing in acting and directing. He is a member of the comedy music band Throwing Toasters, and has opened for Weird Al Yankovic. In 2018 Grant was inducted into the Podcast Hall of Fame for the work he's done for his company Saturday Morning Media, a trans-media company that focuses on quality family friendly content.

Erik Kuska
with Mr. Window
2010

Erik Kuska
1971–present

Career: 2008–Present. Erik Kuska is an animator, writer, actor and puppet builder. In 1996, before discovering puppetry, Erik was an animator for many of the finest animation studios in Los Angeles. He created the show *"Wabbit"* for the Cartoon Network/Warner Brothers, as well as working as a storyboard artist for *"American Dad!"* Erik also was a character layout artist for *"The Simpsons Movie."* His feature film credits included *"Hercules," "The Road to El Dorado"* and *"The Prince of Egypt."* But he gave all of that up for a new career in the puppet world. "As enjoyable as making cartoons is," he says, "you don't get to enjoy how an audience will react to your work."

In 2008, while working full time in the animation industry and taking improvisation classes, Erik took a puppetry course from Michael Earl. Erik says he has never smiled so much, and was soon performing birthday/music puppet shows and appearing at puppet slams in the Los Angeles area. Very shortly he was teaching puppetry for Michael at the Puppet School in Sherman Oaks, which led him to joining the Los Angeles Guild and the Puppeteers of America, and teaching workshops at national puppet festivals. He is especially proud of his teaching work.

Erik primarily works with hand (Muppet) and rod puppets. He performed the roles of Clocky and Mr. Window in the Los Angeles revival of *"The Pee-wee Herman Live"* show on stage. His work can also be seen as the puppeteer for Tom Servo on the new Netflix version of *"Mystery Science Theater 3000"* with fellow manipulator Russ Walko.

Erik graduated from Northern Illinois University with a Bachelor of Fine Arts degree in Electronic Media. His mentors have included Michael Earl, Russ Walko and Disney legend Walt Stanchfield. For influencers, he lists Jim Henson, Frank Oz, Don Sahlin, Jerry Juhl, Art Gruenberger and Grant Baciocco. Erik has also studied writing with the Groundlings, the Pack Theater and ACME.

DEREK LUX
with White Rabbit & Mad Hatter
2017

Derek Lux
1983–present

Career: 2011–present. Born and raised in San Francisco, Derek Lux has been enamored with puppets since a young age, from the Muppets to Ronn Lucas. After seeing a performance by Kevin Menegus, he joined the San Francisco Bay Area Puppeteers Guild and over the course of the next two years attended workshops on puppetry skills. In junior high school he put aside puppetry in pursuit of theater and acting. But in his late 20s, as an actor in Los Angeles, Derek revisited his childhood passion and decided to make it a lifelong career. He started as a puppet builder and soon fell in love with puppeteering as well.

During his time in Los Angeles, Derek interned with Sean and Patrick Johnson of Swazzle, which gave him the necessary basics for building theatrically. Derek's puppetry schooling includes the O'Neill National Puppetry Conference, the Stan Winston School of Character Arts and training with Michael Earl. He eventually taught puppet building at Earl's Puppet School. In 2013 he won a Los Angeles Stage Alliance Ovation Honor Award for puppet design with Christian Anderson in *"Shrek the Musical."* After working on a handful of projects in the film and television industry, in 2017, Lux relocated back to the Bay Area and formed DLUX Puppets with his wife and partner Lauren. The two have taken all of his puppetry and performance skills and combined them to create the family shows *"Alice in Wonderland"* and *"Peter Pan"* as full stage, live puppet performances. Derek is the writer, director and builder of puppets, while Lauren is an actress and education director for the company. To create the background sets, DLUX uses Steve Axtell's "Live Virtual Sets" product that allows for digitally projected images that help tell the story in a virtual sense. In 2019, Derek and his family once again relocated, this time to Las Vegas.

Derek has been influenced by Jim Henson and puppeteer Norman Schneider. His mentors include Steve Axtell and Art Gruenberger. Derek was also a longtime cast member of Steve Silver's *"Beach Blanket Babylon,"* the longest running musical revue in history and a San Francisco institution, where he played Donald Trump.

Russ Walko

Career: Early 2000–present. Russ Walko has built and performed puppets for such notable companies as Jim Henson's Creature Shop, the Chiodo Bros. and Swazzle. His credits include *"Kidding," "Crank Yankers," "The Muppets," "Dark Crystal: Age of Resistance," "The Simpsons," "Community," "The Happytime Murders"* and *"Mystery Science Theater 3000"* where he puppeteered the robotic sidekick Tom Servo. Recently, Walko was a suit performer (playing Conky) and puppet builder for the stage production of *"Pee-wee Herman Live."* Today, Russ runs his own company, Puppet Garage. Being both a puppeteer and builder, he focuses on the performance quality of puppets he creates.

Alex U. Griffin

Career: Mid 2000s–present. Alex is a cinematographer and a photographer with a passion for the puppetry arts. He was cinematographer for Sam Hale's *"Yamasong: March of the Hollows"* and Christine Papalexis' *"Amaterasu."* Alex is also a performer and film coordinator for Heather Henson's Handmade Puppet Dreams. In his spare time he acts as film columnist for the Puppetry Journal, writing articles and reviews on the digital and film world of puppetry. Alex has had movies shown at Cannes, Slamdance and BAM Film Festivals as well as many other prestigious venues. He has also been a photographer for many Puppeteers of America festivals.

ᔐ 11 ᔐ

California Puppet Theaters, 1928–present

Pⓔʀᴍᴀɴᴇɴᴛ puppet theaters in cities and amusement areas have been an important part of California's puppet history. They have not only supplied visitors with quality puppet entertainment, they have also acted as a place where puppeteers could congregate and meet and receive instruction and technique. Many local guilds use these theaters as a place to hold monthly meetings. The locales have included theaters in storefronts, boardwalks, permanent buildings in playgrounds, zoos and amusement parks, as well as some businesses containing theaters, workshops and party areas.

Throughout the century, we have seen people constantly looking to entertainment venues to forget their own problems. And puppetry as a novel and unusual entertainment has filled that need. Puppet shows have reflected the temperament of the time period, and often represented the feelings of the populace at that moment (such as Punch and Judy). Elements of popular literature and film representing a certain period in pop culture are often included in the performances given at successful puppet theaters. The puppet theater has always been a good way to bring the written word to life in a visual and artistic manner.

As puppetry thrives, more and more puppetry centers have arisen in cities and states across America. Each one has been supported by the Puppeteers of America, and each one has offered a way to help promote the puppet arts and let puppet companies present their shows in a welcoming format. California puppet theaters have been strong and often long lasting — but running a theater in one location is very difficult. It requires obtaining a space, rent and/or sponsorship, advertising and a repertoire of successful shows to keep an audience returning.

In this chapter, we spotlight eleven prestigious puppet theaters and programs which have inspired others and influenced our puppet culture. Yet, there were other theaters that came and went over the years. The following is a short list of a few of these puppet companies and places where puppets entertained and enthralled:

The first California puppet theater was co-directed by Blanding Sloan and Ralph Chessé in 1928. For four years, under the banner of the Marionette Guild Theater, they featured puppet productions by such unique artists as John Carter Ford, R. Bruce Inverarity, Vera Von Pilat and Enola Barker. Starting in Blanding's studio, the theater eventually ended up on Merchant Street in San Francisco.

From 1932–1934, Harold and Robert Hestwood performed marionette productions of Walt Disney cartoons with the Hestwood Marionettes at Bullock's Wilshire department store. Nick Nelson took over from the Hestwoods, under the name of the Olvera Puppeteers, and continued the tradition until the mid '40s. Wayne Barlow performed Disney and other marionette productions for nine years (1934-1942) at J.W. Robinson's department store. Other Los Angeles stores featuring puppeteers were the May Company and 5th Street Store. Sometime in the '30s, leading into the '40s, Jack Shafton ran a successful marionette theater on the Venice Beach Pier.

In 1947 in Santa Barbara, you could find the magical Tantamount Theater run by John Ralph Geddis and François Martin, featuring puppet spectacles, dance recitals, poetry readings and the occasional film presentation. After five years the theater moved to Carmel Valley and flourished there until its demise in 1978, twenty-six years later.

After the Turnabout Theatre closed its doors in 1956, Harry Burnett, Forman Brown and Richard Brandon moved the whole theater to San Francisco for a limited run at Polk and Turk streets under the sponsorship of the Town Hall Organization, and then onto Mason Street. Afterwards they resettled the theater in San Diego's Balboa Park for another limited run. Meanwhile in Monterey, Daniel Llords of Llords International successfully ran a theater in the tourist district for several years starting in 1959.

In 1961 in the San Fernando Valley, Sid and Marty Krofft opened their legacy show *"Les Poupées de Paris"* in the Krofft Theatre at Nat Hart's Gilded Rafters restaurant. The show then moved to P.J.'s in West Hollwood, eventually ending up in Lake Tahoe and San

Francisco for a limited run. From 1961 through the early '70s *"Les Poupées"* traveled the country, in various forms, offering puppet training for many future puppeteers.

In 1972, Virginia Austin Curtis opened her Puppet Theatre Workshop in Sierra Madre. For several years she sponsored puppet performances from local companies and hosted puppet events. Also of note are the Jax Marionettes (Jack & Sandy Spottswood), who performed marionette shows for a few years in the '70s at a theater on the pier at the Santa Cruz Beach Boardwalk.

At this point, location-based puppet theaters waned for several years, not picking up again until the 1980s. In the late 1980s and early '90s, Steve Overton opened and performed at his Olde World Puppet Theatre in Pacifica. And in 2008 Theodore Dawson had success with his Zanzibar Fairytale Puppet Theater, first at the Sir Francis Drake Hotel in San Francisco and then in Oakland, with seasonal Christmas runs of *"Cinderella."*

There were also puppet theaters related to colleges and their programs. Perry Dilley had a small theater at Mills College in Oakland where he taught puppet arts, and Lewis Mahlmann presented college puppet productions at San Francisco State in the 1970s. Michael R. Malkin and Mel Helstein developed well-known puppetry programs for many years at Cal Poly State University and UCLA. Also of note is Richard Bay, who for 30 years taught a puppet performance elective at California State University in Sacramento.

And then there were the many puppet companies who found a home at major amusement parks and tourist attractions, such as Angela Combs Canright's troupe in Santa's Village of Scotts Valley. Although featured for a limited time, some of these puppet productions were very elaborate. Bob Mills ran a puppet theater at the Tinker Bell Toy Shop in Disneyland, from 1958–1962. Starting in 1968, and for the next five years, Universal Studios Hollywood featured the artistry of the Tony Urbano Marionettes. Tony then moved to Knotts Berry Farm for two years, where René Zendejas also ran a successful attraction for eight years. In the mid 1980s James Rowland of Apuppetsho Productions created a popular marionette show at the Puppet-Tree Theater at Six Flags Great America Park in Santa Clara. Six Flags Magic Mountain Park in Valencia also featured annual puppet presentations. Christine Papalexis had a three year run performing puppets at the Queen Mary ship in Los Angeles, sponsored by Dreyers Ice Cream. And at a story book park similar to Children's Fairyland and Happy Hollow, Fairytale Town in Sacramento featured seasonal appearances by Richard Bay and Art Gruenberger.

California zoos in Los Angeles, Oakland, San Diego and San Francisco have also presented popular puppet attractions. And don't forget the state and county fairs where the Lesselli Marionettes, Laurie Branham and Nancy Mitchell found a yearly home entertaining the crowds. Meanwhile at the California Renaissance Pleasure and Great Dickens Christmas Fairs you could find Brian Patterson and Bruce Schwartz presenting *"Punch & Judy"* and other favorites. And in San Francisco at the Cannery and Pier 39 on Fishermans' Wharf were Bob Hartman and Steve Hansen busking their talents nightly and passing the hat.

Because of these artists' groundbreaking efforts, you can find many fortunate puppet companies performing annually at festivals, shopping malls and community venues, much like Tony Urbano did for twelve seasons at the Laguna Beach Festival of Arts where Bob Baker had carried on for five earlier seasons.

As mentioned before, many puppet theater histories have been lost in the pages of time, or not yet rediscovered and added to the continually expanding internet. If you find any of these lost gems, don't hesitate to write about it on the web, or highlight your findings in a local guild or puppet newsletter. But for the present, we hope you enjoy the theaters we have included for your reading pleasure. *"All the world's a stage,"* and we need more of them!

Above: BOB BROMLEY
Violinist

Right: HARRY BURNETT
Southern Belle

TEATRO TORITO
Olvera Street
1931-1932

WALTON & O'ROURKE
Olvera Street
1935

Olvera Street Puppet Theaters
Dates of Operation: 1930–1939, nightly year 'round

Olvera Street in Los Angeles was a magnet for puppeteers performing in the 1930s. Many troupes and artists became famous performing for the celebrity and tourist crowds. But by 1930, Olvera Street was quickly falling into decay. Christine Sterling, Harry Chandler and the Los Angeles Chamber of Commerce began the rescue of this historic area, with the aim of revitalizing the original Mexican feel of the community. They invited artists and puppeteers, Mexican vendors and others to help inspire tourism.

The first puppeteers to perform on Olvera Street were the Yale Puppeteers. From 1930 to 1931 (and a short run in 1934), located at #27 Olvera Street, they ran the *"Teatro Torito,"* or theater of the little bull, an homage to the bullfighter pictured on their elaborate puppet curtain. Bob Bromley began his apprenticeship with Harry Burnett, Forman Brown and Richard Brandon. The trio were known for having celebrities who saw their shows sign with chalk on the walls of the theater. This helped to pique the interest of visitors.

When the Yale Puppeteers left to go to New York, Bromley took over the theater with his partners Wayne Barlow and C. Ray Smith. They were known as the *"Famous Olvera Puppeteers"* and entertained with night club-style marionettes from 1932–1935. The 1933 earthquake caused a decline in tourism, so Bob toured as the Famous Olvera Puppeteers until 1935. Nick Nelson rejoined the company in 1934 and they moved the theater to Bullocks Department Store, where the new "Olvera Puppeteers" produced shows until it disbanded sometime in the mid '40s.

The last puppet theater, located at #21 Olvera Street, was run by the famous marionette team of Walton & O'Rourke. Paul and his partner Michael presented fast-paced adult musical revues from 1935–1939. Their theater was simply known as the *"Olvera Street Puppet Theater."*

Other prominent puppeteers who found themselves pulling strings on Olvera Street include Bob Baker, Bob Jones, Nick Nelson, Virginia Curtis, Frank Paris and René Zendejas. Many years later *La Golondrina* Mexican restaurant on Olvera St. returned to having puppets perform for diners with René Zendejas and Bob Baker supplying elaborate marionette productions.

CATALINA ISLAND PUPPET THEATER
1933

Catalina Island Puppet Theater
Dates of Operation: 1933–1936, summer seasons

One of the more unusual "puppet only" theaters was not located in California proper, but rather on an island off the coast in the Gulf of Santa Catalina. The only way to get there was to take the *S. S. Catalina* from Los Angeles to the island's city of Avalon. The theater was located in a Spanish patio named "Paseo El Encanto," that eventually became a glamorous casino built in 1929. The theater featured marionette revue shows for a sophisticated adult audience. This was the realm of the Nickabob Puppets!

Nick Nelson and Bob Jones, who worked for the Olvera Street puppet theaters, along with their manager (and Bob's brother) Bill Jones, established this marionette showcase. Bill heard about a new project on Catalina Island and sold casino builder D. M. Renton on the idea of puppets entertaining tourists before they entered the casino. Renton, and William Wrigley Jr., a member of the Wrigley chewing gum family, loved the idea. They designed a 125-seat theater on the side of the patio, and the puppeteers supplied the stage and performances. Since the boat docked with at least 2,400 tourists each trip, the puppets were soon playing to standing room only crowds. By August of that first year, Bob and Bill bought out Nick's interest in the company and decided to go it alone while Nick returned to the Famous Olvera Puppeteers. Their shows featured grand opera, jazz and ballet music, drawing audiences of adults as the shows were too advanced for youngsters to understand or enjoy.

The theater ran for the next four summers. Since it was seasonal, Bob and Bill used to joke they wintered on Olvera Street and summered on Catalina. After the theater closed, Bob went on to become a production cameraman for Walt Disney in 1937. When Disney learned he was a puppeteer, Bob was put in charge of character development for *"Pinocchio,"* building the first actual Pinocchio puppet used for animation and promotion as well as constructing all of Geppeto's toys.

TURNABOUT THEATRE
1940s

Turnabout Theatre

Dates of Operation: 1941–1956, year 'round nightly at Nine! (save Monday)

716 North La Cienega Boulevard, in Los Angeles, was the home of the ever-popular Turnabout Theatre. Run by the Yale Puppeteers Harry Burnett, Forman Brown and Richard Brandon, Turnabout was unique and exciting because it featured both a marionette show and a live revue show. Over its fifteen-year career Turnabout became known as the "place to go" while visiting Los Angeles.

The theater had a stage at either side of the room: one marionette and one "live" stage. Each of the 77 old time street car seats, with a reversible back, could accommodate two audience members. Thus, if you were in the front row for the first act marionette show, you were in the back for the second act live revue show. Audience members just flipped the seat back to reverse the bench's direction. Because after all, "Turnabout is fair play!" Rather than being numbered, seats had clever names such as "Salt & Pepper," "Sweet & Low," "High & Mighty" and "Hot & Bothered." The theater also featured interior walls where visiting celebrities signed their autographs, and even some amusing life-sized dummies sitting in the balcony who, along with their seats, turned on command to view either show.

Harry Burnett created all the marionettes used in the puppet theater, while Forman Brown wrote all the puppet plays, music and revue songs. Dorothy Neuman, another partner in the company, directed and costumed the live revue shows. A host of entertainers joined the Yale Puppeteers singing in the revue section. They included film actress Elsa Lanchester, Dorothy Neuman, Frances Osborne, Lotte Goslar, Bill Buck, Leota Lane and Odetta Holmes. Forman's songs were highly popular and satirical and featured Forman live on the piano. In 1975 there was a record album called *"Turnabout–A Satirical Revue"* which featured songs and original artists from the show. There is also a documentary film: *"Turnabout: The Story of the Yale Puppeteers"* directed by Dan Bessie. When the theater eventually closed, over 4,535 performances had been given.

MARIE HITCHCOCK PUPPET THEATER
2015

Marie Hitchcock Puppet Theater
Dates of Operation: 1947–1982, semi-seasonal schedule. 1983–present, year 'round

The Marie Hitchcock Theater is one of the oldest puppet theaters in the United States. It is located on the south side of Balboa Park in the Palisades area of San Diego. The theater was originally part of a building erected for the California Pacific International Exposition in 1935. After the exposition closed in 1936, the building did not stay empty for long. Acting on the recommendation of Leo B. Calland, the first Parks and Recreation director, the building was divided into three sections: a little theater, a recital hall and an arts and crafts center.

The 234-seat theater, planned for family entertainment, officially became the Marie Hitchcock Puppet Theater in 1986. Although Marie and her sister often presented semi-seasonal shows in the theater starting in 1947, for years the building was used for many other theatrical and official presentations as well as being home to the San Diego Junior Theater Workshop from 1951–1971. In 1964, the fledgling San Diego Puppetry Guild, under the guidance of its members and Marie, painstakingly began the process to recognize the Balboa Park building as an official "Puppet Theater only." They convinced the Recreation Department to produce an annual six-week summer series of puppet shows, with Marie continuing to perform during all the major holiday seasons. In 1976, six weeks became eight weeks. In 1983 more puppeteers were added to the roster of performers. Now puppet shows could be enjoyed all year, rather than just during summers and holidays. In 1986, the guild's dream was achieved and the puppets moved into their own private theater building, with its new name.

In 2001, the San Diego Balboa Park Puppet Guild was formed. The new guild took over directorship of the theater from the original San Diego Guild of Puppetry. Directors have included Tom Jenson and Joe Fitzpatrick. Other professional puppeteers who have lent their talents to this co-op theater include Don Ave, Nick Barone, Ellen Galpin, Genevieve Engman, Lynne Jennings, Mary Johnson, Pamelia McIntire, Shirley McManus and Pat Platt.

VAGABOND PUPPET THEATER
1954

Vagabond Puppet Theater
Dates of Operation: 1950–2015, summer seasons

Not all puppet theaters were contained in buildings. The Vagabond Puppet Theater, one of the longest running recreational programs of its kind, performed throughout the city of Oakland in recreation centers, public parks and libraries.

When the WPA Works project ended in 1941, Ralph Chessé crated and shipped the puppets to the Oakland Parks Department, where they remained unused until 1950. Then Joyce E. Lobner revived the shows and performed for four years under the troupe heading of the Stardust Puppeteers. In 1954, Lettie Connell Schubert took over the program and the Vagabond Puppet Theater was born. The theater's trailer, which resembled a circus wagon, provided a fine training ground for many local puppeteers. The WPA puppets were retired and new ones created for the smaller performance proscenium of the traveling trailer. In 1957, Jerry Juhl and Frank Oznowicz joined Lettie's program and became directors from 1961- 62, after she stepped down.

From 1963 to 1969, the program was directed by Ruth Sinclair and Pearl Dailey. From 1970–1972, Bruce Chessé, son of Ralph Chessé, took over. In 1973, the reins were passed to Richard and Julie Greene of the Puppet House, who favored hand puppet shows with lots of gimmicks and surprises. Puppeteer, educator and actor Earl Rhue guided the talents of Vagabond from 1976 until 1980. After working alongside Earl since 1976, Blake Maxam took over as director in 1981. Blake ran the program for a total of 32 years while at the Oakland Recreation Department, only missing three years due to other department commitments.

During the three years of Blake's absence (1985–1987), directorship was passed from Randal Metz of the Puppet Company to Daniel Taurines of Geppetto's Puppets to Fred Jackson and Earl Rhue. After Blake's return in 1988, Vagabond Puppet Theater continued until its closure in 2015. The puppets are currently in storage, with plans for curation possibly at the Oakland Museum.

Children's Fairyland
STORYBOOK PUPPET THEATER
1957

Children's Fairyland's – Storybook Puppet Theater
Dates of Operation: 1956–today, year 'round with
seven different shows each year.

The Storybook Puppet Theater is the oldest continuously running puppet theater in America. Opened in 1956 in Children's Fairyland amusement park in Oakland, the theater presents three shows a day with a year 'round schedule. Fairyland itself is located in Lakeside Park. The theater structure, made to look like an open book, was designed by Fairyland architect William Russell Everitt with help from puppeteers Ralph Chessé, Lettie Schubert and Wolo von Trutzschler. Their input ensured a performance space that is easily adaptable for all forms of puppetry. The theater includes lighting, storage, workshop and a scenic fly gallery.

Directors have included Frank and Dorothy Hayward (1956–1958), Tony Urbano (1959–1962), Luman Coad (1963–1966), Lewis Mahlmann (1967–2005) and Randal Metz (1991–present). Lewis and Randal co-directed the theater from 1991–2005 under the name of M Plus M Productions. This theater, unlike some other amusement park puppet theaters, requires the director to be an independent contractor. This allows the shows and puppets to be owned by the puppeteer rather than the city or park. The director is responsible for the production of seven shows a year and for outreach into the schools and community to bring puppets to children of all ages, beyond the park.

Fairyland's motto is "We bring children's literature to life!" Therefore, its shows come from original stories, fairytales, novels, operas, ballets and ethnic tales from around the world. Well-known puppeteers who have lent their talents to Fairyland include Nick Barone, Bob Brown, Forman Brown, Roger Dennis, John Gilkerson, David C. Jones, William Stewart Jones, Jerry Juhl, Elizabeth Luce, Blake Maxam, Pamelia McIntire, Bob Mills, Mike & Frances Oznowicz, Frank Oznowicz, Pat Platt, Bruce Sedley, Charles Taylor and Jesse Vail. As of this writing, the repertory of puppet theater shows numbered above 150 productions.

Children's Fairyland and the puppeteers of the Storybook Puppet Theater were honored to receive the Puppeteers of America Award for outstanding contributions to the field of puppetry in 1999.

GENIILAND PUPPET THEATER
1961

Geniiland Puppet Theater
Dates of Operation: 1958–1977, year 'round.

In 1958 Jean Cease, whom everyone called "Genii," opened her first party puppet theater in the San Fernando Valley. After a year she moved to a larger storefront, and then later in 1960 to an even bigger location in Sherman Oaks. But the crowds grew larger and larger and so did Genii's needs. Ultimately in 1967 the final Geniiland Theater opened at 14837 Besemer Street in Van Nuys. It was a unique theater because it was on a reserved schedule only and no tickets were sold to the public for performances. Working year 'round, a staff of 4–5 costumed helpers and performers catered to the needs of private birthday celebrations.

The theater decor and format were designed by Dr. Richard G. Adams, a noted children's theater director and designer. The unique children's party center had a fully-equipped puppet theater covering three walls of the room, and featured complete party catering and dispensing of birthday presents. Geniiland was a complex of fantasy with a birthday mushroom throne, talking trees, and puppet characters who shook hands with visiting children. Genii, dressed in her genie costume, would sing and tell stories while introducing her cast of colorful puppet friends. Her motto was: "Children's birthday parties at popular prices!" It was Genii's belief that puppet shows in private homes could never achieve the proper magic and make-believe spectacle so necessary to children's theater.

Genii's favorite puppets were marionettes and hand puppets. Her complex also housed a colorful lobby, a gingerbread office, large workshops and storage. The theater could also be rented for adult birthdays or performances for fundraising events. When not at the theater, Genii provided a complete touring stage where shows were given in clubs, churches, restaurants and festivals. Many a youngster, at the tender age of 16, would stumble into Genii's world and years later proudly walk out as a professional puppeteer. After a record run of close to twenty years, Genii stopped fulfilling wishes and closed the doors to this enchanted wonderland.

Happy Hollow Park & Zoo
CASTLE PUPPET THEATER
1961

Happy Hollow Park & Zoo Castle Puppet Theater
Dates of Operation: 1961–2008 & 2011—present,
year 'round.

The Castle Puppet Theater in San Jose is one of the oldest city-run puppet theaters in California. Located in Happy Hollow Park & Zoo in Kelley Park, puppet shows are presented three times a day at 12:00pm, 2:00pm and 4:00pm. The castle building itself is designed to be used for hand, rod & marionette puppets.

This park does not have a professional puppeteer running the programs. For years, the shows were heavily designed by city employees who had an interest in puppetry. Since the city pays the salary of the director, all puppets, props, scripts and ideas are the sole property of the City and Happy Hollow. Historical records indicate only two professional puppeteers have guided the theater and its productions: Jesse Vail (1997–2004) and Judy Roberto (2006–2017).

The theater is shaped like a castle, with a portcullis proscenium opening. The puppeteers' workshop, storage and some park offices are located in the small castle structure. The park relies upon a revolving repertory of past shows, with the shows designed to be quickly exchanged so on any given day two different puppet shows can be seen. In 2007, the fans of the puppet theater raised funds for renovations and some new equipment such as a sound and lighting system and a mechanical roll up proscenium.

In 2008, Happy Hollow exchanged its fairytale park setting for more carnival-like rides and zoo activities. Almost all of the original park sets were sold off, with the exception of the puppet theater and a dragon fairytale train excursion. Both park and puppet theater were closed from 2008–2010 for renovations, during which new storage buildings and workshops were constructed for the puppet theater's 50-year anniversary. Past puppet theater directors have also included Christine Costello, Mike Rudd, Ron Skolman and countless other Park & Recreation supervisors.

BOB BAKER MARIONETTE THEATER
1960s

Bob Baker Marionette Theater

Dates of Operation: 1963–present, year round.

The Bob Baker Marionette Theater is the longest running puppet theater in Los Angeles. Opened in 1963, it was first located at 1345 West First Street in downtown Los Angeles. Bob Baker, with business partners Alton Wood and Helen Crail, envisioned a magical place where families could see quality puppetry on a regular schedule.

White iron gates led to a courtyard and a welcoming, trumpeting clown statue. Inside, the spacious high-ceilinged auditorium had rich red carpets and proscenium curtains, lighted by sparkling chandeliers. The theater was host to full theatrical lighting, a scenic fly gallery and state of the art sound. Children's seating was on the floor at the sides and back, in what they call "theater in the round," with chairs for adults behind them. Shows were basically a musical revue presented by at least 75 colorful marionettes. Sometimes a theme, such as Christmas, circus or a day at the farm was worked into the presentation. The marionettes played in the entire open center of the room and moved among the children, dancing and singing. Adjoining the enormous theater area were office spaces, storage facilities and a large workshop and party room. Up until 1989, the audience was invited backstage into the workshop where a detailed tour of "how to make a puppet" was given to happy throngs.

Since Bob's death in 2014 the theater has been run by a group of dedicated enthusiasts, all trying to keep Bob's legacy alive. In 2009, the theater was declared a Historic-Cultural Monument of Los Angeles, with the help of the L.A. Puppet Guild. Throughout the years, countless California puppeteers helped pull the strings at Bob's, including Michael Earl, King Hall, Ron Martin, Bob Mason, Kevin Menegus, Randal Metz, Bob Mills, Christine Papalexis, Frank Paris, Tom Ray, Roy Raymond, Don Sahlin, Jesse Vail and Greg Williams, among many others.

In 2018 the original theater closed. As of 2019, in Highland Park, a 10,000-square-foot former vaudeville theater, provides a permanent home for the legacy of Bob Baker, an American pioneer in the art of puppetry.

PUPPET PLAYHOUSE
1965

Puppet Playhouse
Dates of Operation: 1965–1981,
January–May & September–December

Located at 3903 Voltaire Street in a small shopping center in San Diego, next to a local 7-11, Pat Platt's Puppet Playhouse catered to birthday party shows and regularly scheduled public performances. Inspired by her friend Genii (Jean Cease) whose Geniiland Puppet Theater was so popular in the Los Angeles area, Pat decided to fill the same void in the San Diego area. "No Fuss, No Mess" parties was Pat's mantra.

A birthday at the Playhouse included puppet-style decorations, pizza, drinks, ice cream and cake, and a special "crowning" ceremony. The child was seated in a throne chair and garbed in a jeweled crown and suitable cape. After the show, through a special hidden door, a puppet handed out the birthday gifts and supervised children hitting a piñata. Pat usually hosted dressed as Mother Goose. When not catering a party, the Playhouse played three shows a day at regularly scheduled times for the public. Pat also presented workshops in puppetry, worked with local high schools to hire and train their puppeteers, and traveled with road shows when necessary. The theater had an unusual yearly schedule because Pat liked to close for the summer season while she built new shows, traveled and made necessary repairs.

Pat's unique and well-loved puppets were created by using the shapes of vegetable gourds. Unlike other puppet productions in popular southern California theaters, her shows were always stories from classical literature. Over the successful run of the Playhouse, she and Fairyland puppeteer Lewis Mahlmann often exchanged puppet shows to expand the offerings of their yearly schedules. Several of Pat's shows are still produced as part of the Children's Fairyland Storybook Theater offerings.

STEVE MELTZER
Santa Monica Puppet Center

Santa Monica Puppetry Center
Dates of Operation: 1997–2009, year 'round

The Santa Monica Puppetry Center was the dream child of puppeteer Steve Meltzer, who moved to Los Angeles in 1979 and discovered puppetry in 1989. He was a 3rd and 5th grade teacher and had a degree in Elementary Education and Psychology from Earlham College as well as a theater degree from the University of Southern California.

Originally opened in 1997 in a small building which had theater seats screwed to the floor, the Center thrived for 15 months until the building was torn down. Steve then collected the seats, puppets and props, and moved to a small location on 2nd Street. After ten successful years, he was forced to move once again to a new location on Broadway near 10th Street.

The Center ran largely as a one-person operation, presenting Steve's informal, ever changing, vaudeville-style musical revue for all ages *"Puppetolio."* The show featured marionettes, hand puppets and ventriloquist creations and was performed more than 300 times yearly. Eccentric puppets were cast in comic vignettes accompanied by songs and old-fashioned recorded music. Steve composed new music, sang and played guitar. Other Center performance highlights included the final shows of ventriloquist legends Paul Winchell and Ricky Layne, sold out engagements of Phillip Huber and his marionettes, and a special seminar by the creators of *South Park*, Trey Parker and Matt Stone, focused on their all-marionette movie *"Team America: World Police."* The Center was also home to the Santa Monica Puppetry Festival in 2008, which featured actress Leslie Caron talking at showings of her movies *"Gigi"* and *"Lili."*

The Center served as a workshop for building puppets and ventriloquist figures and creating, repairing and restoring all puppet related items. It also featured a puppet museum with over 400 curated figures, and was home to puppet classes for children. Each performance, birthday party celebration or school outing included a "Behind the Strings" tour of the puppet theater world. The Santa Monica Puppetry Center closed in 2009 after Steve's passing.

Alex Evans

Career: 2007–present. Alex is the executive director for the new Bob Baker Marionette Theater. The theater, which became a nonprofit in 2018, is now a collective of many talented young artists and performers, where the older puppeteers teach the new puppeteers, largely through oral history. At nineteen, Alex began his career with an interest in animation and special effects. Mentored by Bob Baker, his apprentice duties included puppeteering, digitizing the music library and archives, reorganizing the office and producing a film on the history of Bob Baker. The new theater is located at 4949 York Blvd, Los Angeles.

Bibliography

A Century of Stop Motion Animation, Ray Harryhausen & Tony Dalton. Watson-Guptill Publications. 2008.

Alan Cook: A Puppet Collector's Odyssey, Alan Cook, Jacqueline Marks and Dmitri Carter. Edited by Paul Eide. International Puppetry Museum. 2017.

An Incomplete History of the San Francisco Bay Area Puppeteers Guild, Lettie Connell Schubert (1996) and Randal J. Metz (2010) SFBAPG.Org. Website.

American Puppetry Collections, History and Performance, Phyllis T. Dircks. McFarland & Co, Inc. 2004.

Archives of the *Puppetry Journal.* Puppeteers of America quarterly magazine. 1949 - 2019

A Timeline of Puppetry in America, A Puppeteers of America Inc. publication, Paul Eide, Alan Cook and Steve Abrams. 2003.

A Wandering Showman, I, David Lano, Michigan State University Press. 1957.

Bil Baird... He Pulled Lots of Strings, Richard Leet, Charles H. MacNider Museum, 1988.

Bob Baker and His Marionettes, The Beginning, Gregory Paul Williams. Self published. 2010.

Breaking Out of Show Business: What I've Discovered by Not Being Discovered, Michael Paul Ziegfeld. Post Hill Press. 2014.

Children's Fairyland Archives.

Co-Creation: Fifty Years in the Making, Conrad Bishop & Elizabeth Fuller. The Independent Eye. WordWorkers Press. 2011.

Creating a Fairyland, 60 Years of Magic at Children's Fairyland, U.S.A., Tony Jonick and Randal J. Metz. Rappid Rabbit Publishing. 2011.

Disneyland Line, Disney Newsletter. Sept 6,1991. Vol 23 No 37

Dummy Days, Kelly Asbury. Angel City Press. 2003.

Gregory Paul Williams - Puppet Studio, on line puppet history articles.

GUMBY Imagined: The Story of Art Clokey and His Creations, Joan Rock Clokey & Joe Clokey. Dynamite Entertainment. 2017.

IMDb - Movies, TV and Celebrities Website.

International Puppetry: The California Connection. Curatorial Statement by Alan Cook. 1994 Palos Verdes Art Center exhibit booklet.

Lettie C. Schubert personal puppetry files.

Los Angeles Guild of Puppetry Newsletter Archives.

Marionettes, A Hobby For Everyone, Mabel & Les Beaton. Thomas Y. Crowell Company. 1948.

Martin Stevens - His Book, edited by Luman Coad. Charlemagne Press. 2002.

"My Adventures at Fairyland" by Tony Urbano, 2002. A personal memoir.

"My Life, Dreams & Adventures" by Lewis Mahlmann, 2007. A personal memoir.

Muppet Wiki - Fandom Website.

Other Voices - Ventriloquism from B.C. to T.V. Stanley Burns. Published by Stanley Burns. 2000.

Paul McPharlin and the Puppet Theater, Ryan Howard. McFarland and Company, Inc. 2006.

Personal Correspondence & Websites for many of the puppeteers.

Presenting Marionettes, Susan French. Art Horizons, Inc. 1964.

Pufnstuf & Other Stuff, David Martindale. Renaissance Books. 1998.

Puppeteers of America programs from National and/or Regional conventions.

Puppets: Art & Entertainment, Puppeteers of America, Inc. Garamond Pridemark Press, Inc. 1980.

Puppets in America 1739 to Today, with an account of the first American Puppetry Conference, Paul McPharlin. Puppetry Imprints. 1936.

Puppets, Puppets, Puppets! An Exhibit of Puppets From Around the World. Curatorial Statement by Alan Cook. 1977 Walnut Creek Civic Arts Gallery.

Ray Harryhausen, An Animated Life, Ray Harryhausen & Tony Dalton. Billboard Books. 2003.

Say Kids! What Time Is It? Notes from the Peanut Gallery, Stephen Davis. Little, Brown & Company. 1987.

San Diego Guild of Puppetry Newsletter Archives.

San Francisco Bay Area Puppeteers Guild Newsletter Archives.

Shadow Woman, The Extraordinary Career of Pauline Benton, Grant Hayter-Menzies. McGill-Queen's University Press. 2013.

Sid & Marty Krofft's Les Poupées de Paris, Show program. Salzer Productions. 1961.

Small Wonder, Forman Brown. Scarecrow Press. 1980.

Stevens' Course In Puppetry, Martin Stevens. Charlemagne Press. Reprinted 1997.

Storybook Strings - 50 Years of Puppetry at Children's Fairyland's Storybook Puppet Theater, Randal J. Metz. Rappid Rabbit Publishing. 2003.

Strings, Hands, Shadows, A Modern Puppet History, John Bell. The Detroit Institute of the Arts. 2000.

Subplot - Memoirs of Chicago's Kungsholm Miniature Grand Opera, Gary Jones. Charlemagne Press. 2018.

The Art of the Puppet, Bil Baird. The Macmillan Company, New York. 1965.

The Contribution of Puppetry to the Art Life of Los Angeles, Helen Long Luitjens. Masters Thesis for the University of Southern California. 1943.

The Holdens: Monarchs Of The Marionette Theatre, John McCormick. Society for Theatre Research, London. 2018.

The Marionette Actor, Ralph Chessé. George Mason University Press. 1987.

The Puppet Theater in America: A History 1524 -1948 & Puppets in America since 1948, Paul McPharlin & Marjorie Batchelder McPharlin. Plays Inc. 1969.

The World Encyclopedia of Puppetry Arts - UNIMA online. Union Internationale de la Marionnette.

Tony Sarg: Puppeteer in America 1915-1942, Tamara Robin Hunt. Charlemagne Press. 1988.

Traditional and Folk Puppets of the World, Michael R. Malkin. A. S. Barnes & Co. 1977.

"Under the Puppet" - Saturday Morning Media, podcasts by Grant Baciocco, www.saturdaymorningmedia.com/category/shows/utp/ 2017 - 2019.

Wikipedia Encyclopedia & Online Resources.

MITCHELL MARIONETTES
Golden State Milk

Index

M

University of North Texas, 149
University of Oklahoma, 111
University of Ottawa, 197
University of Santa Clara, 203
University of South Carolina, 177
University of Southern California, 75, 121, 245, 323
University of Texas, 98
University of Toronto, 197
University of Wales, Newport, 277
University of Washington, 38
University of Wisconsin-Milwaukee, 177
Urbano, Tony, 49, 51, 57, 77, 91, 93, 131, 135, 143, 165, 169, 182, 207, 225, 226, 230, 233, 235, 239, 241, 257, 299, 300, 313
USDA Forest Service, 197

V

Vagabond Puppets, 72, 87, 95, 101, 129, 131, 141, 191, 224, 311
Vail, Jesse, 113, 169, 191, 285, 313, 317, 319
Van Volkenburg, Ellen, 12, 15, 38, 68
vaudeville, 3, 7, 11, 12, 40, 59, 67, 69, 70, 100, 289, 319, 323
Venice Beach Pier, 298
Venterprise. *See* Zendejas, René
ventriloquism, 1, 10, 43, 45, 53, 69, 71, 79, 93, 133, 139, 149, 171, 186, 195, 199, 217, 226, 231, 255, 323
Ventriloquist Association Festivals, 217
Vienna Staatsoper, 155
Vietnam War, 145, 146, 185
Vines, Robert, 167
Virginia Serenaders, 7
Von Pilat, Vera, 298
von Trutzschler, Wolo, 45, 87, 313
Vorkapich, Slavko, 121

W

Walden Marionettes. *See* Fredericks, Jack & Christopher
Waldo control system, 230, 245
Walko, Russ, 293, 296

Walton & O'Rourke, 40, 45, 49, 69, 72, 79, 135, 303
Walton, Paul, 40, 49. *See* Walton and O'Rourke
War Horse, 288
Ward, Jay, 97, 135
Warner Bros. Cartoon Studio, 97
Washington Arts Project, 38
Wayang Kulit, 193
  Balinesian, 247
  Indonesian, 105
Weber, Richard, 184
Webisodes, 289
Weird Al Yankovic, 291
Welles, Orson, 40
Wells, H.G., 40
Wences, Señor, 71
West Virginia University, 273
West, Adam, 133
West, Mae, 89
Western University, 251
Weta Workshop, 287
Wetzel, Liebe, 281
Whitaker, David, 105
White House, 53, 93
White, T.H., 39
Whiting Milk Company, 103
Who's Who in Entertainment, 77
Whom the Gods Destroy, 21
Whorls of Wonder Puppet Theater. *See* Naylor, Mary
Wilcox, Caroly, 215
Williams, Greg, 319
Williams, Robin, 189
Williamson, Helga, 137
Winchell, Paul, 71, 93, 99, 217, 323
Winston, Stan, 199, 231, 261
Wohlwend, Heidi, 284
Wolo. *See* von Trutzschler, Wolo
Wood, Alton, 51, 98, 146, 319
Wood, Charles Erskine Scott, 17
Woodstock, 145
Works Progress Administration (WPA), 17, 27, 33, 38, 39
World of Sid & Marty Krofft, 67
World Trade Center, 261, 287

About the Authors

KEVIN MENEGUS is the founder of the Fratello Marionettes, based in the Bay Area. The Fratello Marionettes tour throughout the West Coast and beyond, performing their large-scale marionette productions.

RANDAL J. METZ is the founder of the Puppet Company, based in the Bay Area. Randal is the resident puppeteer at Children's Fairyland in Oakland. The Storybook Puppet Theater is the oldest continuously running puppet theater in the U.S.

LETTIE CONNELL SCHUBERT
Moods for Small Mimes
circa 1960

www.ingramcontent.com/pod-product-compliance
Lightning Source LLC
Chambersburg PA
CBHW050636150426
42811CB00052B/856